Response to Intervention

RESPONSE TO INTERVENTION

A Guide for School Social Workers

Edited by
James P. Clark
Michelle E. Alvarez

OXFORD
UNIVERSITY PRESS

2010

OXFORD

UNIVERSITY PRESS

Oxford University Press, Inc., publishes works that further
Oxford University's objective of excellence
in research, scholarship, and education.

Oxford   New York
Auckland   Cape Town   Dar es Salaam   Hong Kong   Karachi
Kuala Lumpur   Madrid   Melbourne   Mexico City   Nairobi
New Delhi   Shanghai   Taipei   Toronto

With offices in
Argentina   Austria   Brazil   Chile   Czech Republic   France   Greece
Guatemala   Hungary   Italy   Japan   Poland   Portugal   Singapore
South Korea   Switzerland   Thailand   Turkey   Ukraine   Vietnam

Published by Oxford University Press, Inc.
198 Madison Avenue, New York, New York 10016

www.oup.com

Oxford is a registered trademark of Oxford University Press.

Library of Congress Cataloging-in-Publication Data
Response to intervention : a guide for school social workers/edited by
James P. Clark and Michelle Alvarez.
p.   cm.
Includes bibliographical references and index.
ISBN: 978-0-19-538550-2
1. School social work—United States.   I. Clark, James P.
II. Alvarez, Michelle.
LB3013.4.R47 2010
371.7—dc22
2009028721

Printed in the United States of America
on acid-free paper

ACKNOWLEDGMENTS

I have deeply appreciated the persistence and continuous support of my co-editor, Michelle Alvarez, in the development of this book. Her insistence that we describe the contributions of school social workers to the development of Response to Intervention (RtI) systems has been unwavering and uncompromising.

The school social work staff at Heartland Area Education Agency 11 in Johnston, Iowa, have contributed extensively to the content of this book. They are my heroes and the primary source of my inspiration to develop and promote data-based decision making and problem solving in school social work practice. I am forever grateful for their dedication to improving the educational experiences of students, and for their patient support in allowing me to serve as their supervisor.

So many others have played key roles in providing me with opportunities to develop problem-solving and RtI systems—Jean Purdy, the first Supervisor of School Social Work Services at Heartland Area Education Agency 11, who hired me in my first school social work position; Frank Vance, a truly visionary leader and Chief of the Bureau of Special Education at the Iowa Department of Education, who hired me many years ago as a state school social work consultant; Iowa Department of Education colleagues Jeff Grimes, Greg Robinson, and Jim Reese, with whom I worked to develop a state-wide problem-solving system in Iowa; Isadora Hare, senior staff at the National Association of Social Workers, who taught me how to link policy and practice; and Lana Michelson, Chief of the Bureau of Student and Family Support Services at the Iowa Department of

Education, a long-time colleague and friend who has challenged and supported me in so many ways over many years.

Finally, my family has made me who I am and they have tolerated the results graciously. To them I am forever grateful. Most of all, I am thankful for the constant presence of Beverly, the love of my life, whose calm and patient manner have enabled me to accomplish much more than I ever thought possible.

James P. Clark

I would like to acknowledge the contribution to the field of Response to Intervention and student services, including school social work, of the staff at Heartland Area Education Agency11, Johnston, Iowa. Noted as an evidence-based model of RtI in the Individuals with Disabilities Education Act 2004, AEA11 has paved the way for other school districts to learn from their accomplishments. They have been gracious in authoring many chapters in this book and include many school social workers who have implemented RtI before its inclusion in legislation. I would also like to acknowledge Mr. Jim Clark, my mentor of many years and my current co-editor. Jim is a visionary and a true leader in our field who is not afraid to challenge our way of thinking about the provision of school social work services. Finally, I would like to recognize Dr. Susan McDowell-Riley, Evansville-Vanderburgh School Corporation in Indiana, for believing in me and keeping me in the conversation about RtI, and my husband Marvin and children—Kipp, Karolina, and Kristian—for their continuous support of my many projects.

Michelle E. Alvarez

CONTENTS

CONTRIBUTORS

Michelle E. Alvarez, MSW, EdD
Associate Professor of Social Work
Minnesota State University, Mankato

Valerie Bostick, MAT
Director of Early Childhood Education
Evansville Vanderburgh School Corporation

James P. Clark, MSW
Assistant Director of Compliance Monitoring
Heartland Area Education Agency 11

Beth Dedic, MSW, LISW
Program Assistant for Special Education
Heartland Area Education Agency 11

Daniel Diehl, PhD, LCSW
President
Diehl Evaluation and Consulting Services, Inc.

Lucille Eber, EdD
Director
Illinois Positive Behavioral Interventions and Supports
(PBIS) Network

Angelisa Braaksma Fynaardt, MS, PhD
Professional Learning and Leadership Consultant
Heartland Area Education Agency 11

Joseph R. Gianesin, MSW, PhD
Full Professor of Social Work
Springfield College

Jennifer Gilmore, MSW
Program Assistant for Special Education
Heartland Area Education Agency 11

Erika W. Joye, PhD, NCSP
Trainer/Research Specialist
Why Try, Inc.

Brenda Coble Lindsey, EdD, LCSW
Clinical Associate Professor and Chair—School Social Work
Specialization
University of Illinois at Urbana-Champaign

Wendy Marckmann, MSW
Program Assistant for School Social Work Services
Heartland Area Education Agency 11

Christopher Pierson, PhD
Assistant Director of Human Resources
Heartland Area Education Agency 11

James C. Raines, PhD, ACSW
Associate Professor of Social Work
Illinois State University

John Richardson, MSW, LISW, ACSW
Professional Learning and Leadership Consultant
Heartland Area Education Agency 11

Kate M. Scates, MSW
Coordinator of Family Support Services
Evansville Vanderburgh School Corporation

W. David Tilly III, PhD
Director of Innovation and Accountability
Heartland Area Education Agency 11

Andrea Timm, MSW
School Social Worker
Heartland Area Education Agency 11

Margaret White, MSW, LCSW
Technical Assistance Coordinator
Illinois Positive Behavioral Interventions and Supports (PBIS) Network

RESPONSE TO INTERVENTION

Introduction and Overview

JAMES P. CLARK & MICHELLE E. ALVAREZ

This book is designed to provide school social workers with a working understanding of Response to Intervention (RtI) practices and systems. School social workers will be challenged to take on the role of system change agents in the adoption, implementation, and evaluation of RtI systems that improve the educational outcomes for all students. Because RtI includes the development of school-wide supports for *all* students, school social workers will need to expand their repertoires of knowledge and skills beyond assessment of and services to individual students who are at risk or experiencing educational problems. For many practitioners this represents a significant paradigm shift requiring a concomitant shift in practice that includes the development of knowledge and skills required to assist in the design and implementation of school-wide support systems. School social workers will need to be able to conduct system-level assessments and use these data to design differential interventions and supports that are able to be directly measured, monitored, and evaluated for their effectiveness. This does not mean that school social workers should totally abandon their direct service work with students. Rather, a more balanced approach is needed in which considerably more attention is directed to system improvements that will use resources more efficiently and lessen the extent to which individual and group interventions are needed.

WHAT IS RESPONSE TO INTERVENTION?

Response to Intervention (RtI) is a multitiered framework for organizing evidenced-based practices in a systematic process for the purpose of determining what interventions ensure the academic, social, emotional, and behavioral success of all students. In this approach, student performance data are continuously used to match high-quality instruction and supports to the needs of all students. The specific focus of this book is on the use of RtI to address the social, emotional, and behavioral needs of students in elementary and secondary schools.

National policy support for the use of RtI has recently been explicitly stated in the reauthorization of the Individuals with Disabilities Education Act (IDEA) of 2004. As a result, implementing federal regulations for IDEA now require states to permit the use of a process that examines whether the child responds to scientific, evidence-based interventions as part of the information reviewed to determine whether a child has a specific learning disability (SLD). Though the specific reference in IDEA is to evaluation procedures to determine special education eligibility for students with learning disabilities, the benefits of this approach extend far beyond those students requiring special education programs and services. In the role of system change agents, school social workers have the opportunity to lead efforts to develop school-wide systems that incorporate RtI principles and practices and that ensure the educational success of all students. In advocating systemic improvements, school social workers will be effective only if they are knowledgeable about RtI and are proficient in the skills needed to practice in RtI systems.

THE CHALLENGE

To advocate effectively and lead efforts to adopt and implement RtI systems, most practitioners will need to acquire or revitalize the knowledge and skills needed to continually practice data-based decision making. The social work profession has long claimed to be rooted in both science and art. However, to a great extent, considerably more emphasis has been given to the artistic delivery of services such as the use of rapport, relationships, and effective communication as the foundations for effective helping, with relatively less attention given to the scientific dimensions of practice. The strong focus on evidence-based practices and data-based decision making in RtI systems demands greater emphasis on the scientific features of practice than ever before. Developing and using data systems and procedures that document needs and the effectiveness of interventions at the individual and systems levels require the artful application of scientific methods to school social work practice. In effect, RtI represents an opportunity to expand the scope of school social work practice by applying systems theory, functional assessment practices, and an ecological perspective to efforts to improve behavioral and academic results. As such, school social workers will need to effectively and efficiently integrate RtI into their practice.

UNDERLYING BELIEFS

The following beliefs about RtI and school social work practice have guided the development of this book:

- RtI is an approach that is highly consistent with social work values and school social work practice standards and should be viewed as an organizing framework for school social work practice.
- The scientific method can and should be applied to efforts to solve educationally relevant social, emotional, and behavioral problems.
- School social workers should be active participants in supporting the adoption and effective implementation of RtI at state and local levels.
- The implementation of RtI should enhance problem solving and positive educational results for all students and should not promote the labeling and categorizing of any students.
- Social, emotional, and behavioral competence is a matter of teaching and learning on a par with academic competencies. Therefore, RtI should promote an instructional approach to improving students' social, emotional, and behavioral adjustment and performance.
- School-wide, group, and individual student performance data (academic and behavioral) should be systematically used to make decisions about resources needed to ensure student success.
- School social workers should use functional behavioral assessment procedures to inform the design, implementation, monitoring, and evaluation of behavioral interventions.
- The effectiveness of interventions and programs developed for students by school social workers must be documented with data.

ORGANIZATION OF THE BOOK

Chapter 1 traces the evolution of RtI policy and practice beginning with the Elementary and Secondary Education Act (ESEA) of 1965. The influence of policy shifts on practice throughout subsequent decades is described, concluding with the explicit policy support for RtI articulated in the Individuals with Disabilities Education Improvement Act of 2004. A three-tiered RtI model is presented as an organizational framework for the book. This framework is used to organize subsequent chapters into four sections. Sections I, II, and III are organized in relation to each of the three tiers of the RtI framework. Each of these sections includes a chapter describing the tier followed by chapters that present case examples to illustrate how specific programs, practices, or data collection systems might be implemented in that tier. Case examples presented here have several limitations. First, because these programs, practices, and data collection systems were not initially designed with the intent of being implemented within a comprehensive RtI framework, the reader may note that they have a less than perfect or natural fit with the three-tiered model presented here. However, this is the current state of practice, and it illustrates the formidable challenge inherent in using this framework to orchestrate the efficient and effective use of an array of programs and practices in a well-functioning and coherent RtI system. Second, programs and practices presented in the case examples vary in the extent to which they are considered evidence based. They range from promising practices to those that have established strong data to support their claim to be evidence-based. Finally, outcome data that are presented in case examples are intended to illustrate the application of the problem-solving process that includes progress monitoring and evaluation of the effectiveness of the program or practice. The examples are not experimentally designed and the data are not intended to establish an evidence base for the particular program or practice.

Section IV includes a chapter describing the use of RtI data in making special education eligibility decisions; a chapter describing the identification, selection, and use of evidence-based programs and practices; and a chapter presenting critical information on how to support the adoption and sustained implementation of RtI systems. The final chapter concludes with a challenge for school social workers to become advocates for the adoption, implementation, and sustainability of RtI systems.

THE NEED FOR THIS BOOK

The scant attention to RtI in the school social work literature has been a major impetus for the development of this book. Though some topics relevant to RtI such as evidence-based practices are addressed in the literature, it is astounding that in the past decade no articles exclusively focusing on RtI have been published in school social work journals. Only two very recently published book chapters on RtI can be found in the school social work literature (Massat, Constable, & Thomas, 2009; Lindsey & White, 2009). Both of these chapters are in the same book.

Because the knowledge base generated from school social work is lacking, the reader will note that most of the supportive material cited in this book is from the education, school psychology, and applied behavior analysis literature. However, all authors of chapters in this book have been involved directly in the development and implementation of RtI systems. Additionally some authors have extensive experience with designing state and local RtI policies, procedures, and practices, and some have extensive experience practicing as school social workers in RtI systems.

Despite the virtual absence of attention to RtI in our literature, school social workers most assuredly have much to contribute to the systemic improvements that RtI demands. But we will need to become more substantive and visible contributors to the innovations needed to drive these improvements. We will need to act on our claim that we are change agents who use systems theory and thinking to ensure successful outcomes for students and that this role and perspective is what distinguishes us from other professions. After all, isn't this or shouldn't this be the heart of school social work? Let this book serve as a rallying cry for school social workers to rise to this challenge.

REFERENCES

Lindsey, B., & White, M. (2009). Tier 2 behavioral interventions for at-risk students. In C. R. Massat, R. Constable, S. McDonald, & J. Flynn (Eds.), *School social work: Practice, policy and research* (665–673). Chicago, IL: Lyceum Books.

Massat, C. R., Constable, R., & Thomas, G. (2009). Response to intervention (RtI) and the school social worker. In C. R. Massat, R. Constable, S. McDonald, & J. Flynn (Eds.), *School social work: Practice, policy and research* (523–531). Chicago, IL: Lyceum Books.

Response to
Intervention

1

THE EVOLUTION OF RESPONSE TO INTERVENTION

JAMES P. CLARK & W. DAVID TILLY III

A comprehensive understanding of Response to Intervention (RtI) as a matter of current policy and practice is best acquired by considering its historical development. In this chapter we will describe the policy and practice precursors to RtI. Key legislation and policy initiatives at the federal level that have shaped the need and readiness for RtI will be identified, including the Elementary and Secondary Education Act (ESEA) of 1965 and its subsequent reauthorizations, the Education of All Handicapped Children Act of 1975, the Regular Education Initiative in the 1980s, the Individuals with Disabilities Education Act (IDEA) in the 1990s, and most recently the No Child Left Behind Act of 2002 and the Individuals with Disabilities Education Improvement Act of 2004. Changes in practice prompted by shifts in policy emphases will be identified as well.

A conceptual framework that includes key features of RtI systems will also be presented along with a rationale for adopting RtI that challenges prior assumptions about assessment, instruction/intervention, and curriculum. A systematic problem-solving approach to school social work practice is proposed as an essential methodology for ensuring effective results in RtI systems.

THE PURSUIT OF EQUAL ACCESS

The Elementary and Secondary Education Act (ESEA) of 1965, Public Law 89-10, was one of the first national education policies designed to address

3

emerging concerns that some students were not sufficiently benefiting from public education. Federal funding was provided to states primarily to support remedial reading and math instruction for economically disadvantaged students. The Act also included programs to involve families in supporting their children's educational progress. Assessment practices at this time focused on the identification of students who met the criteria for being considered *economically disadvantaged* and who were determined to be discrepant from peers on standardized measures of academic performance. The role of social workers was to facilitate the involvement of parents in supporting their children's educational progress in these programs.

A beginning support for securing access to public education for students with disabilities was present in the reauthorization of ESEA a few years later in 1969, when for the first time limited federal funding was provided to states for hiring special education teachers. More significant policy attention to guaranteeing the right of access to public education for students with disabilities came in 1975 with passage of the Education of All Handicapped Children Act, Public Law 94-142. The law guaranteed a free, appropriate public education (FAPE) in the least restrictive environment (LRE) for all students with disabilities who needed special education.

Because of the unprecedented mandate to afford access to public education to a large number of students previously turned away from their neighborhood schools, the "child find" provisions of the new law challenged states to develop systems for identifying, or "finding," students who were eligible to receive a full continuum of special education programs and services. Infrastructures that included procedures for efficiently and reliably identifying eligible students were rapidly developed by states. Identification systems at this time relied heavily on teacher referrals that were typically based on teacher perceptions about low-performing students. Assessment practices and procedures were mostly descriptive, generating information that enabled decisions to be made about whether characteristics of individual students matched the criteria established for the various categories of disability delineated in the law. Thus, the primary emphasis was on conducting assessments that enabled entitlement decision making—that is, determining which students had disabilities, needed special education in order to benefit from their education, and thus were entitled to access specially designed instruction and the due process protections guaranteed in the law. Typical assessment practices utilized a standard battery of assessment procedures consisting mostly of standardized instruments to measure current academic and behavior performance. This assessment battery approach had the primary purpose of informing eligibility decisions by describing characteristics of the students and matching them to preestablished criteria for specific disability categories. The social history or social developmental study was the school social work contribution to the typical assessment battery at this time (Clark & Thiede, 2007).

The daunting tasks of "child find" caused greater emphasis to be given, and resources directed to, placing students in special education programs, with comparatively less emphasis and resources devoted to the quality and effectiveness of specially designed instruction provided during special education placements. These "refer-test-place" identification systems proved effective in meeting the initial child find mandate of the new law, but concerns about whether assessments were resulting in valid classifications of students began to emerge in the late 1970s and early 1980s. In a National Research Council (NRC) study examining the validity of special education classification, Heller, Holtzman, and Messick (1982) argued that three criteria must be addressed to assure that a special education classification is valid: (1) the quality of the general education program, (2) the value of the special education program in producing important outcomes for students, and (3) the accuracy and meaningfulness of the assessment process in the identification of a disability.

The classification of students as learning disabled was particularly contentious at the time and was exacerbated by the inclusion of the discrepancy approach in the federal implementing regulations of Public Law 94-142 that were established in 1977. Using the discrepancy approach, a student was identified as having a learning disability if standardized assessment instruments were able to document that he or she demonstrated significantly low levels of achievement when compared with students of general intelligence. The discrepancy approach was accepted in the regulations due to the absence of any widely accepted methodology for diagnosing learning disabilities.

Concern over whether all students who were entitled to special education services were actually being identified as well as the more specific concern of whether students who were identified were being accurately categorized into specific disability categories (in particular, learning disabilities) continued into the 1980s. This decade also spawned one of the first education policy initiatives that turned systemic attention to how and where students entitled to special education were being educated. Concerned with how separate regular education and special education had become in response to the mandates of Public Law 94-142, in 1986 Assistant Secretary of Special Education and Rehabilitation Services Madeleine C. Will launched the Regular Education Initiative (REI). While recognizing the accomplishments of special education efforts in the first decade of implementation following the enactment of Public Law 94-142, Will stated strong criticism of pull-out programs, concern for the fragmentation of separately functioning special education and regular education systems, the stigmatizing effects of labeling and special class placement on students with disabilities, and the failure of these fragmented systems to respond in more timely ways to the needs of struggling learners (Will, 1986).

Proponents of the REI advocated the inclusion of students with disabilities in regular education and the need for regular education to assume primary responsibility for educating all students (Stainback & Stainback, 1984; Wang, Reynolds, & Walberg, 1986; Reynolds, Wang,

& Walberg, 1987). Though vaguely defined, the REI provoked vigorous debate among policy makers, researchers, educators, and advocacy groups regarding the responsibility of the general education system for educating students with disabilities as well as many other marginally performing students who were served in various categorical programs, such as students at risk, or remedial academic programs. The "full inclusion" movement that briefly followed the REI in the late 1980s and early 1990s attempted to apply the principles of the REI in an absolute manner by proposing that all students with disabilities be educated in regular education settings regardless of the nature or severity of their disability (Sailor et al., 1989). These initiatives helped set the stage for turning the attention of policy makers, educators, and researchers from ensuring that students with disabilities had access to special education programs and services to a concern for whether access was improving their educational outcomes.

RESEARCH, INNOVATION, AND THE PURSUIT OF RESULTS

Beginning in the late 1980s and continuing into the 1990s, researchers scrutinized factors thought to be barriers to the effectiveness of special education programs and services. This included assessment practices designed to facilitate differential diagnosis, classification, and disability labeling that were being used in decision making for special education eligibility (Macmann et al., 1989; Aaron, 1997; MacMillan, Gresham, & Bocian, 1998). Research also focused on the rigid application of eligibility criteria and its effect on denying or delaying special education eligibility decisions and the provision of services needed to ensure educational success.

System change initiatives designed to improve the delivery and effectiveness of services were also launched in the late 1980s and early 1990s. These initiatives applied concepts and practices espoused by the REI along with findings from research on assessment and decision-making practices. The design of these change initiatives actually proved to be the early experimental iterations or precursors of RtI. Some of these initiatives featured large-scale, and in some cases statewide, implementation of innovations in assessment and decision-making procedures and practices.

In the late 1980s and into the mid-1990s the Renewed Service Delivery System (RSDS) initiative was implemented statewide in Iowa. RSDS was one of the most comprehensive special education systemic reforms attempted at the time, resulting in significant changes in practice and policy (Tilly, Grimes, & Reschly, 1993; Grimes, Kurns, & Tilly, 2006). Affirming the concerns of the REI, the RSDS initiative cited the separation and fragmentation of general education and special education evidenced in the overreliance on pull-out programs along with separate general and special education curriculums among the major issues establishing the need for improvements. Other issues included overreferral and overidentification of students determined to be eligible for special education, rigid requirements of laws and regulations that limited the benefits of special education services and service options to those deemed eligible, overemphasis on the use of standardized eligibility assessments, and an emphasis on process rather than outcomes in evaluating the effectiveness of special education.

To address these concerns, the RSDS initiative promoted infrastructure designs that supported the integration of special education, compensatory education, and general education resources and personnel. This set the expectation for special education and compensatory education personnel to provide early intervention and support to teachers working with students experiencing learning and behavior problems in general education. Building Assistance Teams were established to organize these efforts (Clark, Tilly, Atkinson, & Flugum, 1992). Practices that supported the meaningful involvement of parents in decision making and the delivery of services were also emphasized (Clark, Cunconnun, & Riesen, 1989).

A problem-solving approach to addressing learning and behavior problems was a central feature of innovative practices included in the RSDS initiative. Problem-solving practices included the development of individually tailored interventions based on functional assessments that facilitated an understanding of the underlying causes of learning and behavior problems. Direct and frequent progress monitoring of intervention effects was expected, and procedures were established to enhance the use of progress monitoring data in making decisions about intervention effectiveness or changes needed in intervention implementation. The design and implementation of high-quality interventions based on functional assessment data were established as critical elements in effective implementation of problem-solving practices (Tilly & Flugum, 1995). Problem-solving practices also focused strongly on significant and measurable outcomes for students and less on process requirements.

Another example of a large-scale system change initiative was the Minneapolis Public Schools' implementation of a three-stage problem-solving process in the early 1990s. The problem-solving model supported the use of intervention implementation data to determine which students were eligible for special education (Marston, 2001; Marston, Muyskens, Lau, & Canter, 2003). The process was implemented by classroom teachers in Stage 1. In Stage 2 a Problem-Solving Team including general education, compensatory education, and special education personnel became involved in assessment and intervention development. In Stage 3 a special education eligibility evaluation was conducted. A noncategorical identification procedure was used in which students determined to be eligible for special education were not classified into disability categories such as learning disabled, mentally retarded, or emotionally disturbed. Instead, eligible students were designated as "students needing alternative programming." Reschly and Starkweather (1997) found that prereferral interventions implemented in this process were typically of better quality than those in the prior system, and students requiring special education were identified sooner.

The research and innovation initiatives of the 1980s and 1990s led to improvements in service delivery system infrastructures and professional practices in a number of states. These improvements included practices that shaped what has become RtI. Systematic problem-solving approaches were developed that utilized functional assessment procedures, direct and frequent monitoring of well-designed interventions, and data-based decisions about the effectiveness of interventions. In codifying changes resulting from its system reform initiative (RSDS) in 1995, the state of Iowa defined "systematic problem solving" in its state administrative rules of special education (Iowa Department of Education, 1995) and also defined "general education interventions" as a required component of the process of identifying students for special education eligibility. As a result, the use of RtI data became a required component of state-defined eligibility standards for special education (Iowa Department of Education, 2006).

The research and innovations of the 1980s and 1990s also significantly influenced the reauthorization of the Individuals with Disabilities Education Act (IDEA) in 1997. Provisions of the new IDEA clearly shifted the focus of special education from ensuring access to a free appropriate public education (child find) to an imperative for results. Of particular importance and relevance to the development of RtI systems for addressing student behavioral needs were provisions for disciplining students with disabilities that included requirements for conducting functional behavioral assessments and developing behavior intervention plans. Explicit direction was given to individualized education program (IEP) teams to provide "positive behavioral interventions" for students with disabilities who had behavioral problems. An expectation that school social workers assist with the development of positive behavioral intervention strategies was added to the definition of social work services in schools. Tilly et al. (1998) encouraged states to adopt policies that supported implementation of functional behavioral assessment practices "throughout the special education decision-making process" (p. 18).

The inclusion of provisions for functional behavioral assessment and positive behavioral interventions in the newly reauthorized IDEA was evidence of the emergence of the applied science of positive behavior support (PBS). As documented by Carr et al. (2002), PBS had initially evolved within the field of developmental disabilities drawing on decades of research and practice in applied behavior analysis, the normalization/inclusion movement, and person-centered values. The application of applied behavior analysis knowledge and procedures to behavioral assessment and intervention development for individual students was a significant contribution to addressing the behavioral needs of students with disabilities. The application of PBS in a three-tiered school-wide model was influential in shaping the system design of RtI for addressing the behavioral needs of all students. The continued development of individual and school-wide applications of PBS also significantly impacted the next

IDEA reauthorization, further installing these concepts and practices into national educational policy.

In response to national concern regarding the state of special education, on October 2, 2001, George W. Bush established the President's Commission on Excellence in Special Education. The Commission's report titled "A New Era: Revitalizing Special Education for Children and Their Families" was issued on July 1, 2002 (U.S. Department of Education Office of Special Education and Rehabilitative Services, 2002). Citing dismal outcomes for students with disabilities such as dropout rates twice that of nondisabled peers and low rates of employment following graduation, as well as other problems such as overidentification of minority students (p. 3), the Commission's findings included the following:

1. IDEA is generally providing basic legal safeguards and access for children with disabilities. Too often, simply qualifying for special education becomes an end-point—not a gateway to more effective instruction and strong intervention.
2. The current system uses an antiquated model that waits for a child to fail, instead of a model of prevention and intervention.
3. Special education and general education are considered to be separate systems. General education and special education must share responsibilities for students with disabilities.
4. Parents do not have adequate options and recourse when the system fails them.
5. The culture of compliance has diverted energy from educating every child.
6. Identification methods lack validity and as a result many students are misidentified and many are not identified early enough or at all.
7. Children with disabilities require highly qualified teachers.
8. The current system does not always embrace or implement evidence-based practices.
9. The focus on compliance and bureaucratic imperatives instead of academic achievement and social outcomes fails too many children with disabilities.

Major recommendations of the Commission included the following:

1. Focus on results, not on process.
2. Embrace a model of prevention, not a model of failure.
3. Consider children with disabilities as general education children first.

Of particular relevance to RtI is the Commission's strongly worded statement regarding the identification of students with disabilities:

A key component of the identification process . . . should be a careful evaluation of the child's response to instruction. Children should

not be identified for special education without documenting what
methods have been used to facilitate the child's learning and
adaptation to the general education classroom. In the absence of this
documentation the Commission finds that many children who are
placed into special education are essentially instructional casualties
and not students with disabilities. (p. 26)

Clearly the Commission's report challenged policy makers and educators
to create systems that provide flexible and responsive supports to students
experiencing academic or behavioral difficulties by intervening early and
efficiently, and by using scientifically based instructional interventions
when providing supports and interventions.

Recommendations of the Commission have become explicit in the
2004 IDEA reauthorization as well as in the final implementing regulations issued August 14, 2006. For example, § 300.307(a)(3) of the final
regulations requires states to permit the use of a process that examines
whether the child responds to scientific, evidence-based interventions as
part of the information reviewed to determine whether a child has a
specific learning disability (SLD). In explanatory comments the U.S.
Office of Special Education Programs notes,

> The Act requires that LEAs be permitted to use a process that
> determines if a child responds to evidence-based interventions.
> Further, there is an evidence base to support the use of RtI models to
> identify children with SLD on a wide scale, including young children
> and children from minority backgrounds. These include several
> large-scale implementations in Iowa (the Heartland model; Tilly,
> 2002); the Minneapolis public schools (Marston, 2003);
> applications of the Screening to Enhance Equitable Placement
> (STEEP) model in Mississippi, Louisiana, and Arizona
> (VanDerHeyden, Witt, & Gilbertson, in press); and other examples
> (NASDSE, 2005). (*Federal Register*, August 14, 2006, p. 46647)

When viewed in the context of other long-standing evaluation procedure
requirements in the Act and regulations, these new provisions provide
unprecedented national policy validation and support for the concept of
RtI in the IDEA.

The 2004 IDEA reauthorization also contained language that intentionally aligned federal special education policy and accountability with
some key provisions of Public Law 107-15, the No Child Left Behind Act
of 2001 (Reauthorization of the Elementary and Secondary Education
Act). For example, the reauthorized IDEA stated that

> in making a determination of eligibility under paragraph (4) (A), a
> child shall not be determined to be a child with a disability if the
> determinant factor for such determination is—(A) lack of

appropriate instruction in reading, including the essential components of reading instruction (as defined in section 1208(3) of the Elementary and Secondary Education Act of 1965 [20 USCS § 6368(3)]). (20 USC 1414(b)(5)(A))

Though this particular provision addresses reading instruction, both No Child Left Behind (NCLB) and IDEA have now stated the expectation that evidence-based instructional approaches are to be used with all students. As a result of this policy imperative, the challenge for schools is to develop systems for ensuring efficient and effective delivery of these evidence-based practices and programs.

ESSENTIAL CONCEPTS AND FOUNDATIONS OF RtI SYSTEMS

Batsche et al. (2005) have defined RtI as "the practice of providing high-quality instruction and interventions matched to student need, monitoring progress frequently to make decisions about changes in instruction or goals and applying child response data to important educational decisions" (p. 3). Burns and Gibbons (2008) have defined RtI as "the practice of providing high quality instruction matched to student needs and using rate of learning over time to make important decisions" (p. 189). Clark et al. (2006) have defined RtI as "the application of the scientific method to solving educationally relevant problems. RtI is a framework for organizing evidenced-based practices in a systematic process for the purpose of determining what interventions enable learning." Brown-Chidsey and Steege (2005) define RtI as "an objective examination of the cause-effect relationship(s) between academic or behavioral intervention and the student's response to the intervention" (p. 2).

The themes of these definitions are evident in the following essential RtI components:

(1) *High-quality instruction/intervention.* This includes the use of evidence-based practices that enhance the probability of high learning rates.

(2) *Learning rate and level of performance.* This includes decisions about the type and intensity of instruction/interventions that are needed to ensure that students advance to desired levels of performance within acceptable periods of time.

(3) *Important educational decisions.* Learning rate and level of performance data are used in decisions about the level and intensity of instruction/interventions that are needed to ensure attainment of acceptable levels of performance. (Batsche, et al., 2005, pp. 5–6)

Also congruent with these definitions are the core principles of RtI proposed by Batsche et al. (2005):

1) We can effectively teach all children.
2) Intervene early.
3) Use a multi-tier model of service delivery.
4) Use a problem-solving method to make decisions within a multi-tier model.
5) Use evidence-based, scientifically validated interventions/instruction to the extent available.
6) Monitor student progress to inform instruction.
7) Use data to make decisions.
8) Use assessment for the purpose of screening, diagnostics, and progress monitoring. (pp. 19–20)

The definition of RtI along with these essential components and core principles is clearly consistent with the values of the social work profession. These elements are also consistent with established national school social work standards (National Association of Social Workers, 2002). For example, standard 12 states, "School social workers shall conduct assessments of student needs that are individualized and provide information that is directly useful for designing interventions that address behaviors of concern." Standard 13 states, "School social workers shall incorporate assessments in developing and implementing interventions and evaluation plans that enhance students' abilities to benefit from educational experiences." These standards set an expectation that school social workers will take an ecological perspective in conducting functional assessments that enhance the understanding of educationally relevant problems and that generate data that are useful in designing and implementing interventions. Interventions are expected to clearly identify outcome criteria and include methods for evaluating effectiveness. These are all practices integral to RtI.

OVERVIEW OF A THREE-TIERED SERVICE DELIVERY MODEL

Multitiered school-wide RtI models (typically three or four tiers) seem to be the most common organizational scheme used to efficiently deliver varying intensities of instructional supports and interventions that ensure the academic, social, emotional, and behavioral success of all students (Adelman & Taylor, 1998; Batsche et al., 2005; Sugai & Horner, 2006). The model proposed here is three-tiered (see Figure 1.1). This three-tiered system is structured to address academic and behavioral needs by differentiating supports and interventions using student performance data. The focus in this book is on the behavioral component of this system.

In Tier 1, universal, preventive, and proactive behavioral supports are provided to all students across all settings. These supports are provided to

Response to Intervention System

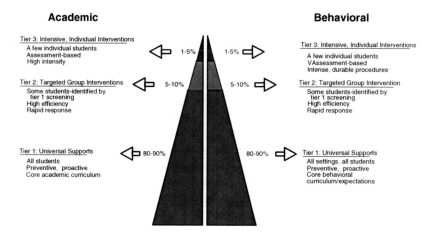

Figure 1.1   Response to intervention.

Source: Copyright 2002 by the National Association of School Psychologists, Bethesda, MD. Use is by permission of the publisher. www.nasponline.org. *Interventions for Academic and Behavior Problems II: Preventive and Remedial Approaches*, Chapter 12, School Environments, Figure 2, Continuum of Behavioral Support: Designing School-Wide Systems for Student Success (p. 320).

ensure that the behavioral competencies expected of all students are identified, taught, and reinforced. The concepts of curriculum, instruction, and assessment that comprise the academic component of the school's program are just as relevant to its behavioral component. Curriculum essentially defines *what* is taught, that is, what students will know and be able to do. Instruction is *how* the curriculum is taught, that is, the methods, approaches, and strategies used to teach the curriculum. Assessment is the data collection that is needed to determine whether the instruction has been effective, that is, whether the knowledge and skills identified in the curriculum have actually been acquired by students. In Tier 1 universal supports ensure that the behavioral curriculum, such as school-wide behavioral expectations, is clearly identified; that instruction is provided to ensure that this curriculum is taught to all students; and that assessment data are collected to determine which students have successfully acquired the behavioral knowledge and skills expected of all students as defined in the curriculum. Applying universal supports in this manner means that behavior is viewed as a matter of teaching and learning, just as it is in the academic components of the school's curriculum.

If instruction is minimally effective in Tier 1, assessment data will typically indicate that 80%–90% of students have acquired adequate levels of performance in the core behavioral curriculum. A continuous goal of building an effective school-wide system is to increase the percentage of students who are successful in the core curriculum while reducing the percentage of students requiring targeted group interventions and intensive individual interventions, as well as special education. The percentage of students successful in Tier 1 is an indicator of the quality of the core curriculum and the effectiveness of instruction.

Students who are not sufficiently benefiting from universal supports in Tier 1 are identified using screening procedures and are provided targeted group interventions in Tier 2. Typically, 5%–10% of students will require this level of intervention. This includes efficient, rapid response interventions typically provided to small groups of students with similar needs. While instruction becomes more intensified or differentiated in Tier 2, the focus continues to be on teaching the core curriculum/expectations that have been defined for all students. Assessment data are collected to determine which students have adequately benefited from targeted group interventions, which students have made progress, and which students will require even more individualized interventions in order to acquire the knowledge and skills identified in the core curriculum.

Tier 3 provides intensive, individual interventions to the 1%–5% of students who have not adequately benefited from universal supports in Tier 1 or targeted group interventions in Tier 2. Intensive individual interventions are also focused on the same behavioral knowledge and skills defined in the core curriculum/behavioral expectations. The design of intensive interventions is based on functional behavioral assessment data. Interventions are evidence-based and matched to the specific problem behavior. Progress is monitored directly and frequently, for example, hourly, daily, or weekly. Monitoring data are collected and displayed on graphs or charts. The need to modify interventions is based on decision rules applied to these data.

Some students may require special education, but decisions about eligibility are based on data generated from supports and interventions provided across the three tiers. If interventions are well designed, implemented, and documented, in many cases little if any additional evaluation data will be needed to make a special education eligibility decision. However, requiring intensive individualized interventions in Tier 3 does not in itself demonstrate special education eligibility (see Chapter 12).

The differential support and interventions provided to students across the tiers is continuously driven by screening and progress-monitoring data. Because decisions about matching evidence-based interventions to student needs are based on data, the tiers do not represent a linear process. Rather, they represent differentiated levels of intensity of supports and interventions that are needed to ensure success for all students. For example, a student who exhibits a sudden onset of intense problematic behavior in Tier 1 may immediately need intensive individualized interventions in Tier 3. Some students may be successful with the short-term application of Tier 2 targeted group interventions and return to universal supports in Tier 1.

PROBLEM SOLVING AND STANDARD PROTOCOL METHODOLOGIES

Two approaches or methodologies have been most frequently proposed for delivering supports and interventions in RtI systems: standard protocol and problem solving. Standard protocol approaches have typically been used for addressing academic problems, particularly with group interventions for reading (Vellutino et al., 1996; Torgesen et al., 2001). As these evidence-based standard treatments or protocols are often provided to groups of students, they can be a viable component of Tier 2 targeted group interventions.

Problem-solving methodology derives from the scientific method and includes four basic steps: (1) problem identification and definition, (2) problem analysis, (3) intervention plan development and implementation, and (4) evaluation of the plan's effectiveness (Clark, 1998; Tilly, 2002). Systematic use of this process is applied to decision making across the tiers and ensures that evidence-based practices and interventions are designed and implemented with integrity and monitored to ensure their effectiveness with individuals or groups of students. Problem-solving teams can coordinate the use of this process across the three tiers as well as with standard treatments for groups of students and interventions for individual students. However, the emphasis throughout this book will be on the use of problem solving as an overarching methodology for managing the efficient and effective delivery of supports and interventions across the three tiers.

CONCLUSIONS: CHALLENGES AND OPPORTUNITIES

RtI has a long and rich history and has been shaped over the past two decades by bold national policy initiatives; rigorous and penetrating research; innovative system change initiatives; and vigorous debate among practitioners, researchers, and policy makers. In many respects its merits are constantly being evaluated, spawning improvements in design and application that are incorporated into new iterations of changing delivery systems. As a result, its evolution continues.

For school social workers, RtI represents both significant change and many opportunities. It would not be accurate to assume that RtI is simply another framework within which school social workers can continue to practice in ways they have traditionally practiced. Social work practice has long purported to incorporate both science and art. RtI places great emphasis on the use of science by requiring the identification and use of evidence-based practices and the application of the scientific method in a problem-solving process. For most school social workers the demand for incorporating a greater degree of science into practice will be a challenge to traditional ways of working. Opportunities await for school social workers to take on leadership roles in designing, implementing, and evaluating RtI systems by drawing on ecological and systems theory concepts. The ultimate challenge will be to artfully apply scientific knowledge to improve the helping system of schools. Chapters that follow will provide many details about how to operationalize the overview of the three-tiered model introduced here.

REFERENCES

Aaron, P. G. (1997). The impending demise of the discrepancy formula. *Review of Educational Research, 67,* 461–502.

Adelman, H. S., & Taylor, L. (1998). Reframing mental health in schools and expanding school reform. *Educational Psychologist, 33*(4), 135–152.

Batsche, G., Elliott, J., Graden, J. L., Grimes, J., Kovaleski, J. F., Prasse, D., Reschly, D. J., Schrag, J., & Tilly, W. D. (2005). *Response to intervention: Policy considerations and implementation.* Alexandria, VA: National Association of State Directors of Special Education.

Brown-Chidsey, R., & Steege, M. W. (2005). *Response to intervention: Principles and strategies for effective practice.* New York: Guilford Press.

Burns, M. K., & Gibbons, K. (2008). *Implementing response-to-intervention in elementary and secondary schools.* New York: Routledge Taylor and Francis Group.

Carr, E. G., Dunlap, G., Horner, R. H., Koegel, R. L., Turnbull, A. P., Sailor, W., Anderson, J. L., Albin, R. W., Koegel, L. K., & Fox, L. (2002). Positive behavior support: Evolution of an applied science. *Journal of Positive Behavior Interventions, 4*(1), 4–16.

Clark, J. P. (1998). Functional behavioral assessment and behavioral intervention plans: Implementing the student discipline provisions of IDEA '97. *Section Connection, 4*(2), 6–7.

Clark, J. P., Cunconnun, R., & Riesen, Y. (1989, October). *Promoting meaningful parent involvement in the renewed service delivery system.* Des Moines: Iowa Department of Education.

Clark, J. P., & Thiede, C. (2007). School social work practice with students with disabilities. In L. Bye & M. Alvarez (Eds.), *School social work: Theory to practice* (261–285). Belmont, CA: Thomson Brooks/Cole.

Clark, J. P., Tilly, D. W., Atkinson, P. J., & Flugum, K. R. (1992). *Building assistance teams: Interventions and outcomes.* Research Report #22. Des Moines: Iowa Department of Education.

Clark, J. P., Timm, A., Gilmore, J., & Dedic, B. (2006, March 30). *Response to intervention: A problem-solving approach to enabling learning.* Paper presented at the 100th Anniversary of School Social Work Conference sponsored by the School Social Work Association of America, Boston, MA.

Grimes, J., Kurns, S., & Tilly, W. D. III. (2006). Sustainability: An enduring commitment to success. *School Psychology Review, 35*(2), 224–244.

Heller, K. A., Holtzman, W. H., & Messick, S. (Eds.). (1982). *Placing children in special education: A strategy for equity.* Washington, DC: National Academy Press.

Iowa Department of Education. (1995). *Administrative rules of special education.* Des Moines, IA: Iowa Department of Education.

Iowa Department of Education. (2006). *Special education eligibility standards.* Des Moines, IA: Iowa Department of Education.

Macmann, G. M., Barnett, D. W., Lombard, T. J., Belton-Kocher, E., & Sharpe, M. N. (1989). On the actuarial classification of children: Fundamental studies of classification agreement. *Journal of Special Education, 23*, 127–149.

MacMillan, D. L., Gresham, F. M., & Bocian, K. M. (1998). Discrepancy between definitions of learning disabilities and school practices: An empirical investigation. *Journal of Learning Disabilities, 31*, 314–326.

Marston, D. (2001, August 28). *A functional and intervention-based assessment approach to establishing discrepancy for students with learning disabilities.* Paper presented at Learning Disabilities Summit, Washington, DC.

Marston, D., Muyskens, P., Lau, M., & Canter, A. (2003). Problem-solving model for decision-making with high incidence disabilities: The Minneapolis experience. *Learning Disabilities Research and Practice, 18*(3), 187–200.

National Association of Social Workers. (2002). *NASW standards for school social work services.* Washington, DC: Author.

Reschly, D.A., & Starkweather, A. (1997). *Evaluation of an alternative special education assessment and classification program in the Minneapolis Public Schools.* Ames: Iowa State University.

Reynolds, M. C., Wang, M. C., & Walberg, H. J. (1987). The necessary restructuring of special and general education. *Exceptional Children, 53*(5), 391–398.

Sailor, W., Anderson, J. L., Halvorsen, A. T., Doering, K., Filler, J., & Goets, L. (1989). *The comprehensive local school: Regular education for all students with disabilities.* Baltimore: Paul H. Brookes.

Stainback, W., & Stainback, S. (1984). A rationale for the merger of special and general education. *Exceptional Children, 51*(2), 102–111.

Sugai, G., & Horner, R. (2006). A promising approach for expanding and sustaining school-wide positive behavior support. *School Psychology Review, 35*(2), 245–259.

Tilly W. D. III. (2002). School psychology as a problem solving enterprise. In A. Thomas & J. Grimes (Eds.), *Best practices in school psychology IV* (pp. 25–36). Bethesda, MD: National Association of School Psychologists.

Tilly W. D. III, Grimes, J., & Reschly, D. J. (1993, September–December). Special education system reform: The Iowa story. *Communique*, pp. 18–19.

Tilly W. D. III, & Flugum, K. R. (1995). Ensuring quality interventions. In A. Thomas & J. Grimes (Eds.), *Best practices in school psychology* (3rd ed., pp. 485–500). Washington, DC: National Association of School Psychologists.

Tilly, W. D. III, Kovaleski, J., Dunlap, G., Knoster, T. P., Bambara, L., & Kincaid, D. (1998). *Functional behavioral assessment: Policy development in light of emerging research and practice.* Alexandria, VA: National Association of State Directors of Special Education.

Torgesen, J. K., Alexander, A. W., Wagner, R. K., Rashotte, C. A., Voeller, K. S., & Conway, T. (2001). Intensive remedial instruction for children with severe reading disabilities: Immediate and long-term outcomes from two instructional approaches. *Journal of Learning Disabilities, 34*, 33–58.

U.S. Department of Education, Office of Special Education and Rehabilitative Services. (2002). *A new era: Revitalizing special education for children and their families.* Washington, DC: Author.

Vellutino, F. R., Scanlon, D., Sipay, E., Small, S., Pratt, A., Chen, R., & Denkla, M. (1996). Cognitive profiles of difficult to remediate and readily remediated poor readers: Early intervention as a vehicle for distinguishing between cognitive and experiential deficits as basic causes of specific reading disability. *Journal of Educational Psychology, 88,* 601–638.

Wang, M. C., Reynolds, M. C., & Walberg, H. J. (1986). Rethinking special education. *Educational Leadership, 44*(1), 26–31.

Will, M. (1986). Educating children with learning problems: A shared responsibility. *Exceptional Children, 53,* 411–415.

SECTION I

Tier 1 Universal Supports

Figure I.1[a]

In Tier 1 universal behavioral supports are provided to all students across all settings. These supports are designed to be preventive and proactive, and to ensure that the behavioral competencies expected of all students are identified, taught, and reinforced. Behavior is viewed as a matter of teaching and learning just as it is in the academic components of the school's curriculum.

This section includes a chapter that describes the essential components of implementing universal supports in Tier 1, two chapters that provide examples of school-wide behavior screening tools that can be used to determine the effectiveness of these supports, and a case example illustrating the implementation of a Tier 1 school-wide program. In Chapter 2, Braaksma Fynaardt and Richardson present a comprehensive description of the critical features of universal supports. They identify the critical components for implementing these supports along with the knowledge and skills school social workers need to actively participate in implementation. The use of two school-wide behavior screening tools is illustrated in Chapters 3 and 4. In Chapter 3 Pierson and Dedic describe the recently developed School-Wide Efficient Behavior Screening (SWEBS), and in Chapter 4, Coble Lindsey and White identify behavior screening implementation issues and describe the use of the School-Wide Information System (SWIS), a Web-based system used to analyze office discipline referral information. In Chapter 5 Gianesin describes the implementation of the Signs of Suicide (SOS) program as a Tier 1 school-wide suicide prevention program.

2

TIER 1
UNIVERSAL SUPPORTS

ANGELISA BRAAKSMA FYNAARDT & JOHN RICHARDSON

The mission of our educational system is to produce students who are academically and socially competent and prepared for a productive adulthood. Administrators and teachers are facing increased demands and accountability measures. Schools need to increase students' academic achievement, maintain high levels of daily student attendance, and increase the number of students graduating from high school. Schools are also focused on decreasing the incidence of suspensions and expulsions and dropout rates. School staff members are being asked to achieve these tasks in the face of changing student demographics, multiple competing initiatives, and decreasing resources. Response to Intervention (RtI) is an approach that allows schools to efficiently and effectively use resources to meet the needs of a variety of students. This chapter provides the identification of the critical features of the universal level of RtI for social-emotional-behavioral development along with the critical components for implementation of Tier 1.

TIER 1 DEFINITION AND DESCRIPTION

At the universal level of RtI, procedures to address school-wide social-behavioral issues and a system to support academic and social success must be developed and implemented for all students. Preventive and proactive behavioral supports are provided to all students across all settings within a school. To meet the needs of all students, Tier 1 universal supports must

21

address several critical features within the school-wide setting. The key hallmarks of Tier 1 supports are the development of processes and procedures to (1) establish clear and consistent school-wide social-emotional-behavioral expectations, (2) teach the school-wide expectations to all students, (3) acknowledge students for demonstrating the expected behaviors, (4) develop clear and consistent response to behavioral violations, and (5) use data to evaluate the impact of school-wide efforts (Colvin, Kameenui, & Sugai, 1993; Lewis & Sugai, 1999; Office of Special Education Programs, 2004; Oswald, Safran, & Johanson, 2005).

Defined Expectations

The first critical features in implementing RtI for behavior is to clearly articulate the expected behaviors and social skills required for students to be successful. Just as the expected skills sets are identified for academic content areas through standards and benchmarks, the expected behaviors and skills must be defined within the domain of social-emotional-behavioral skills. This process can take various forms within the school setting. Some schools may have identified standards and benchmarks for social domains (e.g., standards and benchmarks for guidance counselors). Others may have skills sets identified by the social skills program used to teach all students appropriate social-emotional skills. For example, Providing Alternative THinking Strategies (PATHS) has an identified scope and sequence of skills and corresponding instructional lessons to use with all students (Kusche & Greenberg, 1994).

A team of school-based personnel is responsible for defining behavioral expectations in the framework of positive behavior supports (PBS), one of the best-articulated models of RtI for behavior (Horner, Sugai, & Horner, 2000; Safran & Oswald, 2003; Sugai & Horner, 2006; Turnbull et al., 2002). The team identifies three to five broad, school-wide expectations that apply to all students in all locations (e.g., be respectful, be responsible, and be safe). School-wide expectations should be positively stated as opposed to a list of negative rules (e.g., don't hit, don't run, don't spit). The intent of the positive focus is it to shift the role of staff members from policing students and delivering punishment for behavioral infractions to being supportive encouragers of expected behaviors. The school-wide expectations should be posted in multiple areas throughout the school (e.g., classrooms, hallways, cafeteria).

Teaching Expected Behaviors

The second critical feature of RtI for behavior is to teach the expected behaviors and specific social skills to all students. The broadly stated behavioral expectations and/or standards and benchmarks need to be further defined as specific, observable behaviors. In the PBS framework, the team is primarily responsible for identifying specific, observable behaviors that correspond to each of the three to five school-wide behavioral expectations for

		School-Wide Behavioral Expectations		
		Be Responsible	Be Respectful	Be Safe
Locations	Classroom	• Bring materials for class • Turn in homework	• Raise hand to speak • Listen to speaker	• Walk • Keep hands and feet to self
	Hallway	• Pick up trash and throw away	• Use quiet voices • Open & close locker doors quietly	• Walk • Keep hands and feet to self
	Cafeteria	• Put tray, utensils, and garbage in appropriate locations • Clean up spills	• Use quiet voices • Say please and thank you	• Use eating utensils as intended • Walk • Keep hands and feet to self

Figure 2.1   Sample teaching matrix.

each location in the school. For example, "be safe" in the classroom may be defined as following teacher directions. The same expectations in the hallway may be defined as using "walking feet." School staff may use a teaching matrix (Sugai et al., 2005) to assist with defining specific behavioral examples of the expectations. For each location-expectation combination on the matrix, school personnel should identify the best example of the expectation in the location and an example that addresses the most problematic behavior in that location. The matrix may then be used to guide instruction. See Figure 2.1 as an example of a completed teaching matrix.

If schools have identified standards and benchmarks for the social content domain, the administrator or a group of school staff members needs to ensure that specific behaviors or skills sets are also identified. For example, the state of Illinois has identified one of their social learning standards as "Use communication and social skills to interact effectively with others." This learning standard has been further defined for early elementary students as "Identify ways to work and play well with others and demonstrate appropriate social and classroom behavior" (Illinois State Board of Education, 2007). In this example, the benchmarks or subskills for this learning standard would need to be more clearly delineated for staff members to understand the specific and observable behaviors that correspond to the learning standard, to provide explicit instruction to all students, and to provide appropriate consequences for the behaviors. School staff may find it useful to use a matrix similar to the teaching matrix identified within PBS to clearly identify the social-emotional standards or benchmarks and the corresponding specific skills expected of all students.

Once specific behaviors or social skills are identified, the skills must be taught to students in the school. Just as all students in the school should receive academic instruction, all students should receive instruction to enhance their social-emotional-behavioral skills. The instruction should be direct and explicit, following a similar format as direct instruction for academics. The direct instruction format should include the steps of (1) defining the skill, (2) modeling the skill, (3) providing opportunities for guided and independent practice of the skill, and (4) supporting ongoing practice and maintenance of the skill (Heartland Area Education Agency, 2008; Horner, Sugai, Lewis-Palmer, & Todd, 2001; Kame'enui & Carnine, 1998; Langland, Lewis-Palmer, & Sugai, 1998; Sugai, 1992). The instructor should first identify the school-wide expectation(s) or concept(s) being taught. Often the rationale for the skill should also be provided to students. For example, "Today we are going to learn about being respectful in the hallway. Being respectful means that you are considerate of others. It is important to be respectful in the hallway because other students are in class and trying to learn."

Instruction should include modeling of the expected behaviors or social skills (Heartland Area Education Agency, 2008; Horner et al., 2001; Kame'enui & Carnine, 1998; Langland, Lewis-Palmer, & Sugai, 1998; Sugai, 1992). The behavior examples modeled in the lessons are taken from the expectations-setting matrix developed within the PBS framework. If a site is not implementing PBS, specific examples of the social-emotional-behavioral skills will need to be identified and included as examples of expected behaviors in the instructional lessons. Students should also see nonexamples of the expected behaviors during the lesson so that they learn to discriminate between acceptable and unacceptable behaviors.

Once the teacher has taught and modeled the expected skills, the students should be given an opportunity to practice the expected behaviors. The teacher should facilitate guided practice and independent practice of the social skills and/or expected behaviors. The teacher should also provide corrective feedback to remediate errors and acknowledgment to reinforce the demonstration of the expected behaviors. Practice opportunities should be repeated over an extended period of time to ensure mastery of the skills and automaticity in demonstrating the behaviors.

Once students have been given multiple practice opportunities, the instructor should be monitoring student performance during real life scenarios. The teacher should assess student performance to ensure mastery and maintenance of the expected behaviors and social skills. If the students have not mastered the expected skills, the teacher should provide additional instruction and/or practice until the students can fluently demonstrate the expected competencies.

Developing an Acknowledgment System

Once students have been taught the behavioral expectations, they need to be acknowledged for demonstrating the expected behaviors. The Tier 1 system should include a positive reinforcement system to "catch" students behaving appropriately so as to establish and maintain desired behaviors. The school staff should determine the type and frequency of rewards that will be provided to students. The developmental level of the students should be taken into consideration as the acknowledgment system is created. For example, it may be appropriate for a kindergarten student to earn stickers as a reward. However, high school students would typically not be interested in earning stickers. High school students are more interested in earning things like a special parking spot or tickets to the football game or dance. The types of rewards available should match the developmental age of the students. The acknowledgment system may include a variety of rewards (e.g., access to preferred activities, social recognition, school-wide celebrations) and may be delivered to individual students, groups of students, classrooms, grade levels, or all students in the school. It is often beneficial to include students in the process of determining the available rewards, particularly at the secondary grade levels.

Regardless of the rewards chosen, the system must be easy and efficient for all staff members to use. All staff should be acknowledging students for demonstrating expected, appropriate behaviors and/or social skills. It is important to ensure that staff members are delivering the reinforcement contingent upon specific student behaviors and that staff members are providing verbal feedback along with the given reward. For example, Mrs. Smith is handing out STAR tickets when students demonstrate expected behaviors. She is focusing on increasing the rate at which students raise their hands to be called upon during instruction. Mrs. Smith would hand the STAR tickets to students when she sees them raise their hands to participate and would provide specific verbal feedback paired with the STAR ticket. The verbal feedback should be specific and should refer to the expected school behavior(s).

Developing the Consequence System

The fourth component of the Tier 1 level of RtI is the development and implementation of a corrective consequence system. Although the intention of the universal levels of supports is to design an environment that elicits appropriate behaviors and prevents problem behaviors, some students will continue to demonstrate problem behaviors at school. A system must be put into place that provides students with corrective consequences for demonstrating behavioral errors. The consequence or discipline system should clearly identify staff responses for behavioral infractions. School staff may consider grouping behaviors with similar severity levels or similar impact on the classroom environment to create a leveled consequence system. The team may then identify consequence options for each group of behaviors, ensuring that the intensity of the consequence options matches the intensity and severity of the behaviors. Figure 2.2 is an example of an elementary school's leveling system.

Level 1 Behaviors	Level 2 Behaviors	Level 3 Behaviors
Noncompliance Disruption of instruction Disrespect Minor destruction of property	Physical aggression Harassment Abusive language	Major destruction of property Theft Alcohol or drugs Weapons
Level 1 Possible Consequences	**Level 2 Possible Consequences**	**Level 3 Possible Consequences**
Student conference Verbal warning Parent contact Loss of recess Loss of privilege Restitution or apology Overcorrection	Level 1 consequences Behavior contract Administration, parent, student, teacher conference In-school suspension Out-of-school suspension Bus suspension	Level 2 consequences In-school suspension Out-of-school suspension Bus suspension Contact law enforcement Expulsion
<u>MANDATORY</u> 1st & 2nd offense – Staff administers consequence 3rd offense – Complete minor discipline report; staff administers consequence 4th offense – Complete major discipline report and send to office; principal administers consequence	<u>MANDATORY</u> Complete major discipline report and send form to office; principal administers consequence	<u>MANDATORY</u> Complete major discipline report and send student and form to office; principal administers consequence

Figure 2.2   Example of consequence level system.

Given the focus on instruction within an RtI model, the consequences provided for problem behaviors should include a teaching component. The teaching component may range from reminding the student of the social-emotional-behavioral expectation to actually reteaching and practicing the expected behavior(s) in the actual location(s) in the school. Regardless of the types of consequences, the system should be easy for staff to use, and all staff members should consistently use the system.

Along with identifying staff response to behavioral infractions, the team will need to identify when and how staff members will document inappropriate behaviors. One of the primary data sources within the Tier 1 level of RtI is behavior incident data or discipline data. Information collected about the behavioral incident should include date and time of the incident, student's name and grade, classroom teacher's name, referring person's name, location of the incident, and consequence given. Some schools also choose to identify the potential function of the student's behavior on the referral form. These data should be entered into a database and should be used by the team to guide decision making about program effectiveness. More information will be provided in the following section about using behavior incident data.

Using Data

IMPLEMENTATION INTEGRITY   Data should be collected regarding the implementation integrity of the school-wide system and the impact of the school-wide system on student outcomes. The School-wide Evaluation Tool (SET) is an example of an integrity assessment that addresses the implementation of the universal system within PBS. The SET measures the level of implementation in seven areas: behavioral expectations defined, behavioral expectations taught, behavioral expectations rewarded, systematic response to rule violations, information gathered to monitor student behavior, local management support for school-wide procedures, and district-level support for school-wide procedures (Horner et al., 2004). School personnel should use the results of implementation integrity assessments to monitor the overall level of implementation of the universal prevention system over time and to identify needed areas of improvement.

OUTCOME ASSESSMENT   A comprehensive evaluation plan will include an evaluation of the impact of Tier 1 supports for student social-emotional-behavioral development. Behavior incident or discipline data are an efficient, effective, and naturally occurring way to monitor the impact of the universal system upon student performance. Behavior incident data should be entered into a data system on a regular basis (see Chapters 3 and 4 for examples illustrating the use of data systems). Analysis of the data should be readily available for decision making and should be available in graphic format to allow for the visual analysis of the data. One example of an efficient data system for housing office referral data is the School-Wide Information System (SWIS), available at www.swis.org.

School personnel should regularly review the behavior incident data to determine whether changes need to be made to the school-wide universal system. Behavior incident data may be analyzed regularly to look for trends or patterns. For example, school personnel may use the data to examine the types of problem behaviors being demonstrated, the locations of the problem behaviors, or problematic times throughout the school day. Regularly reviewing the data allows the team to use behavior incident data as a formative analysis tool. An in-depth analysis of these data can help the team determine why a targeted problem may be occurring and assist in developing potential solutions. The use of data in this manner allows for the system to be self-correcting and and ever-evolving.

Behavior incident data should also be reviewed at the end of the year as a summative evaluation measure. End of the year behavior incident data may be used to determine the overall impact of the universal system for the current school year as well as the impact of the universal system over time (e.g., total number of behavior incidents this school year as compared to previous years). Research has shown that schools that implement universal supports for all students experience decreases in the number of behavioral infractions and improved school safety (DePry & Sugai, 2002; Lewis, Colvin, & Sugai, 2000; Lewis, Sugai, & Colvin, 1998; Luiselli, Putnam, & Sunderland, 2002; Mayer, Butterworth, Nafpaktitis, & Suzer-Azaroff, 1983; Nelson, Colvin, & Smith, 1996; Nelson, Martella, & Galand, 1998).

Administrators and school staff members should consider using additional school-wide data to determine the impact of Tier 1 supports on student outcomes. They may want to consider examining the impact of universal instruction and supports upon attendance rates, incidence of suspensions and expulsions, and the number of students who drop out of school. The team may also want to examine the impact of the Tier 1 system on academic achievement. Research is beginning to demonstrate that schools implementing proactive behavioral instruction for all students see decreases in problem behaviors along with increases in academic achievement (Lassen, Steele, & Sailor, 2006; Luiselli, Putnam, Handler, & Feinberg, 2005; Sugai et al., 2005). In addition, schools that are using an RtI approach for academics see larger improvements in academics when academic interventions are combined with positive behavioral support systems (McIntosh, Chard, Boland, & Horner, 2006).

STUDENT IDENTIFICATION   Data may also be used to identify the students who may need more support beyond the level of instruction provided in Tier 1. Schools may use behavior incident data as one screening assessment. A school may identify specific criteria at which a student is targeted as needing additional supports beyond universal instruction and supports. For example, a school may set the criterion for identifying students in need of potential support as any student with four behavior incidents that resulted in the student's being sent to the office for an administrative consequence. Social skills assessments may also be used to identify students who need more support beyond Tier 1. For example, staff may choose to use the Systematic Screening for Behavior Disorders (SSBD; Walker & Severson, 1992) or the School Social Behavior Skills assessment (Merrell, 1993) to identify students in need of additional support beyond universal instruction.

HOW DOES TIER 1 FIT IN THE STRUCTURE OF RtI?

Response to Intervention focuses on providing the instruction and supports necessary for students to achieve socially important outcomes. Applied to academics, RtI is designed to identify and provide the instruction needed to increase every individual student's academic achievement. For social-emotional-behavioral development, RtI also focuses on meaningful outcomes. One intended outcome of the development and implementation of Tier 1 supports is that students learn the social-emotional-behavioral skills necessary to navigate their way through the educational system. Another goal is for students to learn the skills needed to function effectively in social situations and working environments as adults. Providing a broad base of social-emotional-behavioral instruction allows for the development of multiple social competencies to help the majority of students become socially competent, successful adults.

Another key feature of RtI is the use of evidence-based instruction. The universal system of RtI for behavior focuses foremost on the development of core social-emotional-behavioral expectations for all students along with corresponding instruction. Tier 1 supports include direct and explicit instruction on school-wide expectations. Unlike academics, school systems do not always focus on behavioral instruction for all students. For example, some school staff members may simply read the list of rules to students or hand out a school discipline policy as the form of "behavioral instruction" provided to all students. The Tier 1 universal supports place a priority on behavioral instruction equal to that placed on academic instruction. It is this instruction that allows the system to focus on the acquisition of appropriate skills and the creation of a school environment that elicits expected behaviors and focuses on the prevention of problem behaviors.

One hallmark of RtI is to use data to identify the effectiveness of universal instruction and to identify those students who may need more support to be successful in the school setting. The primary data source for evaluating the effectiveness of universal instruction is behavior incident reports or discipline referrals. However, a complete RtI system for behavior uses multiple sources of data to evaluate the overall effectiveness of the universal instruction provided to all students. An evaluation system focuses on decreasing incidents of behavior problems while increasing academic engaged time and academic achievement.

KEY CONSIDERATIONS FOR IMPLEMENTATION

Administrative Participation and Support

Administrators must be actively involved and supportive for the universal level of supports to be implemented successfully in the school setting. The administrator needs to provide the leadership necessary to develop and implement universal behavior instruction and supports for all students. This administrator must believe in the importance of instruction on social-emotional-behavioral skills and be willing to dedicate the resources needed to provide instruction to all students. The implementation of the universal system has implications for discipline practices in the school setting. The administrator will be impacted and needs to consistently use the discipline practices identified in the universal system. In addition, the administrator needs to hold staff members accountable for using the practices and procedures identified in the universal system for behavior.

Staff Consensus

The second key consideration for implementing Tier 1 universal behavior supports is staff consensus. In developing and implementing Tier 1 supports for behavior, one is potentially identifying alternate procedures and practices adults will have to use every day with every student in the school. The system first focuses on changing adult behaviors before impacting student behaviors. It is important for the administrator or team responsible for developing the universal system to seek staff consensus to support the implementation of universal practices and procedures. Sugai et al. (2005) recommends having a minimum of 80% of staff willing to support the implementation of school-wide PBS procedures. Without staff consensus for Tier 1, the implementation of the universal system will not be consistent across staff members and will not lead to the desired outcomes for all students.

A team may employ different strategies to support the development of consensus for Tier 1. Consensus levels may be increased through sharing information. First, the team should provide basic information about Tier 1 for staff members. In addition, the team should clearly articulate for staff members the rationale for Tier 1, why the school needs the universal system, the potential benefits for the school, the potential benefits for students, and the potential personal benefits for staff members. The team should also consider sharing with staff members research articles or data related to the actual implementation of Tier 1 and corresponding outcomes. Last, it is often beneficial for staff members to visit sites that are currently implementing universal instruction and supports to learn about actual implementation and the effort required for implementation of universal instruction and supports.

Another strategy used to gain consensus is to identify various ways for staff members to ask questions and provide feedback. It is crucial for staff members to be able to ask questions freely about Tier 1 and receive answers quickly. All staff members may not feel comfortable asking a team member questions. In this situation, the team needs to identify a way for a staff member to ask his or her question anonymously and receive an answer.

Consensus is also improved when staff members are able to provide input and feedback during the development stage of the universal system. As the team is developing Tier 1, they should take drafts of the various products and processes to staff members to gain their feedback. Once the feedback is received, the team may modify products or processes if necessary prior to implementation. This opportunity for staff members to impact the development of Tier 1 supports the development of consensus.

Professional Development

The administrator or team responsible for developing the universal system will need professional development on the best practices in implementing Tier 1 supports for behavior. They will need to learn new content and will need time to actually develop the system and determine how best practices can be implemented within the context of the current school setting. In addition to the administrator and leadership team, all staff members in a building will need professional development on the expected school-wide procedures and practices. Staff will need to learn about school-wide expectations, how to provide explicit instruction on expectations, and when instruction will be provided to all students. Staff will also need to learn about the corrective consequence system and how to complete discipline incident reports. Last, the team and/or staff will need professional development on how to use the school-wide data to evaluate the effectiveness of the universal system and identify students who may be in need of more supports.

Resources

The last key feature for implementing the universal system of RtI for behavior is resources. Staff will need to have the tangible resources necessary to implement the universal system. Staff will need a method to post expectations in multiple school locations, like access to posters or paint. To provide instruction, staff will need access to social skills curriculum and/or instructional lesson plans and additional materials needed to provide the instruction. Discipline referral forms or behavior incident reports are another resource required by staff members. Also, the leadership team and/or school staff members will need access to a data system to store and analyze the discipline data.

Time is another critical resource for the implementation of RtI universal supports. Staff will need time to develop the universal system and to learn about it. Instructional time will also need to be identified. Staff will need instructional time dedicated to providing social-emotional-behavioral instruction to all students in a regular and ongoing way throughout the school year.

KNOWLEDGE AND SKILLS NEEDED BY SCHOOL SOCIAL WORKERS

Knowledge of the Key Features of Positive Behavior Support

School social workers will need to become familiar with the key features of universal supports for behavior. They also need to become adept at explaining the key features of the universal system to school staff members and at facilitating the development and implementation process. School social workers should also be aware of implementation examples to know what the best practices look like when actually implemented in a school setting.

Knowledge of Social Skills Assessments and Instruction

School social workers are given a unique opportunity to share their knowledge of social skills assessment and instruction in an RtI system. In Tier 1, social skills assessments may be used as a screening assessment for all students. Social workers may be able to provide support to school staff to identify potential and appropriate assessments by sharing their knowledge and expertise. In addition, they may be essential in analyzing and interpreting the results of the social skills assessments and in identifying supports for students. School social workers should also have experience in providing social skills instruction to students in individual or small group settings. Their knowledge of best practices in providing social skills instruction can be expanded to providing instruction to all students on expected behaviors.

Ability to Understand, Analyze, and Use System-Wide Data

School social workers will need to become aware of the data sources used within the universal system for social-emotional-behavioral support. They must be aware of sources of outcome data as well as implementation assessments. Social workers must also be able to analyze the various data sources so they can evaluate the effectiveness of the universal system as well as identify areas of need. School social workers will need the abilities to present data in a visual manner (e.g., graph format), to clearly explain results, and to use data to guide instructional decisions in order to implement and support RtI Tier 1 practices.

Ability to Work with a Team and Get Along with Others

Last, school social workers will need to be able to work collaboratively with others. It is best and most efficient to have a team of school staff work together to develop and implement the components of Tier 1, and the school social worker is a valuable member of such a team. In this role, the school social worker must be able to model appropriate teaming behaviors. He or she also brings specific content knowledge of behavior as a resource for the team. Therefore, the social worker must be able to balance the expectations of sharing content knowledge or expertise along with listening to others and doing the work. The social worker should also be able to communicate effectively with a wide variety of people on the team and within the school. It is through this collaborative, collective effort that universal supports are best developed, implemented, and sustained.

CHAPTER SUMMARY AND CONCLUSIONS

RtI provides an effective framework for designing and implementing a continuum of supports to meet the social-emotional-behavioral needs of all students in a school setting. In particular, universal supports allow a school system to create an environment that promotes appropriate behaviors through explicit instruction for all students. It includes defining and teaching school-wide expectations, using an acknowledgment system to recognize students who demonstrate expected behaviors, and employing the use of a consistent corrective consequence system. In addition, the universal system includes the collection, analysis, and use of data. It is through the development and implementation of Tier 1 that schools may build a foundation of skills for all students and for Tier 2 and 3 interventions.

REFERENCES

Colvin, G., Kameenui, E. J., & Sugai, G. (1993). Reconceptualizing behavior management and school-wide discipline in general education. *Education and Treatment of Children, 16*(4), 361–381.

DePry, R. L., & Sugai, G. (2002). The effect of active supervision and precorrection on minor behavioral incidents in a sixth grade general education classroom. *Journal of Behavioral Education, 11*, 255–267.

Heartland Area Education Agency. (2008). *Applying effective strategies to social skills assessment and instruction.* Johnston, IA: Heartland Area Education Agency.

Horner, R. H., Sugai, G., & Horner, H. F. (2000, February). A schoolwide approach to student discipline: An alternative to get-tough measures that shows promise for dealing with disruptive students with disabilities. *The School Administrator*, 20–23.

Horner, R. H., Sugai, G., Lewis-Palmer, T., & Todd, A. W. (2001, Fall). Teaching school-wide behavioral expectations. *Emotional and Behavioral Disorders in Youth*, 77–96.

Horner, R. H., Todd, A. W., Lewis-Palmer, T., Irvin, L. K., Sugai, G., & Boland, J. B. (2004). The school-wide evaluation tool (SET): A research instrument for assessing school-wide positive behavior support. *Journal of Positive Behavior Interventions, 6*(1), 3–12.

Illinois State Board of Education. (2007). *Illinois learning standards: Social/emotional learning.* Retrieved August 15, 2008, from http://www.isbe.state.il.us/ils/social_emotional/standards.htm.

Kame'enui, E. J., & Carnine, D. W. (1998). *Effective teaching strategies that accommodate diverse learners.* Upper Saddle River, NJ: Prentice Hall.

Kusche, C. A., & Greenberg, M. T. (1994). *The PATHS Curriculum.* Seattle: Developmental Research and Programs.

Langland, S., Lewis-Palmer, T., & Sugai, G. (1998). Teaching respect in the classroom: An instructional approach. *Journal of Behavioral Education, 8*(2), 245–262.

Lassen, S. R., Steele, M. M., & Sailor, W. (2006). The relationship of school-wide positive behavior support to academic achievement in an urban middle school. *Psychology in the Schools, 43*(6), 701–712.

Lewis, T. J., Colvin, G., & Sugai, G. (2000). The effects of precorrection and active supervision on the recess behavior of elementary school students. *Education and Treatment of Children, 23*, 109–121.

Lewis, T. J., & Sugai, G. (1999). Effective behavior support: A systems approach to proactive schoolwide management. *Focus on Exceptional Children, 31*(6), 1–24.

Lewis, T. J., Sugai, G., & Colvin, G. (1998). Reducing problem behavior through a school-wide system of effective behavioral support: Investigation of a school-wide social skills training program and contextual interventions. *School Psychology Review, 27*(3), 446–459.

Luiselli, J. K., Putnam, R. F., Handler, M. W., & Feinberg, A. B. (2005). Whole-school positive behaviour support: Effects on student discipline problems and academic performance. *Educational Psychology, 25*(2–3), 183–198.

Luiselli, J., Putnam, R., & Sunderland, M. (2002). Longitudinal evaluation of behavior support interventions in public middle school. *Journal of Positive Behavior Interventions, 4*(3), 182–188.

Mayer, G. R., Butterworth, T., Nafpaktitis, M., & Suzer-Azaroff, B. (1983). Preventing school vandalism and improving discipline: A three year study. *Journal of Applied Behavior Analysis, 16*, 355–369.

McIntosh, K., Chard, D.J., Boland, J. B., & Horner, R. H. (2006). Demonstration of combined efforts in school-wide academic and behavioral systems and incidence of reading and behavior challenges in early elementary grades. *Journal of Positive Behavioral Interventions, 8*, 146–154.

Merrell, K. W. (1993). Using behavior rating scales to assess social skills and antisocial behavior in school settings: Development of the school social behavior scales. *School Psychology Review, 22*(1), 115–133.

Nelson, J. R., Colvin, G., & Smith, D. J. (1996, Summer/Fall). The effects of setting clear standards on students' social behavior in common areas of the school. *Journal of At-Risk Issues*, 10–17.

Nelson, J. R., Martella, R., & Galand, B. (1998). The effects of teaching school expectations and establishing a consistent consequence on formal office disciplinary actions. *Journal of Emotional and Behavioral Disorders, 6*, 153–161.

Office of Special Education Programs, Center on Positive Behavioral Interventions and Supports. (2004). *School-wide positive behavior support implementers' blueprint and self-assessment.* Eugene: University of Oregon.

Oswald, K., Safran, S., & Johanson, G. (2005). Preventing trouble: Making schools safer places using positive behavior supports. *Education and Treatment of Children, 28*(3), 265–278.

Safran, S. P., & Oswald, K. (2003). Positive behavior supports: Can schools reshape disciplinary practices? *Exceptional Children, 69*(3), 361–373.

Sugai, G. (1992). Instructional design: Applications of teaching social behavior. *Learning Disabilities Forum, 17*, 20–23.

Sugai, G., & Horner, R. H. (2006). A promising approach for expanding and sustaining school-wide positive behavior support. *School Psychology Review, 35*(2), 245–259.

Sugai, G., Horner, R. H., Lewis-Palmer, T., & Todd, A. (2005). *School-wide positive behavior support training manual.* Eugene: University of Oregon, Educational and Community Supports.

Taylor-Greene, S., Brown, D., Nelson, L., Longton, J., Gassman, T., Cohen, J., Swartz, J., Horner, R. H., Sugai, G., & Hall, S. (1997). School-wide behavioral support: Starting the year off right. *Journal of Behavioral Education, 7*, 99–112.

Turnbull, A., Edmonson, H., Griggs, P., Wickham, D., Sailor, W., Freeman, R., Guess, D., Lassen, S., McCart, A., Park, J., Riffel, L., Turnbull, R., & Warren, J. (2002). A blueprint for schoolwide positive behavior support: Implementation of three components. *Council for Exceptional Children, 68*(3), 377–402.

Walker, H. M., & Severson, H. (1992). *Systematic screening of behavior disorders (SSBD): A multiple gating procedure.* Longmont, CO: Sopris West.

3

TIER 1
CASE EXAMPLE
School-Wide Efficient Behavior Screening (SWEBS)

CHRISTOPHER PIERSON & BETH DEDIC

PURPOSE OF THE CHAPTER

The purpose of this chapter is to introduce the philosophy, rationale, principles, methods, and tools for conducting a universal or school-wide behavioral screening. This will be illustrated through review of potential sources of screening data and an example of how to use School-Wide Efficient Behavior Screening (SWEBS) in a Response to Intervention (RtI) system including ethical and legal cautions.

SCHOOL-WIDE BEHAVIOR SCREENING

What is School-Wide Behavior Screening? What is the philosophy and intent? Behavioral needs of students are often identified after they are well entrenched, which reduces intervention efficacy and increases costs (Feil, Severson, & Walker, 2002). Research has shown that proactive strategies can reduce problem behaviors by half (Taylor-Green et al., 1997). A universal or school-wide behavior screening system can equitably provide all students an opportunity to be identified for behavioral intervention. Furthermore, a properly conducted universal or school-wide behavior screening system can inform the practitioners of the most efficient points of intervention for a given problem—systemic, small group, and/or individual interventions.

School-wide behavior screening is a process of assessing all students, in a variety of areas and through a variety of protocols to further determine those students who may need additional assessment and intervention/support. The results of various school-wide screenings allow students to be sorted into universal, targeted group, and intensive performance levels as well as provide information regarding the overall percentage of students in each of those categories. The identification of students who are adequately benefiting from universal supports or who might need targeted group interventions can then guide school-wide intervention strategies and development. The categories can additionally help the schools match resources to needs of the various groups of students.

The use of school-wide behavior screening improves the delivery of behavioral curriculum and instruction by identifying those students in need of targeted group interventions in Tier 2. School social workers have the training and skills to support and implement RtI in order to provide immediate, efficient, and effective interventions to all students at the identified level of individual need.

School social workers typically spend a lot of time assisting teachers and team members in screening individual students for behavioral and/or social skills concerns. Often, social workers' involvement includes screening, developing a functional behavioral assessment (FBA) and behavior intervention plan (BIP) that are implemented in the general education setting. Additionally, school social workers conduct the same types of activities when they evaluate individual students for entitlement for special education. A great deal of time is often spent looking at one student at a time, frequently at the point of severe problem or crisis. According to Scott (2001), "Identifying the neediest group of students and those who are most at risk of school failure represents the first step in a comprehensive and systemic strategy"(p. 88). In most schools, teachers who have varying levels of tolerance for behaviors refer students for evaluations individually. Therefore, it is preferable to have a system of universal screening in place that gives all students an opportunity to be identified for behavioral or emotional needs (Walker & Severson, 1992).

School-wide behavioral screening protocols allow the school social worker to look at all social/behavioral indicators of all students to see which students may need further assessment or intervention and to determine whether more systemic issues are occurring. Based on the initial screening information, the social worker identifies which students need universal supports, targeted group interventions, or intensive individual interventions. After students are screened the social worker can then work with the school to identify the resources that are available and those that are needed to meet the students' needs. If a large number of students are identified as needing targeted group interventions or intensive individual interventions, there is likely a problem with how effective the universal supports are in meeting the needs of most students.

SCREENING TOOLS AND PROCEDURES

A school social worker can screen all students' behaviors in various ways. Most screening tools have both pros and cons and need to be assessed to compare the amount of effort needed to use them in relation to the outcome/information obtained.

The University of Oregon created the School-Wide Information System (SWIS), a database with which school districts can gather and analyze office referrals and other disciplinary actions (see Chapter 4 for greater information and details regarding the SWIS database). The information that can be gathered can be very beneficial in screening large groups of students and over several years of data collection. Additional advantages include electronic management, quick input/output of data, graphing and charting capabilities, and others. A potential disadvantage of the SWIS database is its failure to identify students who do not display external behavioral concerns. These students may have more internalizing problems such as withdrawal, lack of peer and/or family supports, worry/anxiety, overall sadness, and general social withdrawal.

The Heartland Area Education Agency in Iowa has created the Heartland Educational Assessment Resource Toolbox (HEART), a database available to the 54 school districts it serves. Initially the HEART database was used to house academic information for students. The districts were able to input the test scores that they wanted into this system. Typical test information that was downloaded included Iowa Tests of Basic Skills (ITBS) scores, Iowa Tests of Educational Development (ITED) scores, Northwest Evaluation Association (NWEA) scores, and others. The information was available on all students across time. Charts and graphs can be quickly created from the data in the HEART database. As the agency became more actively involved in RtI processes and procedures as they related to school-wide behaviors, a behavioral component was added, and thus behavioral charts and graphs can be created quickly. As with the SWIS database, HEART has advantages and disadvantages. In general, the pros and cons of the HEART database mirror those of SWIS.

Do behavioral rating scales have utility for school-wide behavior screening? School-wide administration of typical behavior rating scales for screening purposes would not be efficient. For example, with a Conner's Teacher Rating Scale, a teacher needs approximately 10 to 15 minutes to rate one student. In a classroom of 20, that is a minimal teacher investment of 200 minutes for rating, and this does not include scoring time. Other abbreviated rating scales such as the Abbreviated Parent/Teacher Questionnaire (Conners, 1985) and the AML Behavior Rating Scale (Cowen et al., 1975) require two minutes to administer. This is still a teacher time investment of 40 minutes for a 20-member class, not including time to score. Therefore, a typical rating scale is useful for determining significance of behavior of one child at a time but is excessively time-consuming for school-wide administration.

The Systematic Screening for Behavior Disorders (SSBD) developed by Walker and Severson (1992) is one system that is efficient for school-wide administration. The SSBD uses a three-stage, multiple-gate screening system to identify at-risk elementary-age students. During Stage One, the teacher is asked to write down the names of students who match descriptions provided on a list of either externalizing or internalizing behaviors. The teacher then selects 10 students who most closely match each of the behavior profiles. A student cannot appear on both lists. The teacher then rank-orders the students from those who most exemplify each of the profiles to those who least exemplify each profile. The three highest ranking students on each profile (six students total) then are assessed further at the second stage of screening. At this second stage the teacher fills out a checklist of 33 maladaptive behavioral indicators and a 23-item Combined Frequency Index. Normative criteria and cutoff points on the Stage Two instruments are used to determine whether any of the rated students qualify for further assessments in SSBD screening in Stage Three. In this stage, a school professional other than the teacher (e.g., school psychologist, school counselor, resource teacher), uses structured observation and recoding procedures to observe the students who exceeded normative cutoff points in Stage Two. The SSBD is an excellent system for ensuring that each child has had at least some consideration for further assessment. The SSBD's multiple gate screening appropriately increases the level of assessment to match the level of need. The first gate of the screening is very time efficient and later stages provide problem validation. However, the design of the SSBD does not allow for class-wide comparisons on a given item or factor, as students are selected by rank-order of the three worst students for "internalizing" and the three worst students for "externalizing" behaviors. Because of the static number of students who are identified in Stage One, the SSBD is not fully compatible with sorting students into the three performance levels for school-wide data analysis and progress intervention (i.e., school-wide, small group, and individual).

Feil et al. (2002) reviewed the Student Risk Screen Scale (SRSS) developed by Drummond in 1993. This is a system with a protocol presented as a matrix in which all students in a classroom can be rated efficiently. It is based on Likert-type teacher ratings and is used to screen an entire classroom of students for antisocial behavior patterns on seven items: (1) stealing; (2) lying, cheating, sneaking; (3) behavior problems; (4) peer rejection; (5) low academic achievement; (6) negative attitude; and (7) aggressive behavior. Feil et al. (2002) described the SRSS as "brief, research based, easily understood, valid, and cost efficient" (p. 148). The screening results from this instrument can be used for school-wide comparisons.

Kamphaus and Reynolds (2007) have recently designed a brief universal screening tool that can be used in various ways; it works well for whole grade screening or whole school screening for age 3 to grade 12. The new screening tool, the Behavior Assessment System for Children: Second Edition-Behavioral and Emotional Screening System (BASC-2 BESS) can be used to gather information for early identification of problems and help determine the need for individual and/or group intervention strategies. The BASC-2 BESS is focused on Tier 1 screening (universal supports) and yields a total score (a *T* score) from Likert-type items that include externalizing, internalizing, adaptive skills, and school problems. The administration of the protocol takes approximately five minutes or less per child and it offers a rapid and efficient scoring system that can be done electronically. The scale has adequate reliability and validity for screening activities. The advantages of the BASC-2 BESS is that it has forms for teacher, parent, and student; is commercially available; and has software designed to provide scoring, scanning, and reporting information for large groups of children and adolescents. The disadvantage is that the teacher's time investment for a typical classroom of 20 to 25 students would be 100 to 125 minutes for rating.

Student report cards, especially at the elementary level, often have marks for behaviors such as the following: "gets along well with others," "listens," "is attentive," "follows directions." In some districts, these marks are gathered in electronic databases for generation of report cards. There is the potential for these data to be organized in such a manner as to inform the educators of systemic issues and to identify groups of children who may need intervention. However, the disadvantage of using such data is that research-based cut scores would not be available and the reliability of the data is not known. Therefore, if such data were to be used, there would be a need to look to other sources of data (teacher/parent interviews, observations, records reviews, etc.), which would increase the time invested for a screening decision.

THE SCHOOL-WIDE EFFICIENT BEHAVIOR SCREENING (SWEBS)

Pierson (2005) constructed and validated the School-Wide Efficient Behavior Screening (SWEBS) protocol. SWEBS consists of 26 items for which the teacher provides dichotomous responses, that is, the teacher indicates "concerned" or "not concerned" about the student in relation to the item. The items are based on risk indicators from the Iowa At-Risk Standards (Iowa Department of Education, 1996), Early Warning Timely Response (Dwyer et al., 1998), Surgeon General's Report on Youth Violence (U.S. Department of Health and Human Services, 2001), and other behavioral literature. The 26 items cluster into three factors: Conduct (10 items), Social-Emotional Needs (9 items), and Academic Survival Skills (7 Items). The protocol is arranged in a matrix format with all students in the classroom on one form (see Figure 3.1). The presentation and dichotomous nature of the scale enable the teacher to complete the screening of a typical class in less than 20 minutes. The premise behind dichotomous responses of *concerned* or *not concerned* is based on two key points. First, the findings reported in the Surgeon General's Report on Youth Violence reports that presence of individual risk factors are additive.

School-wide Efficient Behavior Screening
(SWEBS)

Date: 9 / 28 / 08 Teacher: Bill Smyth

School: Youngtown Building: West Elementary

	1. Bob	2. Jake	3. Sally	4. Chein	5. Frank	6. George	7. Bobbette	8. Devin	9. Darby	10. Kevin	11. Mamie	12. Margie	13. Sue	14. Nicole	15. Duane	16. Scott	17. Frank	18. Lou	19. Ellen	20. Fred	21. Susan	22. Herman	23.	24.	25.	26.	27.	28.	29.	30.
1. The student has difficulty following school rules.	X																X													
2. The student has few friends or weak social ties.				X													X													
3. The student has peer group that makes poor choices.																														
4. The student is worrisome or anxious.																					X									
5. The student is verbally aggressive toward peers or adults.					X							X																		
6. Significant family stress reported by student or parent (financial, medical, conflict, death/loss).					X																									
7. The student has a poor attitude toward school.																X	X			X										
8. The student has poor academic performance.					X																									
9. The student is dishonest, deceptive, or sneaky.																														
10. The student has difficulty focusing, concentrating, is distractible, or inattentive.												X					X					X								
11. The student appears angry.																	X													
12. The student is physically aggressive toward peers or adults.							X																							
13. The student exhibits sad or flat affect, depression or feelings of worthlessness.	X				X																	X								
14. The student has poor social skills.																														
15. The student is, or perceives to be, a victim of harassment, persecution, or bullying by peers.					X												X													
16. The student does not express feelings or does not express feelings appropriately.												X																		
17. The student has difficulty completing large projects or long-term goals.																														
18. The student makes threats of violence.					X												X					X								
19. The student bullies others.	X																													
20. The student has difficulty adjusting to changes in routine or to transitions.																														
21. The student has demonstrated intolerance for differences or prejudicial attitudes.	X				X							X					X				X									
22. The student has expressed suicidal thoughts or has history of a suicide attempt.																	X													
23. The student is not considerate of other's feelings.																	X													
24. The student has poor organizational skills.																														
25. The student has poor work completion.					X							X					X													
26. The student does not express needs or does not express needs appropriately.																				X										
27. Indicate gender (M= male, F=female)	M	F		M	M	M	F			M	F	F	F	F		M	M	M	F	M	M	M								
28. Grade in school: (K, 1, 2, 3, 4, 5, 6, 7, 8, 9, 10, 11, 12)	3	3	3	3	3	3	3	3	3	3	3	3	3	3	3	3	3	3	3	3	3	3								

Figure 3.1 An example School-Wide Efficient Behavior Screening (SWEBS) protocol.

Second, a dichotomous rating of risk factors is a time efficient and valid method of screening (Pierson, 2005).

The advantage of SWEBS is that it allows for efficient screening for factors of conduct, social-emotional needs, and academic survival skills in a time friendly format. It has adequate test-retest reliability and internal consistency. Interrater reliability is strong in grades K–6, but it has not yet been determined for grades 7–12. SWEBS has appropriate validity when compared to educational status (i.e., general education, at-risk, and special education), presence of behavioral goals, and face validity as reported by teachers (Pierson, 2005). The format is conducive to electronic database management, though a proprietary database has not been developed at this time. The disadvantage of SWEBS is that the screening data obtained by the instrument still need to be validated with other information sources before any high-stakes interventions are considered.

In the context of Response to Intevention (RtI), SWEBS has potential as a low-cost, easily administered screening instrument to inform decision making as to (1) whether the core instructional program (universal supports) is meeting social, emotional, and behavioral needs; (2) which students need something more to supplement core instruction (targeted group interventions); and (3) which students may need intensive individual interventions.

The first step in using the SWEBS is to hold a meeting with all teachers to explain the purpose of the instrument, explain how to complete the protocol, provide protocols listing the students they are expected to rate, explain how the results will be used to screen students for intervention need, and describe confidentiality expectations for screening results. When a student has more than one teacher, the teacher who has the most contact with a student should rate that student.

SWEBS INTERPRETATION PROCEDURES

It is recommended SWEBS screening data be collected and used two to three times per year to provide ongoing screening for individuals and as one source of convergent data for monitoring the effectiveness of the core behavior instruction program (Pierson, 2005). A team of three to five educators can examine the school-wide screening data. Such a team can be made up of the principal, representative teachers, school social worker, or other relevant educational support personnel. It is recommended that a data team first assess need at a *school-wide level* before examining student need at an *individual level*. No Child Left Behind (NCLB) makes schools accountable to their subgroups of students; thus it is important to consider the implications of aggregated and disaggregated data when designing school-wide interventions. An electronic database program (e.g., Excel or Access) that allows for disaggregating data by grade level and by gender could help speed the interpretive process (a proprietary database for SWEBS has not been developed by the author at this time). Data may be disaggregated by ethnicity, socioeconomic status, entitlement in special education, and designation as English Language Learners (ELL). Other sources of disaggregation may also be relevant depending on the data available in each school. Interpretation of disaggregated data can inform decision making for instruction and curriculum modifications so that instruction and curriculum can be differentiated appropriately to the varying needs of each member of the student body.

School-Wide Efficient Behavior Screening data should be electronically managed and reported in various formats to assist in interpretations. The displays can help a data team answer questions such as these: (1) What is the effectiveness of our universal supports in addressing the needs of our students? (2) Are there patterns of need within grade levels or within classes? (3) Are there subsections of our population that have need (e.g., ethnicity, gender)? (4) Are there individual students who may require intervention or further assessment? (5) Would the data suggest interventions for the core instruction, targeted small group interventions, and/or individual interventions? (6) Do the data indicate possible groupings for interventions?

Figure 3.2 is an example of a data report that assists in determining whether the core instructional program is meeting the needs of students

Needs by Grade Level for Total Behaviors							
Grade	Total Students	Number Benchmark (Core)	Percent Benchmark (Core)	Number Strategic (Targeted)	Percent Strategic (Targeted)	Number Intensive	Percent Intensive
ALL	332	271	82%	41	12%	20	6%
K- Total	37	22	59%	8	22%	7	19%
K-Females	19	11	58%	3	16%	5	26%
K-Males	18	11	61%	5	28%	2	11%
1- Total	54	50	93%	3	5%	1	2%
1-Females	27	25	92%	2	8%	0	0%
1- Males	27	25	92%	1	4%	1	4%
2- Total	47	46	98%	1	2%	0	0%
2-Females	18	18	100%	0	0%	0	0%
2- Males	29	28	97%	1	3%	0	0%
3-Total	46	33	72%	9	20%	4	8%
3-Females	27	19	70%	7	26%	1	4%
3- Males	19	14	74%	2	11%	3	15%
4- Total	50	39	78%	7	14%	4	8%
4-Females	24	19	79%	4	17%	1	4%
4- Males	26	20	76%	3	12%	3	12%
5- Total	52	46	88%	4	8%	2	4%
5-Females	21	18	86%	3	14%	0	0%
5- Males	31	28	90%	1	3%	2	7%
6- Total	46	35	76%	9	20%	2	4%
6- Males	20	16	80%	2	10%	2	10%
6-Females	26	19	73%	7	27%	0	0%

Figure 3.2 An example School-Wide Efficient Behavior Screening (SWEBS) data report to assist in systemic analysis.

in each grade level. In Figure 3.2, evidence-based cut scores (Pierson, 2005) were used to identify which students showed more concern areas than expected. The report shows the percentage of students meeting expectations (benchmark or core), those at risk (strategic or targeted intervention), and those with intensive needs. If the core instructional program were working properly, one would typically expect to see 80% to 90% of students scoring in the benchmark or core range because they are benefiting from core curriculum and instruction (universal supports). The "Total Behavior" score in Figure 3.2 shows 82% of the students are within benchmark expectations and thus appear to be benefiting from the universal supports. However, the data also suggest that there may be need for improvements in kindergarten, third, and possibly fourth grade since fewer than 80% of the students in those grades are meeting the expectation (benchmark or core). The data also suggest that sixth grade females may also need additional supports to meet expectations. SWEBS factor scores (e.g., Conduct, Social-Emotional Needs, and Academic Survival Skills) can also be presented in this manner to provide insight into school-wide, grade-wide, or class-wide issues; however, these scores do not in themselves answer the question of what needs to be done or which individuals may need support. Other SWEBS reports (below) can indicate which students may need further assistance.

Figure 3.3 illustrates how school-wide data from SWEBS can be displayed for examining need across subgroups. These types of data are appropriate for examining the aggregate of a subgroup when the groups are large enough that an individual's results cannot be inferred from the display. One rule of thumb is

SWEBS Scores Disaggregated						
Disaggregation	Total Number	% of Total	Mean Academic Survival	Mean Conduct	Mean Social-Emotional Needs	Mean Total Score
ESL	0	0	NA	NA	NA	NA
F/R Lunch	37	11%	1.30	1.00	1.16	4.81
Regular Ed.	260	78%	0.38	0.29	0.27	1.17
Special Ed.	29	9%	2.34	1.52	1.69	7.76
At risk	45	13%	1.53	0.64	0.98	4.11
Caucasian	278	84%	0.72	0.44	0.50	2.13
Hispanic	5	1%	1.20	0.80	0.60	3.20
Asian	40	12%	0.57	0.33	0.20	1.58
Black	9	3%	0.56	1.22	1.33	4.56
Native American	1	suppressed due to low number	suppressed due to low number	suppressed due to low number	suppressed due to low number	suppressed due to low number

Figure 3.3 An example School-Wide Efficient Behavior Screening (SWEBS) data report to look at subgroup needs.

to suppress the results in a table if the subgroup is less than 5 or 10 individuals. Most states also have restrictions on who can have knowledge of individual data such as free/reduced price lunch status. Comparing across the scores of the subgroups can help to expose groups that may not be having their needs fully met by the core curriculum and instruction. For example, the students of free and reduced price lunch status in Figure 3.3 have SWEBS scores much higher than the typical "general education" students, and thus students of low socio-economic status may need more supports.

Figure 3.4 illustrates how individual results can be displayed to show the need within a grade level based on the ratings of students on the Academic Survival Skills factor. Researched-based (Pierson, 2005) cut scores are used to help determine the expectations as to how many concerns a student can have before being identified. This allows one to see not only how much of the class is meeting expectations but also which individuals may need more support and how many concerns were identified for each student. The report does not indicate which items an individual was endorsed on or what intervention group-ings would be appropriate, other than by broad factors. Such displays would be repeated for total and each of the factor scores (e.g., Conduct, Social-Emotional Needs, and Academic Survival Skills) (also see Figure 3.5).

The following display is a grouping display (see Figure 3.6). This would be used when school-wide or grade-wide factor reports have indi-cated that a need exists for group interventions. This report would be used to assist in group construction (i.e., which students may need what group instruction). The example below is a list of students from a large elementary school who were endorsed by the teacher for having difficulty following school rules. This information, along with other information at the dis-posal of the educators, would help in group construction.

It would be appropriate for a school-based data team to review the data to determine what school-wide instructional and curricular adapta-tions would be appropriate based on the screening data. It is also sug-gested that the social worker remind the data team that these are

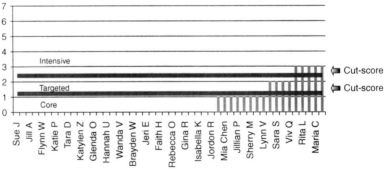

Figure 3.4 An example School-Wide Efficient Behavior Screening (SWEBS) data report to examine need across all grade sections—academic skills.

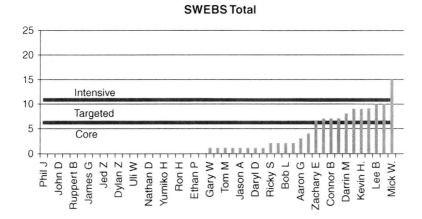

Figure 3.5 An example School-Wide Efficient Behavior Screening (SWEBS) data report to examine need across all grade sections—SWEBS total.

Item 1. The student has difficulty following school rules.					
Name	Gender	Grade	Name	Gender	Grade
John Anderson	M	1	Mykayla Crowles	F	4
Albert Smith	M	2	Sue Winer	F	4
Sara Sing	F	2	James Copper	M	4
Celesta Thomes	F	2	Summer Brown	F	4
Neal Rowles	M	2	Jason Gates	M	4
Scott Mau	M	2	Juan Gomez	M	4
James Knoop	M	2	Ivan Knutson	M	4
Kevin Haney	M	2	Bryan Flatt	M	5
Donald Dudley	M	2	Jerry Thurtell	M	5
Darwin Mott	M	3	Hy Abels	M	5
Jacob Morely	M	3	Mia Chen	F	6
Lee Bash	M	3	Mick Weis	M	6

Figure 3.6 An example School-Wide Efficient Behavior Screening (SWEBS) data report to assist with forming intervention groups.

screening data based on teacher perceptions of behavior and that it should be used with other convergent data such as grades, discipline data, reports of concern by parents, and other indicators before high-stakes decisions are made (e.g., costly purchase of instructional programs or special education entitlement decisions).

LEGAL AND POLICY CONSIDERATIONS

The Individuals with Disabilities Education Act (IDEA) of 1997 made it clear that special education is a service, not a place, and that services must focus on student outcomes. Additionally, educational services were to be offered/provided regarding student needs prior to a student's being labeled with a disability (intervention). The national school social work standards, specifically standard 12, indicate that "school social workers shall conduct assessments of student needs that are individualized and provide information that is directly useful for designing interventions that address behaviors of concern" (National Association of Social Workers, 2002). No Child Left Behind (NCLB) is based on the premise that all children will learn and have access to services based on needs; school-wide screening allows for all children to be considered regarding needs, issues, and services. NCLB further calls for professional development and training for, and involvement of, school personnel, pupil services personnel, parents, and interested community members in prevention, education, early identification and intervention, and mentoring or rehabilitation referral as related to drug and violence prevention (20 U.S.C. § 115 STAT. 1747(D); Pierson 2005). In addition to NCLB, IDEA 1997, and IDEA 2004, there are numerous policy reports and research studies that support the process of RtI and the use of problem solving in schools. The National Institute of Child Health and Development (NICHD) Studies, the National Reading Panel, the National Research Council on Minority Overrepresentation, the National Summit of Learning Disabilities, and the President's Commission on Excellence in Special Education provide policy statements and supports for the implementation of RtI (see Chapter 1 for more information on the policies and supports for the implementation of RtI).

No Child Left Behind also advises schools to use funds to prevent drug use, prevent violence, and engage students in the learning process. Key pieces of the act supporting RtI for behavior and/or school-wide screening include the following:

- Professional development (20 U.S.C. § 115 STAT. 1747(D))
- Early identification, intervention, and assessment (20 U.S.C. § 115 STAT. 1747(D)), (20 U.S.C. § 115 STAT 1748 (E vii), (20 U.S.C. § 115 STAT 1782 (14)), (20 U.S.C. § 115 STAT 1630 (B))
- Referral services, training of teachers by school-based mental health service providers in appropriate identification, and intervention techniques for students at risk of violent behavior and illegal use of drugs (20 U.S.C. § 115 STAT 1748 (E x)
- Programs to rely on the diagnostic-prescriptive model to improve students' learning of academic content at elementary and secondary levels (20 U.S.C. § 115 STAT 1782 (26)
- Local education agencies (LEAs) to create a well-disciplined, learning-conducive environment, which includes consultation between teachers, principals, and other school personnel to identify

early warning signs of drug use and violence and to provide
behavioral interventions as part of classroom management efforts
(20 U.S.C. § 115 STAT 1746 b1Cii)
- The promotion of school readiness through early childhood
emotional and social development (20 U.S.C. § 115 1853
(sec. 5542))
- Use of technology to collect, manage, and analyze data to improve
teaching and decision making (20 U.S.C. § 115 STAT 2083 (E))

The SWEBS provides one means for early identification leading to prescriptive intervention by helping to determine which students are in need of
intervention. It may be one screening tool or a first step in a diagnostic-
prescriptive model that might help improve students' learning of academic
content through improved behavior. It has promise to be part of a needs
assessment to improve behavior in the schools and thus enhance academic
engagement. Finally, SWEBS is a promising tool for collecting and analyzing
data that might help improve teaching and instructional decision making.
Thus, SWEBS is one tool that has promise to help meet the intentions of
NCLB to improve students' academic, behavioral, and social functioning.

According to the Family Educational Rights and Privacy Act (FERPA)
(20 U.S.C. § 1232g; 34 CFR Part 99), parents or eligible students have the
right to inspect and review students' education records maintained by the
school. Generally, schools must have written permission from the parent or
eligible student to release any information from the record. However,
schools may disclose those records without consent to the following:

- School officials with legitimate educational interest
- Schools to which the student is transferring
- Court offiicals when complying with a judicial order to a lawfully
issued subpoena
- Appropriate officials in cases of health and safety emergencies
- Juvenile justice system authorities pursuant to state law (partial
listing; see 34 CFR § 99.31 for complete listing)

According to FERPA provisions, parents must be allowed to see their
child's screening results. The SWEBS results can be shared with school staff
members who have a legitimate educational interest in the child's programming, and the results could be disclosed as an educational record when the
student transfers to another school. Therefore, SWEBS data may be analyzed
by school staff when used for school-wide decision making. Schools considering using SWEBS should consider if their current policies regarding record
access are consistent with ethical use of behavioral screening data. For example,

- How and where will the information be stored?
- Will those with access to SWEBS results have training regarding
issues of confidentiality and appropriate use of data?

- Who will be given access to data and under what conditions?
- Is it the intent that postsecondary institutions (e.g., a military recruiter) will be able to see SWEBS results?

The Protection of Pupil Rights Amendment (PPRA) (20 U.S.C. § 1232h; 34 CFR Part 98) requires schools to obtain active parental consent before minor students are required to participate in any U.S. Education Department–funded survey, analysis, or evaluation that reveals information concerning the following:

- Political affiliations
- Mental and psychological problems potentially embarrassing to the student and his or her family
- Sex behavior and attitudes
- Illegal, antisocial, self-incriminating, and demeaning behavior
- Critical appraisals of other individuals with whom respondents have close family relationships
- Legally recognized privileged or analogous relationships, such as those of lawyers, physicians, and ministers
- Religious practices, affiliations, or beliefs of the student or the student's parents
- Income (other than that required by law to determine eligibility for participation in a program or for receiving financial assistance under such a program)

Parents or students who believe their rights under PPRA may have been violated may file a complaint with the U.S. Department of Education. SWEBS does ask questions of protected areas; however, it is not a survey administered *"to students"* and no information is collected *"from students."* Instead the SWEBS is a behavioral rating scale designed to collect information *from a teacher* about his or her concerns for students. Thus, SWEBS does not meet the threshold for the requirement of active parental consent to screening.

For administration of physical exams or screenings of students, PPRA requires local education agencies (LEAs) to work with parents to develop and adopt policies, unless the LEA or state education agency (SEA) had established comparable policies on or before the date of enactment of NCLB on January 8, 2002. Parents are able to opt out of certain school activities. These activities include a student survey and analysis or evaluation that concerns the eight protected areas. SWEBS does fall under this more ambiguous definition; therefore, opt-out provisions apply. Under this provision, LEAs must notify the students' parent directly, through means such as U.S. mail or e-mail, of the special activities and provide an opportunity for parents to opt their child out of participation in the specific activity. The LEA may make this notification at the beginning of the school year if the approximate dates of the activity have been determined. In summary, parents should be provided a reasonable notification of the planned activities and be provided an opportunity to opt their child out, as well as an opportunity to review any pertinent surveys (Letter to Chief State School Officers, February 2004, United States Department of Education by LeRoy S. Rooker, Director of Family Policy Compliance Office). See Box 3.1 for a model letter of the SWEBS opt-out.

While this analysis suggests that universal screening with the SWEBS is a legitimate educational activity that can be carried out as long as parents

---

Box 3.1   PPRA Model Notice and Opt-out for SWEBS

Dear parent:

The Protection of Pupil Right Amendment (PPRA), 20 U.S.C. § 1232h, requires **[School district]** to notify you and allow you to opt your child out of participating in certain school activities. These activities include a student survey, analysis, or evaluation that concerns one or more of the following eight areas ("protected information surveys"):

1. Political affiliations or beliefs of the student or student's parent;
2. Mental or psychological problems of the student or student's family;
3. Sex behavior or attitudes
4. Illegal, anti-social, self-incriminating or demeaning behavior
5. Critical appraisals of others with whom respondents have close family relationships;
6. Legally recognized privileged relationships, such as with lawyers, doctors, or ministers;
7. Religious practices, affiliations, or beliefs of the student or parents; or
8. Income, other than as required by law to determine program eligibility.

On or about October 15th and April 15th of this school year the **[district name]** plans to screen the behavior functioning, social functioning, and academic survival skills of students grades kindergarten through six. Your child will NOT be asked to complete any survey, be asked any questions, or be aware of the screening process. Instead, your child's teacher will rate your child's behavior against a set of research based statements that reflect risk behaviors for academic failure, behavior problems, or social/emotional problems. Should your child's ratings on this instrument be of concern, your teacher will contact you to discuss the results and how the screening results can be further assessed. You have the right to examine your child's screening results.

If you wish to review the screening questions prior to the scheduled administration dates, please submit a request to **[school official, address]**. **[School official]** will notify you of the time and place where you may review these materials.

If you do not want your child to be screened for behavior, social, and academic survival skills, please contact **[school official]** at **[telephone number, email, address, etc.]** no later than **[date]**.

We strongly encourage this screening. The data obtained will help students needing support to receive instruction or intervention to improve their academic survival skills, behavior functioning, or social functioning. This data can also be analyzed systematically by the administration to help determine needs for instructional programs and instructional staff at your child's school, thus improving the quality of your child's school.

Thank you,

[School official]

are given reasonable notice and opportunity to opt out of screening, schools considering use of the SWEBS should consult their own legal counsel for interpretation in light of their state statutes and regulations.

Pierson (2005) anticipates that although opt-out procedures may prevent some students from being screened, enough students will be screened to allow meaningful interpretation of data for school-wide decision making.

ETHICAL CONSIDERATIONS

Educators using an instrument like SWEBS need to take responsibility to follow the intent of screening. Educators using the SWEBS are cautioned to remember that the SWEBS must be used appropriately in light of the assessment question being asked. The SWEBS is intended to help educators determine which students are at risk for not having their social, emotional, and behavioral needs met.

The SWEBS is *not* intended to be a tool to place students into unproven or ineffective programs. Using the SWEBS solely to place students into at-risk or special education programming without providing effective general education interventions aligned to a validated area of concern would be inappropriate. The intent of the SWEBS is not to seek identification of pathology but to align effective instructional services to student need. While it is important to identify needs for intervention, professionals need to be wary of attaching labels to young children (Webster-Stratton, 1997) or targeting troublemakers (Dwyer et al., 1998).

Educators are cautioned to consider that the SWEBS collects perceptual data regarding students. Perceptions can vary from rater to rater, and students' behavior can vary from setting to setting. If the guidelines in the previous paragraph for the intent and use of the screening tool are followed, the risks of using such perceptual data become more acceptable. Again, the information provided by the SWEBS is not in itself diagnostic, and individual student concerns identified through the use of the SWEBS might be validated by looking at multiple data sources (e.g., discipline records, attendance records, cumulative files, observations, information from parents and teachers, other diagnostic data).

The SWEBS data can be used, in part, to determine how students might be grouped to increase the effectiveness and efficiency of instruction. However, care must be taken since grouping students with high levels of behavior problems can result in students encouraging each other to misbehave (Poulin, Dishion, & Burraston, 2001) and aggressive classroom contexts may sustain loops of aggression and victimization (Leadbeater, Hoglund, & Woods, 2003).

As part of the ethics of evaluation, educators should keep in mind the cultural expectations of the setting and the diversity of the student(s) they are attempting to assess. As with other assessment data, educators must be careful to contextualize the assessment results and validate the findings with other data/assessment sources. Schools tend to reflect middle-class expectations (Payne, 1996), and thus the concern statements are likely to reflect risk factors that inhibit functioning within middle-class expectations. As Payne (1996) noted, "For our students to be successful, we must understand their hidden rules and teach them rules that will make them successful at school and work." Payne also noted, "Two things that help move a person out of poverty are education and relationships."

Finally, the following excerpt stresses the importance of using screening data wisely:

> In short, not all students who have risk factors associated with antisocial behavior or delinquency involve themselves in rule-breaking behavior. Risk and resilience theory suggests that students who do not end up with negative outcomes, despite the existing risks, have some individual resiliency or protective factors with the environment that allow for more positive trajectories (Hawkins, Catalano, & Haggerty, 1993). (Rutter, Giller, & Hagell, 1998, p. 177)

Thus educators should not use SWEBS or similar screening tools to label troublemakers and segregate them from others, but rather to provide interventions to build upon student resiliency and protective factors within the environment.

Can behavioral and academic data be integrated? As indicated earlier, risk factors are additive. Academic struggle would be combined with social/behavioral issues and would be a stronger indication of need for intervention supports. The same could be said for combining these data with behavioral data from a system such as SWIS. Development of electronic systems for both academic and behavioral indicators increases the utility and efficiency of such data-based decisions.

HOW DOES SCHOOL-WIDE BEHAVIOR SCREENING FIT IN THE STRUCTURE OF RtI?

Properly designed and conducted assessments help to inform instruction. The four pillars of assessment are screening, diagnosing, progress monitoring, and summative (outcome) assessments. Assessments should be question driven.

Screening assessments answer the question of who has problems and should err on the side of overidentification. This helps to avoid missing a student who should potentially receive intervention. Diagnostic assessments help to validate and determine how bad the problem is and to identify key skills the student may need to be taught. Progress monitoring assessments inform the practitioner regarding intervention efficacy on a frequent basis so that changes or modification to the intervention can be made. Summative assessments help answer the question "How well did this intervention work?"

Universal or school-wide behavioral screening assessments in an RtI system help to inform the practitioner of who has the problem. Furthermore, it helps to inform the practitioner of the points within the system that will provide the level of change needed. For example, if an assessment question asked of all teachers at a grade level is, "How many students have difficulty remaining on task in the classroom?" differing results can lead to different interventions. For example, if 30% of the students are having difficulty with task behaviors, then there may be a systemic curricular or instructional modification that would enable more students to be productive. If 15% are having difficulty, it might lead to a small group intervention. If only a small percentage (1% to 5%) have difficulty with task behaviors, individualized interventions may be the most appropriate. Such a system view may help avoid inappropriate interventions individually determined, such as referring 30% of the students in a class for evaluation for attention deficit hyperactivity disorder when the curriculum or instructional techniques are driving the children to distraction (Pierson, 2005).

KNOWLEDGE AND SKILLS NEEDED TO IMPLEMENT SCHOOL-WIDE BEHAVIOR SCREENING

To implement a school-wide screening process, school social workers need to be aware of school policies and procedures for testing students, gaining parental permission, and administering the screening tool. If school social workers are employed by an intermediate service provider, they will also need to be aware of these same types of parameters as required by that employer and the school that they are serving. Practitioners will need to be knowledgeable and proficient with reviewing and aggregating large amounts of screening data. Additionally, they will need to be able to analyze and assist school staff in making decisions with the data. School social workers will need to offer resources and referral options to teachers, students, and families for specific needs identified by screening. These social workers must also be well versed in group intervention strategies and have the ability to deliver small group instruction if needed. Additionally, school social workers will need to use their communication and referral skills and their knowledge of community resources to provide linkages for students and families who need or want supplemental nonschool-based services.

CHAPTER SUMMARY AND CONCLUSIONS

This chapter provided information regarding the philosophy and intent of using a universal screening tool in the school or academic setting. Links have been made to the policies and procedures that support the use of RtI and its practice in schools and by school social workers. Additionally, connections have been made to NCLB, IDEA, and other proponents of the problem-solving practice.

Several tools and protocols were presented with information regarding each tool's efficiency, display ability (sorting, graphing, etc.), and the ability to guide intervention/student needs (core, targeted group, or individual/group intensive). The potential limitations of each tool were also offered.

The examples provided in this chapter (see Figures 3.1–3.6) offer a view of how to use and implement the SWEBS model of school-wide screening. Sample graphs and charts were presented to show what information could be gathered through this screening and what the data displays could offer in terms of grouping and student needs.

Following the case example, policies, legal implications, privacy procedures, Acts and ethical considerations were reviewed. The legal and ethical considerations offered should be considered for the implementation of any universal screening procedures.

How universal or school-wide screening fits into the structure of RtI was detailed. Universal screening is a proactive means that allows for all students to be screened with early identification and intervention as an identified outcome. Problem solving based on the screening information allows for the determination of interventions at the needed level (universal, targeted, or intensive) and a discussion about the resources that will be needed to meet students' needs.

The skills and training of the school social worker fit well within the RtI model. The skills and knowledge base necessary for the school social worker to practice within this context were considered and reviewed and clarified.

In summary, school social workers have the knowledge and skills to understand and implement school-wide behavior screening in schools and to work within an RtI structure to support and enhance the educational experience of all children.

REFERENCES

Conners, C. K. (1985). *The Conners rating scales: Instruments for the assessment of childhood psychopathology.* Unpublished manuscript.

Cowen, E. L., Trost, M. A., Lorion, R. P., Dorr, D., Izzo, L. D., & Isaacson, R. V. (1975). *New ways in school mental health: Early detection and prevention of school maladaption.* New York: Human Sciences Press.

Dwyer, K., Osher, D., & Warger, C. (1998). *Early warning, time response: A guide to safe schools.* Washington, DC: U.S. Department of Education.

Feil, E. G., Severson, H. H., & Walker, H. M. (2002). Early screening and intervention to prevent the development of aggressive, destructive behavior patterns among at-risk children. In M. R. Shinn, H. M. Walker, & G. Stoner (Eds.), *Interventions for academic and behavior problems II: Preventive and remedial approaches* (pp. 143–166). Washington, DC: National Association of School Psychologists.

Hawkins, J. D., Catalano, R. F., & Haggerty, K. (1993, September). Risks and protective factors are interdependent. *Western Center News, 7.*

Iowa Department of Education (1996). *Guidelines for serving at-risk students.* Des Moines, IA: Iowa Department of Education, Office of Educational Services for Children, Families and Communities.

Kamphaus, R. W., & Reynolds, C. R. (2007). *Publication Summary Form.* Behavior Assessment System for Children: Second Edition-Behavioral and Emotional Screening System. [Brochure]. Bloomington, MN: Pearson.

Leadbeater, B., Hoglund, W., & Woods, T. (2003). Changing contexts? The effects of a primary prevention program on classroom levels of peer relational and physical victimization. *Journal of Community Psychology, 31,* 397–418.

National Association of Social Workers. (2002). *NASW standards for school social work services.* Washington, DC: National Association of Social Workers.

Payne, R. K. (1996). *A framework for understanding poverty.* Highlands, TX: Process.

Pierson, C. C. (2005). School-wide behavior screening for instructional decision-making. (Doctoral dissertation, Iowa State University, 2005). *Dissertation Abstracts International* (DAI-A 66/08, p. 2797, February 2006).

Poulin, F., Dishion, T. J., & Burraston, B. (2001). Three-year iatrogenic effects associated with aggregating high-risk adolescents in cognitive-behavior preventive interventions. *Applied Developmental Science, 5*(4), 214–224.

Rutter, M., Giller, H., & Hagnell, A. (1998). *Antisocial behavior by young people.* Cambridge, U.K.: Cambridge University Press.

Scott, R. M. (2001). A schoolwide example of positive behavioral support. *Journal of Positive Behavior Interventions, 3,* 88–94.

Taylor-Green, S., Brown, D., Nelson, L., Longton, J., Gassman, T., Cohen, J., Swartz, J., Horner, R., Sugai, G., & Hall, S. (1997). School-wide behavioral support: Starting the year off right. *Journal of Behavioral Education, 7,* 99–112.

U.S. Department of Health and Human Services. (2001). *Youth violence: A report of the surgeon general.* Rockville, MD: U.S. Department of Health and Human Services, Centers for Disease Control and Prevention, National Center for Injury Prevention and Control: Substance Abuse and Mental Health Services Administration, Center for Mental Health Services; and National Institutes of Health, National Institute of Mental Health.

Walker, H. M., & Severson, H. H. (1992). User's guide and administration manual. *Systematic screening for behavior disorders.* Longmont, CO: Sopris West.

Webster-Stratton, C. (1997). Early intervention for families of preschool children with conduct problems. In M. J. Guralnick (Ed.), *The effectiveness of early intervention* (pp. 429–453). Baltimore, MD: Brookes.

4

TIER 1
CASE EXAMPLE
School-Wide Information
System (SWIS)

BRENDA COBLE LINDSEY & MARGARET WHITE

The practice of collecting and analyzing academic data in schools can be applied to school-wide behavioral management approaches. Schools can use the same process by collecting and analyzing student discipline data to identify problem behavior trends and detect building "hot spots" where the greatest numbers of incidents occur (Lewis & Sugai, 1999). This procedure allows schools to identify the circumstances under which problem behaviors are more likely to take place (Scott, 2001). Schools with behavioral data systems in place can use the information to develop school-wide approaches to prevent or reduce future occurrences of problem behaviors. The data can also be used to learn which students exhibit highly challenging behaviors and to tailor effective behavioral interventions to meet their needs.

The key is to implement coordinated processes for evaluating behavioral data. Schools should use the results to inform decision making about programs, curricula, and intervention strategies (Freeman, Smith, & Tieghi-Benet, 2003). This chapter identifies issues that schools should consider before implementing data systems and how to use data to inform decision making about behavioral management approaches. An example of a data system for collecting and analyzing school-wide behavioral data is also presented.

BEHAVIORAL DATA COLLECTION METHODS

Scott and Martinek (2006) suggested that schools consider the following questions when developing a comprehensive data collection and analysis plan:

1. What behaviors are of concern at our school?
2. When are they most likely to occur? (time of day/location/context)
3. What behaviors do we expect our students to display?
4. What rules, routines, and practices can be put into place to encourage these behaviors?
5. How can they be consistently implemented school-wide by students and teachers?
6. What information needs to be collected to assess whether our approach is working?
7. How often should data be reviewed?

These questions can be answered by reviewing data that are currently being collected. In addition, it is essential to obtain multiple perspectives from teachers, parents, and students through surveys, focus groups, or interviews (Benbenishty, Astor, & Estrada, 2008). The results can be used to create a school-wide behavior management plan. It should be disseminated to key stakeholders to create a common understanding of the issues and increase buy-in. The process of determining what and how data should be collected and analyzed is the foundation of a solid data-based decision-making approach.

Office discipline referrals are an effective data source to assess and monitor school-wide behavior intervention efforts (Sugai, Sprague, Horner, & Walker, 2000). The information to be collected should consist of student name, date, referring teacher, time of day, nature of problem, location where offense occurred, and administrative response. Other data to be collected include the number of suspensions, detentions, attendance/truancies, and tardies. This information is already being collected in most schools and provides an efficient way to evaluate the effectiveness of school discipline approaches (Skiba, Peterson, & Williams, 1997; Tobin, Sugai, & Colvin, 2000; Walker, Stieber, Ramsey, & Oneil, 1993; Wright & Dusek, 1998). Data can also be examined to determine discipline trends for vulnerable student populations, including minority students and students with disabilities.

SCHOOL-WIDE INFORMATION SYSTEM (SWIS)

The School-Wide Information System (SWIS) is a Web-based data collection and analysis system designed to evaluate office discipline referral information (Barrett, Bradshaw, & Lewis-Palmer, 2008; Sugai et al., 2000; School-Wide Information System www.swis.org). This type of software can be used to enter, organize, manage, and report school discipline data in a meaningful way. The results can be utilized to identify areas of concern and create easy-to-read charts and graphs that depict data. These findings are used to guide implementation of school-wide behavior approaches. SWIS can also facilitate development of effective behavior intervention plans for students with challenging behaviors by pinpointing situations in which the behaviors are most likely to occur. SWIS provides the means for school staff to thoughtfully evaluate their school behavioral climate and precisely identify areas of concern.

Schools that adopt SWIS are required to have their staff complete training provided by a qualified SWIS facilitator. School staff must also be trained on how to record office discipline referral data to ensure reliability of results. Users connect to SWIS through computers with Internet access and a compatible Web browser. School staff should enter office discipline referral data on a regular basis, usually daily or weekly (Sugai et al., 2000). Each office discipline referral item takes approximately 45 seconds to enter in the online database. SWIS can aggregate data and transform it into simple charts, graphs, and tables that can be shared with school leadership teams, building principals, school social workers, and staff.

The School-Wide Information System allows users to create reports that highlight office discipline referral rates for individual students, classrooms, grade levels, or schools (May et al., 2000). Reports can be generated by type of problem behavior, location, motivation or function of behavior, referring staff, and time of day. Custom reports can also be created to illustrate the percentage of students at each of the three tiers, number of suspension/expulsion days, ethnic/racial background of students receiving office discipline referrals, and the rate of incidents for students with disabilities. School staff should examine data summary reports and use the results to inform decision making about ways to increase effectiveness of school-wide discipline efforts. Irvin et al. (2006) reported that the process of examining SWIS reports increased the efficiency and effectiveness of decision making for Tier 1 implementation efforts. Data should also be shared with school staff so they are aware of successes and challenges associated with Response to Intervention (RtI) implementation.

As can be seen in Figure 4.1, SWIS can generate office discipline data graph reports by location. The graph indicates that the most commonly reported locations in which discipline referrals occur are classrooms followed by the playground. Since students spend most of their school day in classroom settings, this is not unexpected. However, it is important to use the data to prompt further discussion. Are the referrals generated by one student or many students? How can problem behaviors be prevented? Are there strong classroom management skills that engage all students? Are trainings needed on how to deal with specific problem behaviors? Have appropriate behavior expectations been defined, taught, and monitored? Is there a reward system in place to acknowledge students who exhibit appropriate behaviors? Are problem behaviors being rewarded inadvertently? Is there adequate supervision at specific locations? By using data

Referrals by Location

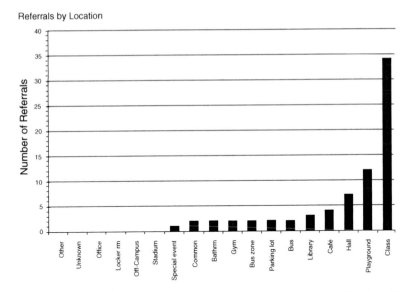

Figure 4.1 Example of School-Wide Information System (SWIS) office discipline data report by location.

in this way, effective strategies can be put in place to reduce office discipline referrals school-wide.

Another important data tool is a SWIS report that examines office discipline referrals by type of problem behavior. Data analysis should begin by identifying the most commonly reported type of problem behaviors. As can be seen in Figure 4.2, disrespectful behavior is the primary reason for most of the office discipline referrals in this example. The data can be used to probe deeper by asking what can be done to prevent the problem behaviors from taking place. By looking more closely at the data, key questions can be asked: When are the problem behaviors occurring? Who is being disrespectful? Are the referrals generated by a few students or many students? Are there procedures in place to define and teach students what it means to be respectful in school? Are students acknowledged for being respectful? What are the consequences for being disrespectful? The answers to these questions can suggest target areas for developing successful strategies that will reduce the likelihood that problem behaviors will occur.

Similar questions should be considered when reviewing data regarding the time of day that most office discipline referrals occur. As illustrated in Figure 4.3, the time frame that generates the greatest number of office discipline referrals in this example is 9:45–10:15 A.M. Further inquiries should be made, such as these: What happens at that time of day? Where are students? Are they at recess? Is there a passing period? If so, is there a great deal of congestion? How can the problem behaviors be prevented during

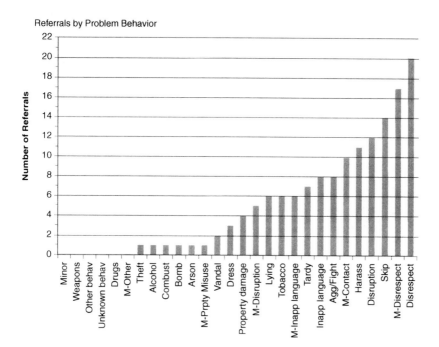

Referrals by Problem Behavior

Figure 4.2 Example of School-Wide Information System (SWIS) office discipline data report by type of problem behavior.

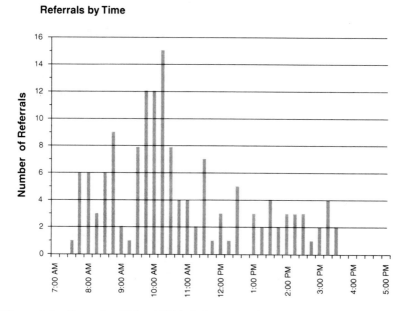

Referrals by Time

Figure 4.3 Example of School-Wide Information System (SWIS) office discipline referral data by time of day.

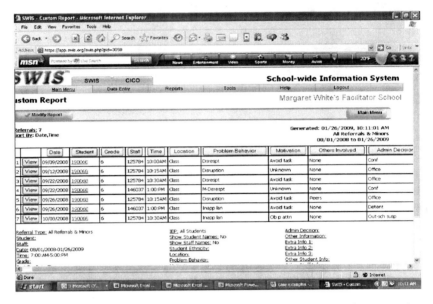

Figure 4.4   Example of School-Wide Information System (SWIS) data report by
student showing motivation (function) of behavior.

this timeframe? Is more adult supervision needed? Are adults actively
supervising students or are they socializing with each other? Have the
appropriate behavior expectations been taught to students?

SWIS can generate custom reports such as the one depicted in
Figure 4.4. In this case, the report identifies the perceived underlying
motivation or function of behavior for an individual student. The student
in this example has a history of exhibiting problem behaviors between
10:00 A.M. and 10:30 A.M. each day. The function of behavior is
identified as task avoidance. These data can be used to investigate further.
Questions can be formulated: What is happening in the classroom during
this time? Is the student trying to avoid the subject taught during that
time because he or she lacks the necessary academic knowledge and skills?
In this case, the student preferred to receive office discipline referrals
rather than read aloud in class.

SWIS data reports can also be created that highlight students with
one or more referrals. The reports can be printed in chart form with
student names to clearly identify students who may require more intensive interventions. Reports can also be created using student identification numbers as illustrated in Figure 4.5. Regardless of which type of
report is produced, it is crucial to examine these types of data reports
monthly to ensure students in need of Tier 2 and/or Tier 3 interventions
are identified.

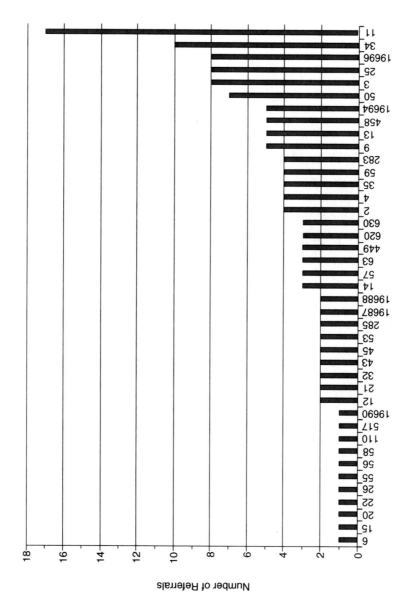

Figure 4.5 Example of School-Wide Information System (SWIS) data report of students with multiple referrals.

USING DATA TO MAKE DECISIONS

In today's No Child Left Behind world, schools must wisely use data to identify students in need and determine whether intervention efforts are successful. School-wide efforts will be better organized, exact, and efficient (Horner, Sugai, & Todd, 2001). There are four guidelines to follow when collecting behavioral data in classrooms, schools, or at the district level.

1. Choose wisely. Collecting data takes time and effort, so limit the type of data to those items that truly improve the value and worth of decisions (Horner et al., 2001). Before beginning data collection, formulate a clear plan on what decisions need to be made, who will make them, and how often data should be collected. Emphasis should always be placed on how to make the process as simple and painless as possible.
2. Time invested now will pay off in the future. Design and utilize a data collection system that is easy to use, allows users to quickly gather information, and facilitates decision making (Horner et al., 2001). Decisions can be made based on identified needs, and progress can be monitored continuously. Ervin et al. (2007) reported a 50% decrease in office discipline referrals in schools that use data to guide implementation of school-wide behavior management plans.
3. Use it or lose it. Schools are required to collect multiple data for reports to district, state, and federal entities. Some or all of the information needed for Tier 1 implementation may already be on hand, which can streamline the collection process (Horner et al., 2001). The data should be reviewed to see how it could be used to enhance school-wide improvement as well as Tier 2 and Tier 3 efforts.
4. Have the right information at the right time. Adjust the data collection and reporting schedule to match the decision-making cycle (Horner et al., 2001). If the school's teams meet weekly, then the data collection process must be designed to provide current data each week.

These principles help schools identify data that are valid indicators of their overall behavioral climate as well as determine which students require additional support (Irvin et al., 2004). Students with challenging behaviors can be recognized and targeted to receive more specialized assistance. Specific interventions can be created by examining trends and patterns over when and where problematic behaviors occur (Tobin et al., 2000). By incorporating these strategies into the development of a school-wide RtI approach, data collection and analysis processes will be useful to key implementers.

CASE EXAMPLE: HIGH SCHOOL RtI TIER 1 SCHOOL-WIDE BEHAVIORAL APPROACH

A high school located in a large city in the midwestern part of the United States was chosen as a case example to illustrate how data-based decision-making processes can be used to guide implementation of RtI Tier 1 interventions. The school has a total student population of 7, 000 with one-third of those students identified as low-income. Approximately 65% of the students are Caucasian, 30% are African American, and the remaining 5% are of Hispanic background. During the 2003–2004 school year, RtI behavioral implementation leadership team members were identified and trained on proper data collection and analysis processes. The school social worker was a member of the team. Leadership team members began preparing for RtI Tier 1 implementation by using SWIS and collecting preliminary data that included the number of office discipline referrals, attendance, tardies, suspensions, and expulsions that occurred within the past year at their school. The data revealed that over 16, 000 detentions were issued to students because they were tardy to school or late to class. As can be seen in Figure 4.6, these tardies represented 60% of all detentions issued and were identified as a chief issue of concern.

The Response to Intervention leadership team members also conducted direct observations to determine school-wide behavioral trends and combined those results with data from office discipline referrals, attendance rates, tardies, suspensions, and expulsions. Team members then discussed the findings by considering the following questions:

1. Who? When ? What? Are the problem behaviors the result of a few students or many students? If most of the infractions are committed by a small number of students, then further investigation is needed. Do families' circumstances impact the ability of students to be at school on time? In this case, the team decided that the tardy problem was experienced by numerous students and a school-wide approach was needed to address the issue.

2. Grade, socioeconomic, and ethnic/racial background. What are the data trends by grade level? Are the students who exhibit the identified problem from one grade level or different grade levels? Are particular socioeconomic or ethnic/racial groups overrepresented? The data revealed that students with tardies were widely represented by all grade levels, socioeconomic, and ethnic/ racial backgrounds. This further supported the leadership team's decision to adopt a school-wide approach to the problem.

3. Are the data reliable? Is there consensus among staff regarding the definition of the problem behavior? In this case, the definition of being tardy was simply "late to school or class." The leadership team determined that the act of being tardy needed further clarification so all students and staff had a common understanding so tardy behavior could be easily recognized when it occurred. Does it mean the student has crossed the doorway into the classroom? Does it mean the student is seated at his or her desk

when the bell rings? Do some teachers allow students to be late to class thereby avoiding an office discipline referral? The RtI leadership team members pondered these questions and concluded that there was no consistent definition of "late to school or class" in their school.

4. Is the problem the result of system issues? In this situation, the leadership members needed to investigate whether students were late to school because of bus transportation and parking issues. They gathered additional information to answer related questions: Do buses consistently run on time? Are teachers informed when a bus is late so students are not marked tardy? Is there adequate parking for students? The team also explored whether there was sufficient time between passing periods for students to get where they needed to go. Is there enough time for students to get from class to class or to go to their lockers then to class? Is there adequate supervision by teachers and staff between passing periods? Do they stand in the doorway to their classroom so they can monitor students and pre-correct them to ensure they arrive at class on time? The RtI leadership team members determined that transportation to/from school and travel time between classes was not part of the problem. However, they noted there was no consistent school-wide effort under way to ensure adequate supervision during passing periods.

5. Is there a particular location or area of the building where students are consistently late? In this case, the team found that the data did not reveal specific tendencies for tardies related to location.

6. What are the behavior expectations in our school? Are students taught the expectations? The RtI leadership team members contemplated whether and how students were informed of what it truly means to be tardy. At their school, there was no common procedure for teaching students behavioral expectations that explain what it looks like to be late to school.

7. What happens to students who do not follow the expected behaviors? Are teachers consistently completing office discipline referral forms and reinforcing the consequences? In this case, the leadership team learned that a key factor was the lack of consistency among teachers because some referred tardy students for disciplinary action while others did not.

The leadership team summarized the findings and used the results to design a school-wide approach intended to reduce the number of tardies in their school beginning with the 2004–2005 school year.

The initial intervention developed by the team required them to clarify the definition of being tardy and establish procedures for what should occur when students were late to class. They decided that students would be considered on time for class when they were seated at their desks in their classroom when the bell rang. Students who entered their classrooms after the bell rang would be considered tardy. New procedures were developed that required teachers to send tardy students to meet with hall monitors who were centrally located on each floor. The hall monitors were to complete the office discipline referral forms, assign detentions, give students a pass, and send them back to class. The hall monitors maintained data on the number of tardy students who received detentions. These data were analyzed weekly and reported to the RtI leadership team.

The school had a continuum of consequences for tardies that included detentions, in-school suspensions, and out-of-school suspensions. While the initial intervention resulted in a reduction in the number of tardies, the number of suspensions increased during the first year of RtI implementation. The leadership team created an additional intervention to combat the increase in suspensions called the Fourth Quarter Final Exam Exemption Incentive. Students were given the option of not taking their final exams if they received passing grades and did not have any tardies during the fourth quarter of school. Data at the end of the 2004–2005 school year revealed a reduction of 2,178 tardies but the number of suspensions remained unchanged.

The RtI leadership team continued to meet throughout the summer of 2005. After reviewing the end-of-year data, they identified a need to further strengthen a school-wide approach to tardies by hosting attendance reward parties. A Tier 1 intervention was developed that rewarded students with good attendance who did not receive any office discipline referrals. These students were invited to attend quarterly school-wide celebration parties. The themed parties featured an extended lunch period with pizza and a disk jockey, Waffle Dogs, a March Madness cookout with the local state representative, and a breakfast burrito party. The team also decided to merge school tardy data collection into the district-wide data system. This allowed the team to gather more detailed data that would be used to evaluate behavioral and academic issues more precisely.

The leadership team members also decided to continue the hall monitor intervention but realized there was a need to focus more closely on students with high numbers of tardies/detentions. This required a reevaluation of the continuum of disciplinary consequences for tardies, and a new Tier 2 behavioral intervention was put in place. Repeat offenders were identified by the data and referred to "First Steps Class." Upon receiving four detentions for being tardy, students were summoned to the office to meet with the assistant principal. A discussion was held to alert them of the need to be on time for class and to determine whether there were contributing factors that caused them to be tardy. Students were then referred to "First Steps Class" that provided them with additional information on problems caused by missing class and helped them to identify underlying

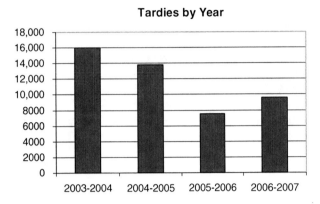

Figure 4.6 The number of tardies by school year.

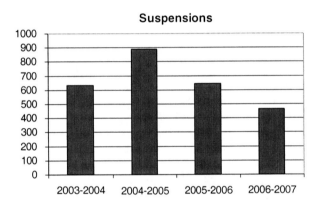

Figure 4.7 The number of suspension days by school year.

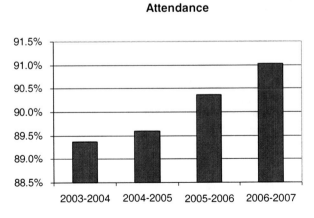

Figure 4.8 The percentage of student attendance by school year.

issues for being late. Students were taught a problem-solving process and encouraged to identify strategies they could use to prevent future tardies. Sample strategies included changing lockers, clarifying when to go to lockers between classes, giving students a map of the building, supplying alarm clocks, dispensing bus tokens, and distributing bus schedules. Students also reviewed their own tardy/detention data, the progression of disciplinary consequences, and their place on the continuum. As can be seen in Figures 4.6 and 4.7, data for the 2005–2006 school year revealed a further reduction in the number of tardies as well as the number of suspensions.

The RtI leadership team continued to monitor data trends and evaluate the progress of interventions designed to decrease tardies/detentions. New Tier 1 behavioral and academic interventions were implemented for the 2006–2007 school year. These interventions included adding a school-wide advisory period to the school day that was used to teach school-wide behavioral expectations. Another intervention was created that permitted seniors to exempt themselves from final exams if their scores from state required NCLB tests met or exceeded the state average. Additional Tier 2 interventions were put in place that assigned mentors to at-risk students and created individualized attendance improvement plans for repeat tardy offenders. A school-wide commitment was made to increase communication between teachers and parents through phone calls and personal contacts. By the end of the 2006–2007 school year, RtI behavioral data showed continued reductions in the number of tardies and suspensions and an increase in attendance.

The RtI team used data illustrated in Figures 4.6, 4.7, and 4.8 to evaluate progress of Tier 1 behavioral interventions. These figures summarize the various sources of data that were used by the leadership team to guide implementation of Tier 1 RtI interventions. The team examined the data on a regular basis, used it to identify areas of concern, and created effective school-wide interventions.

CHAPTER SUMMARY AND CONCLUSIONS

Response to Intervention Tier 1 behavioral interventions can be implemented as part of a systematic approach to promote socially appropriate behavior on a school-wide basis. The case example highlighted in this chapter illustrates how data collected with the SWIS system can be used to examine specific disciplinary problems and develop particular interventions to reduce office discipline referrals. School social workers should become key members of RtI leadership teams and facilitate data-based decision-making procedures. By playing an integral role in the data collection and analysis process, these teams can ensure that a school-wide approach to behavior management is effectively and efficiently implemented.

REFERENCES

Barrett, S., Bradshaw, C., & Lewis-Palmer, T. (2008). Maryland statewide PBIS initiative: Systems, evaluations and next steps. *Journal of Positive Behavior Interventions, 10*(2), 105–114.

Benbenishty, R., Astor, R., & Estrada J. (2008). School violence assessment: A conceptual framework, instruments, and methods. *Children and Schools, 30*(2), 71–81.

Ervin, R., Schaughency, E., Matthews, A., Goodman, S., & McGlinchey M. (2007). Primary and secondary prevention of behavior difficulties: Developing a data-informed problem-solving model to guide decision making at a school-wide level. *Psychology in Schools, 44*(1), 7–18.

Freeman, R., Smith, C., & Tieghi-Benet, M. (2003). Promoting implementation success through the use of continuous systems-level assessment strategies. *Journal of Positive Behavior Interventions, 5*(2), 66–70.

Horner, R., Sugai, G., & Todd, A. (2001). "Data" need not be a four-letter word: Using data to improve schoolwide discipline. *Positive Behavior, 3*(20), 20–22.

Irvin, L., Horner, R., Ingram, K., Todd, A., Sugai, G., & Boland, J. (2006). Using Office Discipline Referral data for decision making about student behavior in elementary and middle schools: An empirical evaluation study. *Journal of Positive Behavior Interventions, 8*(1), 10–23.

Irvin, L., Tobin, T., Sprague, J., Sugai, G., & Vincent, C. (2004). Validity of office discipline referral measures as indices of school-wide behavioral status and effects of school-wide behavioral interventions. *Journal of Positive Behavior Interventions, 6*(3),131–147.

Lewis, T., & Sugai, G. (1999). Effective behavior support: A systems approach to proactive schoolwide management. *Focus on Exceptional Children, 3*(6), 1–24.

May, S., Ard, W., Todd, A., Horner, R., Glasgow, A., Sugai, G., & Sprague, J. (2000). School-wide Information Systems (SWIS). Eugene: University of Oregon, Educational and Community Supports.

National Center for Educational Statistics. (2008). *Digest of Education Statistics.* Retrieved December 1, 2008, from http://nces.ed./gov/.

School-Wide Information System. www.swis.org.

Scott, T. (2001). A schoolwide example of positive behavior support. *Journal of Positive Behavior Interventions, 3*(2), 88–94.

Scott, T., & Martinek, G. (2006). Coaching positive behavior support in school settings: Tactics and data-based decision making. *Journal of Positive Behavior Interventions, 8*(3), 165–173.

Skiba, R., Peterson, R., & Williams, T. (1997). Office referrals and suspension: Disciplinary intervention in middle schools. *Education and Treatment of Children, 20*(3), 295–316.

Sugai, G. (2006, February 13). *School-wide positive behavior support: Getting started.* Retrieved October 2, 2007, from http://www.pbis.org/files/George/co0206a.ppt.

Sugai, G., Sprague, J., Horner, R., & Walker, H. (2000). Preventing school violence: The use of office discipline referrals to assess and monitor school-wide discipline interventions. *Journal of Emotional and Behavioral Disorders, 8*(2), 94–101.

Tobin, T., Sugai, G., & Colvin, G. (2000). Using discipline referrals to make decisions. *National Association of Secondary School Principals Bulletin, 84*(6), 106–117.

Walker, H., Stieber, S., Ramsey, E., & Oneil, R. (1993). School behavioral profiles of arrested versus nonarrested adolescents. *Exceptionality, 1*(4), 249–266.

Wright, J., & Dusek, J. (1998). Compiling school base rates for disruptive behaviors from student disciplinary referral data. *School Psychology Review, 27*(1), 138–147.

5

TIER 1
CASE EXAMPLE
Signs of Suicide (SOS)

JOSEPH R. GIANESIN

School social workers working in a Response to Intervention (RtI) system can make a difference in the lives of students. In this chapter, a case example of a school social worker developing and implementing an evidenced-based Tier 1 intervention is discussed.

The case example takes place in an alternative middle/high school where a school social worker employed in the Chicopee Public Schools, along with graduate social work interns from Springfield College School of Social Work, implemented a program with high school students in classrooms at Chicopee Academy, an alternative middle/high school located in Chicopee, Massachusetts. The evidenced-based program they chose to use is the SOS (Signs of Suicide) program endorsed by the United States Department of Public Health.

BRIEF OVERVIEW OF THE SIGNS OF SUICIDE (SOS) PROGRAM

The SOS Signs of Suicide program for secondary schools is a cost-effective Tier 1 universal support program of mental health screening and suicide prevention, which can be easily implemented by school social workers. The program is a widely studied, evidenced-based program that has been co-sponsored by the National Association of Social Workers. It

70

was one of the first programs to be selected by the U.S. Department of Health and Human Services Substance Abuse and Mental Health Services Administration (SAMHSA, 2008b) for its National Registry of Evidence-based Programs and Practices. It is a school-based suicide prevention program that has been shown to reduce suicidality in a randomized, controlled study (Aseltine & DeMartino. 2004). The SOS program uses an educational component to increase students' understanding and recognition of depressive symptoms in themselves and others, and a self-screening component to help students assess depressive symptoms and suicidal thoughts, prompting them to seek assistance when coping with these issues.

According to Aseltine and DeMartino (2004), "SOS is a school-based prevention program that incorporates two prominent suicide prevention strategies into a single program by combining curricula to raise awareness of suicide and its related issues with a brief screening for depression and other risk factors associated with suicidal behavior (p.446)." The goal of the SOS program is to reduce suicidal behavior among adolescents through two mechanisms: an educational component of the program that increases the students' understanding and recognition of depressive symptoms in themselves and others, and the use of a self-screening component to assess and evaluate the depressive symptoms and suicidal ideations they might be experiencing and then to seek help or assistance from someone at the school or in the community (Aseltine & DeMartino, 2004).

Typically, the SOS program is used as a two-day secondary school-based intervention that includes screening and education. All students are screened for depression and suicide risk and referred for professional help as indicated. Students also view a video that teaches them to recognize signs of depression and suicide in others. They are taught that the appropriate response to these signs is to acknowledge them, let the person know you care, and tell a responsible adult (either with the person or on that person's behalf). Students also participate in guided classroom discussions about suicide and depression. The intervention is designed to prevent suicide attempts, increase knowledge about suicide and depression, clarify the facts and myths about suicide and depression, and increase help-seeking behavior.

The SOS program consists of three components: prevention, intervention, and post-intervention. Prevention includes creating a school team that starts the assessment process, having the school connected to outside agencies and referral sources, providing active support in classrooms, developing the program, providing professional development to teachers and parents, and involving the community. Intervention includes knowing the signs of suicidal behavior and risk factors, making necessary assessments of suicide and referrals, and staying with a child until a relationship is established with an outside agency. Intervention focuses on identifying possible suicidal students, conducting an appropriate and thorough assessment, intervening on behalf of the student with family and support systems, and providing referral and intervention services appropriate to the student's need. Post-intervention includes providing follow-up support to the student and their family ensuring that needed services have been put into place. For those schools where a suicide attempt was successful, follow-up support and services need to be provided to students and school staff who were affected by the suicide. In the post-intervention phase, it is important not to glorify the suicide but rather to connect to the importance of life (Ward, 1995).

SOS PROGRAM STRENGTHS

The implementation materials of the SOS program offer detailed information that can directly assist implementation. The intervention is well described in videos, brochures, and other implementation materials with considerable attention paid to implementing this program in a school setting. The program DVD is racially and culturally diverse, includes a mix of brief presentations of facts and stories from teens who have been suicidal, and is generally an excellent resource that seems appealing to a teen audience. The training manual provides step-by-step guidance for providers in addition to online resources and articles to increase implementer knowledge about depression and suicide. Feedback forms, screening tools, and response cards, along with examples of data that have been collected in other schools, provide guidance on data that could be collected and analyzed for quality assurance (http://www.nrepp.samhsa.gov/programfulldetails.asp?PROGRAM_ID=66#description).

SOS PROGRAM WEAKNESSES

No formal training curriculum is offered to teach implementers the skills required to work with systems to gain support for the program, be an effective trainer, or do effective presentations (although, in Massachusetts, the Department of Public Health did conduct training sessions for implementing the program). Supervision and support for the lead implementer is not addressed, and very little information is provided on how this program can fit into existing high school schedules (SAMHSA 2006; http://www.nrepp.samhsa.gov/programfulldetails. asp?PROGRAM_ID=66#description).

Outcome measures are more qualitative than quantitative although recent research by Aseltine, James, Schilling, and Glanovsky (2007) reported, "Significantly lower rates of suicide attempts and greater knowledge and more adaptive attitudes about depression and suicide were observed among students who were in an SOS intervention group. SOS continues to be the only universal school-based suicide prevention program to demonstrate significant effects on self-reported suicide attempts in a study utilizing a randomized experimental design. Moreover, the beneficial effects of SOS were observed among high school-aged youth from diverse racial/ethnic backgrounds, highlighting the program's utility as a universal prevention program (p. 1)."

EFFICACY STUDIES TO SUPPORT THE SOS PROGRAM

The SOS program is the only school-based suicide prevention program that has been shown in a randomized, controlled study to reduce suicidality (Aseltine & DeMartino, 2004).A random sample of 2,100 students was selected from five high schools in Columbus, Georgia, and Hartford, Connecticut. Participants were randomly assigned to intervention and control groups. Both groups completed self-administered questionnaires three months after the prevention program. There was a significant reduction in the number of self-reported suicide attempts following exposure to the program. Additionally, an increase in knowledge and adaptive attitudes about depression and suicide were also found although no significant effects were observed in suicidal ideation and help-seeking behavior (Aseltine & DeMartino, 2004).

Another outcome study done by Aseltine (2003) on the SOS program reported that it was effective in increasing help-seeking behavior; improving communication among students, teachers, and parents; and identifying students in need of help. There was an almost 60% increase in help-seeking behavior after the implementation of the plan.

COMMUNITY AND SCHOOL DESCRIPTION

Chicopee Academy is an alternative middle school and high school located in Chicopee, Massachusetts, a suburb of Springfield in the western part of the state. One of the oldest communities in that region, Chicopee produces sporting goods, electronic components, machinery, plastics, packaging textiles, electrical equipment, chemicals, surgical products, and more. Over 100 diversified industries are located in Chicopee, including the publication facilities of the *Wall Street Journal*. Although once defined by the predominant nationality of its immigrant occupants, historically largely Polish and French Canadian, these neighborhoods are now occupied by people of many cultures. The most recent census reported a median income for a household in the city was $35, 672, and the median income for a family was $44, 136.

Chicopee Academy was established in September 2005. It was designed to serve high school students in three main classifications: (1) students with behavioral disturbances in both general and special education; (2) students with emotional disturbances in both general and special education; (3) students in out of district placements who are transitioning back to the district and require specialized services and support to help them succeed.

Chicopee Academy Program serves approximately 100 students from the Chicopee Public Schools in grades 6–12. The school is staffed by a team of highly trained teachers and school social workers who help students toward personal success through individualized educational planning and clinical support. The school strives to involve families and to form home/school/community partnerships to support students.

The students who attend the school have had significant problems in adjusting to their regular school environment and have been largely unsuccessful at school. Problems with attendance, discipline, and behavior are common among this population. At least 75% to 80% of the population has experienced some type of traumatic incident or exposure to violence.

Chicopee Academy, like many of its educational counterparts, has limitations and gaps in existing programs. The amount of student need far exceeds the staff's ability to meet those needs. The school is different from its normal high school counterparts that have a diverse population of students. Chicopee Academy services students, who are at high risk of dropping out, have behavior problems that interfere with their ability to get the most out of school, and experience substantial family problems. Demographically, the school serves a low-income population as evidenced by 87.5% of the student population receiving free or reduced price lunch. The school district in general has been impacted by changing demographics that include an increase in a low socioeconomic Latino population for whom English is a second language. In many instances, the parents of these students have become disillusioned with school systems based on their own past unfavorable experiences or their child's experiences. If their student is referred to Chicopee Academy, it is likely for disciplinary or behavioral problems. Their experiences with the school system are highly likely to have been negative. The challenges to meet the needs of these students and their families are to hire a diverse faculty and staff who have bilingual skills, to train staff to be both culturally and trauma sensitive, and to engage positively parents who have been alienated from school.

SCHOOL SOCIAL WORKERS

The Chicopee School District and administration recognized the value of school social workers in an alternative school and chose to staff the school with three school social workers. Of these, two have the title school social worker/school adjustment counselor and the other is a behavioral interventionist. The school social workers have an alliance and partnership with the Springfield College School of Social Work, which provides graduate student interns for the school. The school social workers provide supervision for graduate interns placed at the school.

Currently, Chicopee Public Schools has implemented Response to Intervention (RtI) district-wide. Chicopee Academy has been at the forefront of implementing the concept of RtI at Tier 1, Tier 2, and Tier 3 levels as the leadership saw it as an approach that increased the opportunity for all students to meet academic achievement standards through early intervention with students whose academic and/or behavioral needs placed them at risk. Since the school was recently reorganized, using evidenced-based interventions at the start made staff and faculty collaboration much easier to implement. For Chicopee Academy, the students were at such high risk to begin with, any other alternative would have been unsuccessful.

Chicopee Academy is like many high schools as it provides individual and group counseling for students through normal channels, such as the school social workers/school adjustment counselors. In addition, the district contracts with several outpatient counseling agencies to provide school-based outpatient therapeutic services for students who have emotional and mental health problems. With the formation of a new alternative program, Chicopee Academy seized upon the opportunity to create a school that has as a theme: a safe and positive school climate. The commitment to that theme has brought a major change in the culture of the school. Students and staff alike feel supported and safe after many institutional and classroom attempts to facilitate a change in the culture of the school. Because of the student population and the commitment to these students, administrators and staff began to work diligently to collaborate with recognized experts in the fields of child and family violence, trauma, and suicide prevention and intervention. The school also developed partnerships with specialists on community violence and created partnerships with local community mental health providers. One such provider was the Department of Public Health and the SOS Program.

CHICOPEE ACADEMY AND THE NEED FOR A SUICIDE PREVENTION/INTERVENTION PROGRAM

Suicide among high school–age young people is a serious public health problem. According to the National Center for Health Statistics (http://www.cdc.gov/mmwr/preview/mmwrhtml/mm5635a2.htm 2007), the suicide rate for youth and young adults, aged 15 to 24, has tripled since 1950. Suicides among young people nationwide have increased dramatically in recent years. Each year, thousands of teenagers commit suicide. It is considered the third leading cause of death for 15- to 24-year-olds, and the sixth leading cause of death for 5- to 14-year-olds.

Many of the students who attend this alternative school have high psychosocial risk factors that complicate their ability to deal with depression, mental illness, and family problems. The administration and staff at Chicopee Academy used the data from attendance records, disciplinary reports, crisis incidents, and referrals to the school social workers to implement an evidenced-based program for addressing depression, self-harm, and suicidal ideations.

DESCRIPTION OF THE RtI SOS PROGRAM AT CHICOPEE ACADEMY

The SOS program was initially piloted at Chicopee Academy by the school social worker and graduate social work interns from Springfield College School of Social Work. The program was initially implemented in two self-contained emotional/behavioral classrooms consisting of eight and seven students, respectively, with significant emotional and behavioral needs, their teacher, and a teacher's aide. A total of 18 students, two teachers, and two teacher aides along with the school social worker were involved in this pilot. The program was so successful that it became a universal, school-wide support implemented at every grade level and classroom.

Prior to implementing the program, the school social worker sent a note home to parents informing them of the purpose of the program and held a parent information meeting to answer questions and provide feedback regarding community resources. Parents who attended the information meeting were shown the video used in the SOS program followed by a discussion of depression symptoms and warning signs of suicidal behaviors. They were also given the parent version of the Brief Screen for Adolescent Depression (BSAD), which is a depression screening tool for teens and adolescents. Parents were told about community resources offering mental health counseling, encouraged to attend the classroom sessions with students and teachers, and given a forum to express their concerns. Following the parent meeting a note was sent home prior to students completing the BASD screening form. No parent objected to their student being screened.

The program was conducted over the course of two weeks. SOS incorporates two prominent suicide prevention strategies into a single program, combining a curriculum to raise awareness of suicide and its related issues with a brief screening for depression and other risk factors associated with suicidal behavior. According to the American Foundation for Suicide Prevention, SOS promotes the concept that suicide is directly related to mental illness, typically depression, and that it is not a normal reaction to stress or emotional upset (SAMHSA, 2008a). The basic goal of the program is to teach students to respond to the signs of suicide as an emergency, much as one would react to signs of a heart attack. Students are taught to recognize the signs and symptoms of suicide and depression in themselves and others and to follow the specific action steps needed to respond to those signs (Aseltine, 2005).

The main teaching materials are a video and discussion guide. Program activities usually include an introduction of the topic and a viewing of a video entitled, *Friends for Life: Preventing Teen Suicide.* The video includes dramatizations depicting right and wrong ways to treat someone who is depressed and suicidal. It features interviews with people whose lives have been touched by suicide as well as interviews with school-based professionals and experts in the child psychiatry and child suicide prevention fields. After watching the video, students are asked to complete the Brief Screen for Adolescent Depression (BSAD)—a seven-question screening instrument for depression, suicidality, and related risk factors. The students themselves score the form.

At Chicopee Academy, students watched the video and were encouraged to talk about their own experiences with others. They showed great interest in the topic and were highly motivated to learn about the material. Discussion topics after the video often were linked with depression and drug and alcohol use. The discussion section follows a curriculum that uses an action-oriented approach instructing students how to ACT (Acknowledge, Care, and Tell) in the face of this mental health emergency. The SOS literature defines ACT as Acknowledge that your friend has a problem; Care: Let your friends know that you are there for them and CARE what happens; and Tell a trusted adult about your concerns (http://staffweb.wwcsd.net/foresterd/SignsofSuicideProgram.htm).

Students whose scores on the BASD were considered a strong indicator of depressive disorder and those who scored in the high range of the instrument were offered counseling both at school and through community resources. Students who answered affirmatively to questions about suicidal thoughts or attempts were strongly recommended to see a mental health professional regardless of their score. Follow-up post-intervention work is done with each of the students who demonstrate any suicidal ideation or strong depression. Often with such screening, students will identify peers who may or may not attend the same school as possibly being at risk for suicide. When Chicopee Academy students identified such friends or acquaintances, the school social workers contacted their colleagues at other schools for follow-up. The identified students received counseling services and referrals for assessment by community providers.

KEY CONSIDERATIONS FOR IMPLEMENTATION

Before implementing any screening program, school social workers should consider the following:

- Population and setting (Defining the population and determining risk and need. Consideration for major stakeholders such as parents, teachers, community, and administration should be taken into account.)
- Screening instrument (Selecting the screening tool and its fidelity)
- Staffing and referral network (Resources, linkages, personnel, protocol, administrative support, etc.)
- Quality assurance (How will the program be monitored, evaluated, and assessed? What are the expected outcomes?)
- Legal and ethical issues (Informed consent, risks, benefits, limits of screening, community support (Joe & Bryant 2007, p. 225)

Other pragmatic considerations are the cost of program materials. The SOS program kits are relatively inexpensive—about $300. Schools implementing this program will need to send key personnel like the school social worker and teaching staff for one to three hours of training and need to designate a site coordinator. Program materials are supplied by the developer and include

- Procedure manual (40 pages)
- Teacher training video (28 minutes)

- Student video (25 minutes)
- Teacher discussion guide
- Student self-screening form and administrator protocols
- Parent version of the student screening form and directions for parent use
- Support materials (anti-suicide posters, handouts, cards, etc.)

For additional program information, contact www.mentalhealthscreening. org.

Another key consideration is measuring implementation fidelity and results of the program. Signs of Suicide has an extensive research base that makes implementation of the instruments fairly simple, as suicide attempts are indicated by a single self-report item. Since the SOS program uses the student self-screening form, students self-identify or identify peers who may be at risk for depression or suicidality. Compilation and record keeping are straightforward tasks in case management. A separate pre-post study of SOS (Aseltine, 2003) reported increases in the number of school-wide referrals for suicidality/depression. Randomized studies of SOS have shown that participants were less likely than comparable students who did not participate in the intervention to report attempting suicide in the past three months (www.nrepplsamhsal.gov/programfulldetails. asp?Progam_ID=66 9/22/08). An experimentally designed study (Aseltine & DeMartino, 2004) found that program participants were 40% less likely to report a suicide attempt in the three months following program implementation than were students in a control group.

Anecdotal reports from students themselves can document the results of the program. For example, Sadie, a senior in a Massachusetts high school participated in an SOS program presentation: "Once you break someone's trust you don't know where you're going to end up yourself. SOS gives students a different perspective; you really see how dangerous it is not to speak out.... When it comes down to losing a friend because they're not talking to you anymore or losing a friend because they lost their life, you know, I think this makes people come out and say, 'This person needs help' " (www.print-this.clickablity.com/pt/cpt?action=cpt&title=Suicide+prevention+program9/22/08).

KNOWLEDGE AND SKILLS SCHOOL SOCIAL WORKERS NEED FOR SOS

School social workers who work with adolescent populations must implement programs that are evidenced based at the appropriate tier. When implementing an SOS program, school social workers are often faced with resistance from administrators, faculty, and parents who believe that providing education on the topic of suicidal behaviors actually increases suicidal thoughts and behavior. No matter how well intended, parents and administrators who resist this type of intervention have little research to substantiate their fears. In fact, according to Joe and Bryant (2007), the growing body of research on suicide prevention programs indicates that suicide-related content does not encourage individuals to consider attempting suicide.

School social workers need to formulate a well-thought-out plan before implementing this type of program. Considerations for implementation include suicide prevention, intervention, and post-intervention. This usually entails finding a program that has the following features: ease of implementation, well-established curriculum, staff development considerations, student friendly content, culturally sensitive and representative content, and instruments to measure implementation fidelity and results.

Although many SOS programs are implemented as a universal support in Tier 1, many school social workers and school administrators would argue that a more efficient use of time and resources would be to specifically target at-risk youth rather than conduct a school-wide screening or implement a school-wide prevention curriculum (Joe & Bryant, 2007). Joe and Bryant argue that suicide prevention screening should be a two-layer system, and this framework should be considered when developing empirically based suicide screening programs and tools. The first layer utilizes a crisis response on the part of the school social worker which includes taking action, making collateral contacts to keep the student safe, notifying parents or guardians, and seeking immediate help from crisis personnel. In layer two, the school provides mental health resources, monitors students at risk, and counsels parents on how to navigate the mental health issues of their child. In either case, these students are identified as having some significant risk factors.

The social worker at Chicopee Academy took a very proactive approach to implementing the SOS program. She reviewed the evidenced-based research on the SOS program. She contacted the Department of Public Health and found an SOS training session to attend. She convinced her principal to support her efforts. After attending the training she developed a flowchart for planning implementation of the program.

OUTCOMES OF THE SOS PROGRAM AT CHICOPEE ACADEMY

The school social worker and the social work interns saw many benefits of the SOS program. Initially, they were able to make important contacts with parents who have had negative experiences with public schools. The effort to inform and educate parents about the program helped develop rapport with them and gain their trust. In addition, the information on available community resources and mental health supports was often unknown to parents before they attended the parent meeting.

For students who participated in the program, these efforts provided confirmation that the SOS program is a potent tool for curtailing suicidal behavior among diverse groups of high school–age youth. The SOS program demonstrated that it continues to be the only universal school-based suicide prevention program for which a reduction in self-reported suicide attempts can be documented. For Chicopee Academy, the results were in real student responses. Five students filled out the response cards indicating they were either extremely depressed or contemplating suicide. Two of the five students required inpatient hospitalization. Additionally, contacts with other school personnel were made as friends of students who did not attend Chicopee Academy were identified as having suicidal ideations. The program was so successful that it has been implemented every year in February since the pilot project began. Qualitative and quantitative data for the program indicate a reduction in crisis interventions and disciplinary referrals. Using evidence-based programs and building a responsive culture in a school that advocates safety and nurturing responses to students in need can benefit all those involved in helping students achieve their full potential. SOS as a Tier 1 RtI universal support merits serious consideration from school social workers, school counselors, and administrators seeking to bolster their school's suicide intervention strategies, health curricula, and prevention portfolio.

REFERENCES

Aseltine, R.H., James, A., Schilling, E.A., & Glanovsky, J. (2007). Evaluating the SOS suicide prevention program: A replication and extension. *BMC Public Health*, 7:161doi:10.1186/1471-2458-7-161.

Aseltine, R. H. (2003). An evaluation of a school based prevention program. *Adolescent and Family Health, 3*(2), 81–88.

Aseltine, R. H., Jr., & DeMartino, R. (2004). An outcome evaluation of the SOS suicide prevention program. *American Journal of Public Health, 94*(3), 446–451.

Joe, J., & Bryant, H. (2007). Evidence-based suicide prevention screening in schools. *Journal of the National Association of Social Workers, 29*(4), 219–227.

National Center for Health Statistics, Centers for Disease Control (CDC). (2007, September 27). *Suicide trends among youths and young adults aged 10–24 years—United States, 1990–2004, 56*(35), 905–908.Retrieved October 1, 2008, from http://www.cdc.gov/mmwr/preview/mmwrhtml/mm5635a2.htm.

SAMHSA (2008a) SOS: Signs of Suicide. *Suicide Prevention Resource Center (SPRC).* Retrieved August 31, 2008 from http://www.sprc.org/featured_resources/bpr/ebpp_PDF/lifelines.pdf

SAMHSA. (2008b). *SAMHSA's National registry of evidence-based programs and practices (NREPP).* Retrieved August 31, 2008, from http://www.nrepp.samhsa.gov/programfulldetails.asp?PROGRAM_ID=66.

SAMHSA. (2006). *Signs of Suicide (SOS) review.* Retrieved August 31, 2008, from http://www.nrepp.samhsa.gov/programfulldetails.asp?PROGRAM_ID=66#description.

Shaffer, D., Garland, A., Vieland, V., Underwood, M., & Busner, C. (1991). The impact of curriculum-based suicide prevention programs for teenagers. *Journal of the American Academy of Child and Adolescent Psychiatry, 30*(4), 588–596.

Shaffer, D., Scott, M., Wilcox, H., Maslow, C., Hicks, R., Lucas, C., Garfinkel, R., et al. (2004). The Columbia suicide screen: Validity and reliability of a screen for youth suicide and depression. *Journal of the American Academy of Child and Adolescent Psychiatry, 43*(1), 71–80.

Ward, B. R. (1995). The school's role in the prevention of youth suicide. *Social Work in Education, 17*(2), 92–100.

SECTION II

Tier 2 Targeted Group Interventions

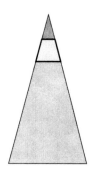

Figure II.1[a]

In Tier 2, targeted group interventions are provided to students who do not adequately benefit from the universal supports and instruction provided to all students in Tier 1. These interventions are more intensive than universal instruction and are typically provided to small groups of students with similar instructional or functional needs. Typically, 5%–10% of students will require this level of support. Though instruction in Tier 2 is more intensified or differentiated, the focus of instruction continues to be on teaching the core curriculum/expectations that have been defined for all students. Chapters in this section describe the essential features of targeted group interventions and the implementation of two targeted group intervention programs.

In Chapter 6, Braaksma Fynaardt and Richardson describe the essential features of targeted group interventions in Tier 2, key considerations in implementation, and the knowledge and skills school social workers need to participate in the design and implementation of these interventions. The implementation of two targeted group intervention programs is provided in Chapters 7 and 8. Joye and Alvarez provide a case illustration of the implementation of the WhyTry program in the Denver Public Schools, and Bostick, Diehl, and Scates describe the implementation of the Reconnecting Youth program in Evansville, Indiana.

6

TIER 2
TARGETED GROUP
INTERVENTIONS

ANGELISA BRAAKSMA FYNAARDT & JOHN RICHARDSON

Three tiers of supports are put in place within the Response to Intervention (RtI) model. The model includes increasingly intensive levels of intervention to help schools efficiently and effectively address students' social-emotional-behavioral development. Tier 1 supports are intended to facilitate the development of an environment that elicits appropriate behaviors and prevents problem behaviors from beginning. The universal system includes defining and teaching students expected social-emotional-behavioral skills, using an acknowledgment system to recognize students who demonstrate appropriate behaviors and employing a system of consistent corrective consequences to address behavioral infractions. The universal system also includes the collection of school-wide data to guide systemic decisions.

Although Tier 1 supports have demonstrated success with approximately 80%–90% of a school's student population (Colvin, Kameenui, & Sugai, 1993; Lewis, Sugai, & Colvin, 1998; Sprague et al., 2001; Sugai, Sprague, Horner, & Walker, 2000; Taylor-Greene et al., 1997), some students continue to demonstrate social-emotional-behavioral problems and may need more supports beyond universal instruction to demonstrate appropriate behaviors at school. The targeted group of students includes approximately 5% to 10% of students who are at risk for developing severe problem behavior (s) due to poor peer relations, low academic achievement, and/or chaotic home environments (Hawken & Horner, 2003; Lewis & Sugai, 1999). Targeted group interventions in the Tier 2 system are designed to meet these

85

students' social-emotional-behavioral needs and to prevent students from developing more serious and chronic patterns of problem behaviors at school.

TIER 2 DESCRIPTION AND KEY FEATURES

Tier 2 targeted group interventions are introduced to students whose behaviors do not respond to the universal instruction provided to all students. These interventions are more intensive than universal instruction and are typically provided to small groups of students with similar instructional or functional needs. Typically, a school will need to develop the Tier 2 system to meet the needs of students who are not benefiting from universal instruction. However, in some rare situations, the number of students needing secondary and tertiary supports may be low enough that the school may be able to meet the needs of all students with individual interventions. The Tier 2 system is primarily designed for use in schools with more students needing behavior support than can be supported via intensive and individual tertiary support. It is also designed for students who are at risk of chronic problem behavior but for whom high-intensity interventions are not essential (OSEP Technical Assistance Center on Positive Behavioral Interventions & Supports, 2004).

While instruction becomes more intensified or differentiated in Tier 2, the focus continues to be on teaching the social-emotional-behavioral expectations that have been defined for all students in Tier 1. Assessment data are collected to determine which students may need Tier 2 interventions, which students have benefited from targeted group interventions, and which students are not successful with a group intervention and require intense, individualized interventions to acquire the knowledge and skills identified in Tier 1.

Targeted group interventions are implemented through a systemic process, which includes the identification of students and their respective instructional needs, the implementation of targeted interventions, and the evaluation of implementation integrity and student progress. A key feature of the targeted system is its continuous availability and rapid access to interventions. This is accomplished by defining targeted intervention(s) and training all staff to access and implement the intervention(s). Staff members receive training prior to student identification so that if and when an intervention is needed, all staff members are able to quickly respond to student needs.

Another key feature of targeted interventions is that they are designed to be easy for any and/or all staff members to implement. The intensity of instruction and supports provided to a student should match the intensity and severity of the problem behavior(s). Targeted interventions should include assessment(s) and instruction that are more intense than universal interventions, yet are less intense than an individualized assessment and intervention plan.

The instruction provided within the targeted system must also be aligned with the universal system. The knowledge and skills that are identified and taught within the targeted system are in alignment with the core, universal behavioral expectations. For example, a school-wide expectation may be that all students are respectful. School staff may have defined respect as "treating others the way that you want to be treated," and may have identified and taught all students that using manners is demonstrating respect at school. A targeted intervention that is more intense than the universal level of instruction may be focused on specifically teaching a group of students when and how to use the phrases "please," "thank you," and "excuse me." The targeted intervention may also include more practice opportunities and more feedback on student performance until the students master the skills.

TIER 2 IMPLEMENTATION PROCESS

The first step in the implementation process is to identify students who may benefit from targeted interventions. Once these students have been identified, one will need to identify students' specific instructional needs and sort students into intervention groups. Last, targeted interventions are implemented and data are collected to evaluate the implementation of the targeted intervention and the corresponding outcomes. These data are then used to make instructional decisions for these students.

Screening Assessment to Identify Students in Need of Tier 2 Support

One hallmark of RtI is the use of screening assessments to identify students who may need Tier 2 supports to be successful in the school setting. Various assessment data and information may be used within an RtI system to identify students who may benefit from instruction or supports beyond Tier 1. Behavior incident data and social skills assessments are the primary measures used to identify students in need of targeted interventions. Teacher, student, or parent referrals may also be used as a mechanism to identify students for Tier 2 interventions.

BEHAVIORAL INCIDENT DATA   The most common and readily available data source to use when considering targeted supports is behavior incident information or discipline reports. Discipline incident data may be used to evaluate the overall impact of social-emotional-behavioral instruction and to identify students who may need targeted intervention support to be successful at school. A general guideline is that students with a moderate number of major discipline incidents (two to five per year) should be considered for targeted intervention supports (Horner, Sugai, Todd, & Lewis-Palmer, 2005).

School staff may want to consider other behavior data as additional screening assessments. Potential data sources include attendance rates, suspension data, detention information, grades, and homework completion rates. For example, if a school-based team or staff member reviews attendance data and identifies a student who is repeatedly missing school, that student may potentially benefit from Tier 2 supports like a mentoring program to get the student connected to school. A student who is new to the district/building may also be a potential candidate for a targeted intervention. For example, a new student may benefit from a "welcome" club in which the new student is able to meet others, tour the building, and learn about the school-wide behavioral expectations.

SOCIAL SKILLS ASSESSMENTS   Social skills assessments may also be used to identify students who need more support beyond Tier 1. Behavior incident data primarily reflect the students who demonstrate externalizing behaviors. It may not accurately screen for or identify students with internalizing behaviors like depression or anxiety. Therefore, some schools may decide to use a formal social skills screening assessment to identify students who may have internalizing or externalizing disorders. For example, staff may choose to use the Systematic Screening for Behavior Disorders (SSBD; Walker & Severson, 1992) or the School Social Behavior Skills assessment (Merrell, 1993) to identify students in need of additional support beyond universal instruction in Tier 1. Once identified, these students could be placed into different targeted invention groups to meet their specific needs.

TEACHER, PARENT, OR STUDENT REFERRALS   Teacher, parent, and student referrals should also be considered as a mechanism to identify students in need of targeted group interventions. It is important that these concerns be validated by behavioral incident data whenever possible. However, teachers and parents may have knowledge that may not be evident in behavior incident reports or certain social skills assessments. If a school is going to include teacher or parent referrals as an identification method, the school must develop a referral form and process. In addition, staff must receive training on the referral process and requirements. Last, if a school is not using a social skills assessment to identify students with internalizing behaviors but is relying upon staff to identify these students, the staff members must receive adequate training on these types of psychological needs to be able to recognize symptoms of internalizing disorders and make accurate referrals.

Schools may also want to consider developing a process for students to refer themselves or other students. Some students may identify within themselves a need for more support to be successful at school. In addition, students may have information about other students that the adults in the school or home are unaware of. Given students' access to personal information about other students, it may be beneficial to identify a mechanism they can use to alert adults to any potential issues so that supports may be provided to these students if needed.

Diagnostic Assessment to Identify Student Needs

Once students have been identified through screening assessments, diagnostic assessments should be completed to determine student specific instructional and functional needs. In Tier 2, it is recommended that a functional behavioral assessment (FBA) be completed to identify the function of the student's behavior and his or her instructional needs. The intensity of the diagnostic assessment or FBA should match the intensity of the problem behavior. Therefore, the FBA that is completed as part of the Tier 2 system may be very brief. For example, the FBA may just include a record review and an informal conversation with the student's teacher. The rigor of this FBA is considerably less than what is needed to develop a Tier 3 intensive individualized intervention (see Chapter 9). A more rigorous FBA will usually include more formal interviews with multiple people (e.g., general education teacher, special education teachers, parent(s), and student), direct observations of the student in multiple settings across multiple days, and more formal assessments of student skills.

Identify and Implement Group Interventions

Another hallmark of RtI systems is that students receive instruction and intervention supports that are matched to their specific instructional and/or functional needs. Once student needs have been identified with diagnostic assessment, specific interventions may be selected to meet student-specific needs. Students should essentially be "sorted" into various intervention groups and students with similar needs should be grouped together to receive intervention services.

For example, 15 students were identified by the screening assessment data as needing supports beyond the universal system. The diagnostic assessment revealed that three students struggled with reading and their behavior was maintained by escape from academic demands to read. The brief functional assessments also revealed that four students struggled with anger management skills. The last eight students demonstrated problem behaviors that were maintained by attention. Students were respectively placed into a reading instructional intervention, anger management social skills group, and the Behavior Education Program (Crone, Horner, & Hawken, 2004) based upon sorting the students into groups with similar needs. It is this process that makes targeted interventions a more efficient use of resources as compared to individual interventions for each of the fifteen students.

Use Data to Guide Instructional Decisions

IMPLEMENTATION INTEGRITY   Prior to implementing the identified interventions, one should identify how implementation integrity will be assessed along with how student progress will be monitored. Interventions need to be implemented as designed to make decisions about the effectiveness of the intervention both for the individual student and for the system as a whole. Implementation integrity checks should ensure that the intervention is being implemented as scheduled (e.g., actually for 20 minutes a day, three days a week) and that the critical features of the intervention are being implemented as designed. Permanent products such as journals, log sheets, and student worksheets can provide proof of implementation fidelity. Other sources of data may include teacher interviews or direct observation of the instruction. Figure 6.1 is an example of a form that may be used to document intervention integrity.

Student: _____   Grade: _____
Teacher: _____   Observer: _____

Directions: Put a checkmark in the column for *each step* for which there is evidence of a permanent product. At the end of each day, *calculate daily integrity* by dividing the number of checkmarks by the total number of steps possible. At the end of the week, *calculate component integrity* by dividing the number of checkmarks for each step by the total number of days per week.

Intervention Step Date	M	T	W	TH	F	Component Integrity %	Permanent Products
							1.
							2.
							3.
							4.
							5.
Daily Integrity %							

Figure 6.1   Sample behavior implementation integrity assessment.
Source: Developed by Heartland Area Education Agency 11, Johnston, Iowa. Used with permission.

PROGRESS MONITORING   A plan must be developed to determine whether the student is making progress prior to targeted intervention implementation. To monitor progress, the specific features of the student's problem behaviors must first be identified. For example, the student demonstrates 25 incidents of talking out per day. Next, an expected or acceptable level of performance must be established. In this example, peer observations were completed and it was determined that the typical peer in the student's same classroom talks out two times per day. Next, a goal must be established for the student's performance. In this example, the goal was for the number of talk-outs to decrease to two per day.

Student progress should be monitored on a regular and frequent basis during implementation of targeted interventions. Progress may be assessed on a daily basis (e.g., incidents per day, per class period, or points earned per day) or on a weekly basis (e.g., incidents per week or points earned per week). Student progress data should be compared to the goal or expected level of performance to guide decisions about the intervention. If the student is not making progress, he or she may need a more intensive, individualized intervention (see Chapter 9). If he or she is making progress as expected and continues to need the targeted intervention support, the intervention may continue as designed. The targeted intervention may need to be modified if the student has made progress but continues to need a less intensive version of the intervention or if the student has not made adequate progress and needs a more intensive version of the targeted intervention.

Last, the targeted intervention may need to be terminated or gradually faded if the student has met his or her performance goal and no longer needs targeted supports to be successful in school.

HOW DOES IT FIT IN THE STRUCTURE OF RtI?

Targeted group interventions in Tier 2 are focused on early identification and prevention, two key features of Response to Intervention (RtI). Various data sources are used for early identification of students who may need more support beyond universal instruction. It is this early identification that allows for instruction and remediation of problem behaviors before they escalate into severe problem behaviors. Thus, the emphasis is on being proactive.

Response to Intervention also focuses on the use of instruction to teach all students the social-emotional-behavioral skills needed to achieve socially important outcomes. The primary purposes of targeted group interventions are to provide the additional instruction and supports beyond universal instruction that students need to be successful and to prevent minor problem behaviors from escalating into more significant, severe problem behaviors. Tier 2 interventions are aligned with the Tier 1 social, emotional, and behavioral expectations and focus on the student's learning important social outcomes.

The use of data to guide decisions is another key feature of RtI systems. Data are used throughout Tier 2 to guide decisions. Assessments are used to identify students who may benefit from targeted interventions, to identify student-specific instructional or functional needs, to monitor student-specific progress, and to monitor implementation integrity. Screening and diagnostic assessment data are used to place students into various targeted interventions. Implementation and progress monitoring data are used to determine whether the student needs continued targeted supports or more intensive intervention supports, or whether he or she would be successful with universal supports.

KEY CONSIDERATIONS FOR IMPLEMENTATION

Administrative Participation and Support

Administrators must be actively involved and supportive for targeted group interventions to be effectively implemented. The administrator needs to provide the leadership necessary to develop and implement targeted interventions and supports for all students. The assignment and coordination of resources and funds necessary for the successful implementation of any targeted intervention is the primary responsibility of the administrator. The administrator must also be fluent in communicating the rationale for, and benefits of, targeted supports to staff, funding entities, and the broader body of stakeholders.

Staff Consensus

The second key consideration for implementing Tier 2 interventions is staff consensus. In developing and implementing Tier 2 supports for behavior, one is potentially identifying alternate procedures and practices that adults may have to use for students who are in need of supplemental supports beyond the universal level of instruction. The staff must thoroughly understand need, rationale, purpose, and intended benefits of the Tier 2 system and the proposed targeted intervention(s). They must also understand the role of data and teacher referrals in the student identification process and how a teacher may access support for individual students if needed. Last, staff members must understand their role in implementing targeted interventions and in collecting and using data to guide instructional decisions.

Professional Development

The administrator or team responsible for developing the targeted system will need professional development to ensure that best practices are used in implementing targeted group interventions. They will need to learn new content and will need time to actually develop the targeted system and determine how best practices can be implemented within the current school structures. In addition to the administrator and leadership team, all staff members in a building will need professional development on the processes and procedures of the targeted intervention(s). All staff should be trained on how to implement basic targeted interventions to ensure rapid access to interventions for students. Training prior to having to implement allows the teacher to have the required skills when needed, preventing any delay in the student's receiving the intervention because the teacher must be trained in the targeted intervention. Last, the team and/or staff will need professional development in how to use progress-monitoring data to evaluate the effectiveness of targeted interventions and to guide instructional decisions for students.

Resources

The last key feature for implementing the targeted system of RtI for behavior is resources. First, the people responsible for developing the Tier 2 system will need time to learn about targeted group interventions and time to work on the development of the system. Staff will also need to have access to the tangible resources necessary to implement targeted interventions. For example, they may need access to professional books, research articles, social skills programs, instructional materials, implementation logs, items to use to reinforce learned skills, electronic data support, and so on. The team will also benefit from access to coaching and consultative supports that can provide technical assistance on the development and implementation of the Tier 2 system.

KNOWLEDGE AND SKILLS NEEDED BY SCHOOL SOCIAL WORKERS

Knowledge of Social Skills Assessments and Instruction

School social workers have a unique opportunity to share their knowledge of social skills assessment(s) and instruction in an RtI system. In Tier 2, social skills assessments may be used as a screening assessment to identify students who may need additional support beyond Tier 1. Social workers can provide support to school staff to identify appropriate assessments, analyze and interpret the results of assessments, and identify supports for students.

School social workers should also have experience with various social skills groups and experience in teaching social skills to students. Their understanding of various targeted intervention options will support the school in making appropriate instructional matches for individual students. Their knowledge of providing social skills instruction also allows them to consult with teachers and provide support for those who are struggling with teaching social skills.

Ability to Understand, Analyze, and Use Data

School social workers will need to become aware of the data sources used within the RtI system. Social workers play a critical role in helping schools use data to identify students who may need support or instruction beyond Tier 1. Social workers also need to know how to complete brief, low rigor FBAs to assist schools with determining student-specific instructional and functional needs. Last, they will need to understand how to use progress monitoring assessment data to guide instructional decisions. Social workers are in a unique position to act as consultants and to help teachers or administrators think about data and understand how data can be used to guide decisions.

CHAPTER SUMMARY AND CONCLUSIONS

Targeted group interventions are a necessary component of a continuum of supports for all students regardless of type, frequency, intensity, or chronicity of student behavioral need. Targeted supports must be developed to meet the need of a group of students exhibiting similar behaviors with the same functional or instructional needs. Targeted support programs must be thoughtfully developed within a school structure. Staff must identify the goal or purpose of the Tier 2 system. They must then identify the data sources that will be used as screening, diagnostic, and progress monitoring assessments. They must also have the resources necessary to implement targeted interventions, monitor their effectiveness, and modify the interventions as necessary. Having the Tier 2 system in place provides a mechanism to respond to identified student needs in a timely manner and, when implemented with fidelity, will prevent students from engaging in behaviors that will necessitate individualized, intensive interventions that are more costly and time consuming.

REFERENCES

Colvin, G., Kameenui, E. J., & Sugai, G. (1993). School-wide and classroom management: Reconceptualizing the integration and management of students with behavior problems in general education. *Education and Treatment of Children, 16,* 361–381.

Crone, D. A., Horner, R. H., & Hawken, L. S. (2004). *Responding to problem behavior in schools: The behavior education program.* New York: Guilford Press.

Hawken, L. H., & Horner, R. H. (2003). Evaluation of a targeted intervention within a schoolwide system of behavior support. *Journal of Behavioral Education, 12*(3), 225–240.

Horner, R. H., Sugai, G., Todd, A. W., & Lewis-Palmer, T. (2005). School-wide positive behavior support: An alternative approach to discipline in schools. In L. Bambara & L. Kern (Eds.), *Individualized supports for students with problem behaviors: Designing positive behavior plans.* New York: Guilford Press.

Lewis, T. J., & Sugai, G. (1999). Effective behavior support: A systems approach to proactive school-wide management. *Focus on Exceptional Children, 31*(6), 1–24.

Lewis, T. J., Sugai, G., & Colvin, G. (1998). Reducing problem behavior through a school-wide system of effective behavioral support: Investigation of a school-wide social skills training program and contextual interventions. *School Psychology Review, 27*(3), 446–459.

Merrell, K. W. (1993). Using behavior rating scales to assess social skills and antisocial behavior in school settings: Development of the school social behavior scales. *School Psychology Review, 22*(1), 115–133.

Office of Special Education Programs Center on Positive Behavioral Interventions and Supports. (2004). *School-wide positive behavior support: Implementers' blueprint and self-assessment.* Eugene: University of Oregon.

Sprague, J., Walker, H., Golly, A., White, K., Myers, D. R., & Shannon, T. (2001). Translating research into effective practice: The effects of a universal staff and student intervention on indicators of discipline and school safety. *Education and Treatment of Children, 24,* 495–511.

Sugai, G., Sprague, J. R., Horner, R. H., & Walker, H. M. (2000). Preventing school violence: The use of office discipline referrals to assess and monitor school-wide discipline interventions. *Journal of Emotional and Behavioral Disorders, 8,* 94–101.

Taylor-Greene, S., Brown, D., Nelson, L., Longton, J., Gassman, T., Cohen, J., Swartz, J., Horner, R.H., Sugai, G., & Hall, S. (1997). School-wide behavioral support: Starting the year off right. *Journal of Behavioral Education, 7,* 99–112.

Walker, H. M., & Severson, H. (1992). *Systematic screening of behavior disorders (SSBD): A multiple gating procedure.* Longmont, CO: Sopris West.

7

TIER 2
CASE EXAMPLE: WHYTRY?

Erika W. Joye & Michelle E. Alvarez

This chapter introduces the reader to the WhyTry? program, describes how it fits within a school context in a Response to Intervention (RtI) framework, and provides a case example of the implementation of the WhyTry? program in Denver Public Schools Denver, Colorado. Implementation of an evidence-based program involves formal training, implementation of the program, use of instruments to measure the fidelity of program implementation, and a continuous evaluation loop. At the individual student level, data collected during program participation can be utilized to measure the student's response to the intervention.

OVERVIEW OF THE WHYTRY? PROGRAM

WhyTry? is a program that promotes social-emotional learning and positive behavior through a multisensory and strength-based approach. WhyTry? uses various learning styles to reach students and promote positive behavior. This curriculum consists of 10 visual analogies (pictures) with solutions and written questions based on the conceptual framework of each picture to help students develop insight, awareness, and application to daily life and challenges. The program also utilizes hip-hop and rock music along with body/kinesthetic challenge activities to reinforce the skills taught in the curriculum including problem solving, team building, and decision-making components of the creative thinking process. The tools provided in the WhyTry? program (visual analogies, music, body/kinesthetic challenge activities) provide a framework that creates a supportive and engaging environment for teaching skills to answer the question "Why try?" The purpose is to

95

teach students that making good decisions can be difficult, but doing so will result in more opportunity, freedom, and self-respect whereas giving up and doing things that hurt themselves and others result in a significant decrease in opportunity, freedom, and self-respect. Such behavioral expectations must be directly aligned with the defined school-wide behavioral expectations in Tier 1. A summary of the 10 visual analogies and core concepts is presented in Box 7.1. Currently, over 5, 000 schools in the United States are using the WhyTry? program. It is also being used in schools in the U.K., Canada, and Australia. Given much of the evidence collected from schools currently usingWhyTry? it appears to be a promising practice. However, more research is needed on this program to improve the evidence-base of student outcomes.

Box 7.1   Summary of the Ten Core Concepts in the WhyTry? Program

1) Channeling Anger, Frustration, and Challenges into Positive Motivation:
   This is a picture of a river with a series of dams that channel and control the flow of water. This analogy helps educators teach students how to convert challenge into positive motivation. In this picture, the water represents life's challenges and frustrations. When presented with these challenges, people have a choice on how to channel that energy. The flood zone represents a choice that has negative consequences. In the flood zone energy dissipates and stagnates, and a person stuck in the flood zone hurts him/herself and others. The other path uses dams to show how a powerful river can be used to create something positive, like electrical energy.

2) The Reality Ride:
   This visual analogy is of a roller coaster representing the reality of life. This analogy provides students insight into the consequences of their decisions. One path leads to extreme highs and lows ending in a crash and often getting stuck in the loop where behaviors are repeated over and over. The other path is harder but worth it and leads to opportunity, freedom, and self-respect.

3) Tearing off Labels:
   This visual analogy is a picture of cans. It teaches students that negative labels must be torn off and encourages students to let their strengths emerge.

4) Defense Mechanisms:
   This visual analogy uses a knight protected in armor to teach students how to make good decisions for protecting themselves when angry, frustrated and scared. It teaches students to choose positive coping mechanisms so they won't hurt themselves or others.

5) Climbing Out:
   This visual analogy illustrates peer pressure by showing crabs trying to climb out of a pot. This shows students how peers can affect them both positively and negatively.

6) Jumping Hurdles:
   This is a picture of a tennis school and a hurdle. The core concept taught in this visual analogy teaches students to overcome problems by following certain steps. The steps are as follows: identify the problem, create options, get help, take action, believe in positive change, and to "jump back up" if they trip.

(continued)

Box 7.1 (Continued)

7) Desire, Time, Effort:
   This is a maze that helps students understand and experience the importance of desire, time, and effort in overcoming challenges.

8) Lift the Weight:
   This visual analogy is a picture of a weight lifter. The purpose is to create a cognitive connection between becoming physically stronger by lifting weights and mentally stronger by following rules and self-discipline. This analogy represents strength based living and how overcoming resistance and challenges can produce opportunity, freedom, and self respect.

9) Getting Plugged In:
   This is a picture of five sockets and a light bulb. This analogy teaches the importance of building a positive support system. Students are taught that connecting with others (parents/caregiver, a positive friend, a teacher, school official and a positive mentor can help them see the light in their future.

10) Seeing Over the Wall:
   This visual analogy of a brick wall and stairs teaches students to see more in life than just problems and challenges. Applying the above eight principles will help them see their potential and dreams with more clarity. When one's view is limited by failure, drugs, anger, fighting, an "I can't" attitude and family problems, hope is hard to see. Through this program students learn one step at a time how to get on top of the wall and see opportunity in life, how they earn freedom to make the most of their opportunities, and as a result how they achieve more self-respect.

Source: Reproduced with permission from WhyTry Organization.

Many of the core components of the WhyTry? program are based on the fundamental principles of solution-focused, strengths-based, and cognitive-behavioral therapy theories. Taken together, these theories have helped inform some of the most thoroughly researched psychological and educational concepts of the late twentieth century. Within the WhyTry? program, students are asked to identify their strengths and skills and to establish how these attributes can aid them in solving their problems. There are rating scales on some of the visual metaphors where students rate their belief in their ability to change. The "miracle" question is also asked. For example, in one lesson students are asked what their lives would be like if they woke up in the morning and all their negative labels were gone. The focus in the WhyTry? program is to help students use strengths to overcome challenges and create freedom, opportunity, and self-respect.

The WhyTry? program provides tools for presenting social-emotional concepts through each of the different learning modalities. This curriculum supports the creation of an interactive, multimodal learning environment. Such an environment is defined as one that uses at least two different learning modalities to represent the content knowledge and includes multidirectional communication between the educator and the learner (Moreno & Mayer, 2007). These environments assist the individual in building a mental representation of the concept and an association to previous knowledge rather than rote memorization of facts (Moreno & Mayer, 2007). To achieve this type of learning environment, WhyTry? uses visual metaphors, music, videos, hands-on activities, and journal activities to reinforce the social/emotional concepts taught in the curriculum. Lakoff (1989) states that the application of one domain of knowledge through another domain of knowledge, such as the use of metaphor, offers new perceptions and understandings. The school social worker leads the student through the visual metaphor teaching the core concept. During this process, the student is asked the questions about his or her life provided on the visual metaphor. The school social worker asks the questions written on the metaphor and then writes the student's answers in the blank spaces provided. The student also has an 8 1/2 × 11 copy of the metaphor on which to write his or her answers. This process facilitates interaction between the school social worker and the student and creates a narrative of the student's life related to the visual analogy.

Another critical component of the curriculum, referred to as "surrendering the one-up, " focuses on relationship building between the school social worker and student using concepts and activities that allow them to connect and form a relationship in which the student becomes the central member. These activities, written into the curriculum, provide positive ways to recognize the student so that he or she feels value and worth despite successes or failures. There is also a gratitude component, which is taught and practiced in the Motivation Formula, one of the visual analogies. A recent study by Froh, Sefick, and Emmons (2008) found that gratitude was associated with optimism, life satisfaction, and decreased negative affect. The strongest relationship found in this study was the relationship between gratitude and school satisfaction.

Currently, the WhyTry? program is implemented in schools, alternative settings, addiction treatment facilities, correctional facilities, and mental health facilities. It is used with children ages 5 to 18, and with adults. As a Tier 2 intervention, the WhyTry? program is taught by the school social worker in a small group with students who have been referred for behavior and/or social-emotional difficulties. Indicators of behavior problems or difficulties are number of office referrals, suspensions, and teacher report. Students may be referred for social-emotional challenges based on parent and teacher report, attendance, and classroom observations of student performance and engagement in school. The Behavior and Emotional Screening System (BESS) provides a reliable, valid, and systematic tool with which to assess behavioral and emotional strengths and weaknesses in children and adolescents (Kamphaus & Reynolds, 2008). This tool may be used with children in grades preschool through 12 and takes approximately 5 to 10 minutes to administer. The BESS provides forms that can be completed by the student, teacher, and/or parent/caregiver. This measure can be administered to all students at a Tier 1 level. Those who are considered in the at-risk or clinically significant range are appropriate for WhyTry? as a Tier 2 intervention. School social workers monitor the students' progress by tracking attendance, office referrals, and suspensions prior to, during, and following the intervention. The social worker may also administer the BESS post-intervention to examine change. An increase in performance in these areas indicates that the student is responding to the intervention. Students are referred for Tier 3 services if they are not responding to WhyTry? as indicated by no change or a decrease in academic, behavioral, and/or social/emotional functioning.

Another component for measuring the effectiveness of the intervention is to examine fidelity of implementation. High fidelity of intervention is significantly correlated with the probability of behavior change (Moncher & Prinz, 1991). Vanderheyden, Witt, and Gilbertson (2007) state, "Implementation is the linchpin of RtI. If there is to be an evaluation of RtI, a series of interventions must be implemented correctly and monitored" (p. 226). Fidelity is the consistency, precision, and accuracy in which an intervention is implemented (Hennessey & Rumrill, 2003; Moncher & Prinz, 1991; Noell et al., 2005). Fidelity is imperative for ensuring sustainable treatments and for validating the treatment results (Moncher & Prinz, 1991; Noell et al. 2005). When fidelity is not monitored, it is impossible to know whether the results are due to unknown variables. Evidence-based interventions are utilized in schools with students who need assistance in a particular area. Training in a program includes a protocol for implementation. The WhyTry? protocol is provided in the form of a manual.

After a few weeks of intervention, progress monitoring may show that the student is not responding to the intervention. The question that often arises from this scenario is where did the system break down? Does this intervention work only in a well-funded research center or university? Was the intervention ineffective for this child? Did the facilitator implement the intervention appropriately? Fidelity measures and monitoring can aid in discovering the answer to the last question. Furthermore using a fidelity measure to monitor implementation will enable immediate feedback to the facilitator that can enhance implementation. Providing corrective feedback to an individual engaged in an intervention regarding the initiation and sustainability of the targeted change can enhance overall success and lead to sustained changes in behavior (Noell et al., 2005). A fidelity measure was recently created for the WhyTry? intervention (see Appendix 7.A). However, there is no information on the psychometric properties of this form. Further evaluation is needed in this area. School social workers may use this measure to assess the fidelity of different components included in the WhyTry? program and monitor students' understanding. This measure may provide informative feedback related to the implementation and response to the WhyTry? intervention (see Appendix 7.A).

Following a required two-day training, the WhyTry? program as used in a Tier 2 intervention is designed to meet one hour, once a week for 12 to 15 weeks. It takes approximately 45 minutes to one hour to go through one analogy and the music, and one hour to complete each of the hands-on activities. The suggested number of students participating in the group is five to twelve with six to eight being the optimal number (Vinogradov & Yalom,

1989). This number of students allows for open communication among the members of the group and provides an adequate amount of group members needed to complete the body/kinesthetic activities within a trusting setting.

PROGRAM OUTCOMES

The outcomes of the WhyTry? program are currently supported by data from pilot studies and school evaluations. These show the program to be a promising practice. A brief summary of those outcomes is presented here. In future studies more rigorous evaluations are needed of the effectiveness of WhyTry? Evaluations examining the outcomes of the WhyTry? intervention show significant improvements among participants in academic achievement and social-emotional attitudes and behaviors. Eggett (2003) studied the effectiveness of the WhyTry? intervention with high school age students identified as being physically, sexually, emotionally maltreated or neglected; these students were enrolled in an alternative education setting and participated in the intervention for one year. The study was conducted in southern California and included a largely Hispanic and African American sample reflective of the demographics of the community. Also, these students had been expelled from their homes. Results showed a significant increase in levels of motivation and a decrease in behavioral problems. Students who participated in the WhyTry? program were more likely to have lower negative attitudes toward teachers and school, a higher locus of control (indicating they were more personally responsible for their behavior), and fewer attendance problems compared to a control group. Teacher rating revealed a significant improvment in motivational attributes. The students also rated their own behavior as improving (Eggett, 2003).

An evaluation in the Rocky Mountain region examined the relationship between the WhyTry? intervention and academic achievement with high school students in grades 10 through 12 (Bushnell & Card, 2003). This study was conducted with a largely Causcasian sample reflective of the demographics of the community. Data on academic achievement were gathered every six weeks during the school year revealing significantly increased GPAs and no change in the number of course failures whereas students in a control group had significantly decreased GPA and increased number of course failures (Bushnell & Card, 2003).

The previous studies discussed focused on a sample of high school age children. The South Los Angeles Resiliency (SOLAR) project results in a pre/post test showed that elementary school students responded to the WhyTry? intervention. Those students who participated in the WhyTry? intervention had significantly higher scores on a measure of student resiliency, a positive change in trying to succeed, a decreased desire to be mean to others, and an increase in asking for help (Acuna, Vega, Meza, Marquez, & Vera, 2008). This evaluation also revealed a significant grade improvement for students participating in WhyTry? (Acuna et al., 2008). Another evaluation conducted by Mortenson and Rush (2007) examined the pre/post outcomes for students in grades K–5. These results show that after participating in the WhyTry? program students had significantly lower emotional and behavior problems as reported by teachers and primary caregivers on the Behavior Assessment System for Children—Second Edition (BASC-2).

There is evidence that WhyTry? also had a positive effect on behavior with students living in group homes in California. A quasi-experimental study examining the impact of the WhyTry? intervention with youth (ages 12–18) living in group homes found that the students who participated in the WhyTry? intervention had significant increases in self-efficacy scores (Baker, 2008). This study also found significant decreases in internalizing problems, social problems, attention problems, rule breaking behaviors, aggressive behaviors, and externalizing problems as measured by teachers on the Achenbach System of Empirically Based Assessment (ASEBA) compared to the control group (Baker, 2008). On the Youth Self Report (YSR) of ASEBA, students reported significant positive changes on the syndrome scale for anxious/depressed, social problems, thought problems, internalizing problems, externalizing problems, and total problems (Baker, 2008). These evaluations provide a foundation for future research on the WhyTry? program. WhyTry? is a promising practice used nationwide. There are several opportunities for future research in examining the effectiveness and practices of WhyTry? in various other settings.

CASE STUDY: *WHYTRY?* AS A TIER 2 INTERVENTION IN DENVER PUBLIC SCHOOLS (DPS)

In DPS, educators are offered the opportunity to participate in professional development units (PDU) offered for a number of education-related topics. During the 2007/2008 academic year, 27 social workers and school psychologists chose to complete a PDU on the WhyTry? program. Participants in the WhyTry? PDU were required to attend a two-day WhyTry? certification training, implement WhyTry? with a small group of students referred for Tier 2 intervention, and collaborate with the WhyTry? training coach and other colleagues about the implementation process. Completion of this PDU fulfilled Denver Public School's mission for highly skilled faculty empowered by professional development, collaboration among the Denver community, performance improvement for all students, and closing the achievement gap by identifying and implementing strategies to enhance learning (Denver Public Schools, 2006).

Demographics of Denver Public Schools

In DPS there are 152 schools. Of these 152 schools, 68 are elementary schools, 18 are K–8 schools, 16 are middle schools, and 15 are high schools. There are 21 charter schools and 6 alternative schools. In October of 2008, there were 75,269 students enrolled in DPS; 65.93% of these students receive free/reduced price lunch. Of those DPS population, 1.11% were

American Indian, 3.41% were Asian, 17.50% were Black, 55.36% were Hispanic, and 22.62% were White. There are several different languages spoken by the students at DPS; 18% are English Language Learners and 40% are Spanish-speaking students. The top five languages spoken by students are Spanish, Vietnamese, Arabic, Russian, and Somali (Denver Public Schools, 2008).

Student Recruitment, Retention, and Program Fidelity

Before beginning the WhyTry? intervention, students were selected for small groups. In DPS, a model for identifying students for small groups and Tier 2 interventions is to use a problem-solving process. The process was designed to assist school officials, teachers, and parents in selecting strategies to improve students' academic, behavioral, and social/emotional performance and outcomes. This group collaborated using a problem-solving approach to identify the specific challenge and choose an evidence-based intervention for the student.

At Tier 1, grade-level data teams screen all students based on academic progress and behavior. Students who struggle at Tier 1 based on data regarding attendance, social, emotional, and/or behavioral difficulties are referred to the problem-solving process for Tier 2 interventions. The following criteria help staff identify students who are not responding to a Tier 1 intervention. Behavior and social/emotional difficulties are identified by teacher/staff observation and/or parent/caregiver observation using a rating scale such as the BESS or a district-created rating scale. Also, the frequency of occurrence of office referrals and suspensions that are in the top 20th percentile among the population of students at the school indicates that the student is not responding to a Tier 1 intervention. Before the initial meeting to discuss Tier 2 interventions, the teacher, parent, and a designated consultant work together to gather a body of evidence on the student's strengths and weaknesses as well as information indicating that the student is not responding to the Tier 1 intervention. This information is presented during the problem-solving process. In this case study, students who were having academic difficulties and behavioral difficulties as indicated by the data were referred for the WhyTry? intervention. At the end of the 12 week WhyTry? intervention, student progress was assessed. If the intervention was implemented with fidelity and there was no improvement, more intensive interventions or referral to special education were recommended.

RESULTS

The following section includes a brief summary of results from the case studies submitted for the PDU. Further information is provided regarding student perceptions and practitioner perceptions of the WhyTry? program.

In this case study, the WhyTry? program was co-facilitated in two small groups by a school social worker and a school psychologist with students in grades 4 and 5. There were three students in one group and five in the other. The group met weekly over the course of a semester (15 weeks). While progress of Tier 1 goals continued to be measured, with this Tier 2 intervention, expanded targeted behaviors were monitored. These behaviors include the frequency of unsafe behaviors (termed "groundings"), and progress in the school's level system was tracked to monitor response to intervention. The level system is an organizational framework for managing students' behavior whereby students gain access to more privileges and independence when they demonstrate increased control (Heward, 2003). Students learn appropriate behavior through clearly defined behavioral expectations and rewards, privileges, and consequences linked to those expectations. There are specific criteria for advancement to the next level where the student(s) enjoy more desirable contingencies.

Unsafe Behaviors

"Groundings, " incidents when a student behaves in an unsafe manner, were tracked daily for each student involved in the WhyTry? small group intervention. Examples of groundings include fighting, disrespect toward teachers or other students, and throwing objects. Students involved in the WhyTry? intervention exhibited on average a 66.4% decline in "groundings" over the course of the intervention. The occurrence of these incidents was used to track the response to the intervention. With a 66.4% decline in the groundings most students responded to the WhyTry small group intervention. However, one of the groups was restructured to support an individual student who was not responding to this intervention based on the number of groundings. He was removed from the group and provided a more intensive intervention based on the challenges he was facing.

Progress in the Level System

Students have the ability to move up the level system by exhibiting consistent positive behaviors. Positive behaviors are defined as following directions, using coping skills (such as counting to 10 or deep breathing when in a pressure situation), speaking respectfully, and staying away from and ignoring conflict with other students. Each student gets points on the level system each day for displaying these positive behaviors. The students gain more privileges as they climb up the level system. In this case study, if a student decreased on the level system she or he was moved to Tier 3 and provided a more intensive intervention. However, as measured by the level system, none of the students significantly decreased on their level throughout the course of the WhyTry? small group intervention. Therefore, they continued in the Tier 2 WhyTry? intervention. Students continued to show increasing amounts of positive behavior as measured and defined in this level system.

Student Reflections

Students were asked several open-ended questions related to their experiences in the WhyTry? group. These qualitative data provide insight into the intervention from the student perspective. They document how the students were conceptualizing the information learned and relating it to current and past experiences. The first question asked the students was what they liked the most about WhyTry? Most students mentioned the body/kinesthetic challenge and the Crab Pot analogy. This answer shows a positive response to the kinesthetic learning strategies, providing insight into the students' learning styles. This information was used to direct future activities and interventions for these students based on their preference for kinesthetic learning. The majority of the students also mentioned liking the Crab Pot analogy. This visual analogy illustrates peer pressure by showing a crab trying to climb out of a pot while the other crabs in the pot pull it back into the boiling water. This shows students how peers can affect them both positively and negatively. One student said that the Crab Pot analogy "helps me think about who puts me down and who helps me up." Students were asked to identify the *WhyTry?* lesson from which they learned the most. There were several different answers. One student said, "I learned the most from the lesson with the tennis shoes (Jumping Hurdles—a problem-solving model). We learned how to fix problems and create options." One student mentioned the Lift the Weight metaphor. In this metaphor, a man is pictured lifting a weight. On one side there is a balloon and the man has no muscles. On the other side the man is lifting a weight and has large and distinct muscles. The metaphor creates a cognitive connection between lifting weight to build strength and having self-discipline to build strength and character. It teaches students that they gain strength by following society's rules, school rules, home rules, and self-discipline. This student said that she could compare level one (student is not following rules and has no privileges) with the side where the man was lifting the balloon and level three (student is following rules and has more opportunity and privileges) to the side where the man is lifting the heavy weight. The student then related this concept to school and used the metaphor to help her follow school rules.

These students were also asked about situations when they used a skill learned in WhyTry? One student said that there was a situation where another student made her mad. She said that she thought about "options of hitting or breathing" and stayed calm. Another student mentioned that he supported a friend when this friend was in trouble. This students said, "I supported him and told him it would be better the next day." This illustrates the use of concepts from the Defense Mechanisms and the Plugging In analogies.

Finally, students were asked about their thoughts on group composition. A theme that arose in the answers to this question was related to consistency. All of the students reported that they did not like it when students were coming in and out of the group. They preferred to have the same group composition that was started at the beginning of the semester through the end of the semester. Many of the students mentioned that it was confusing and that they did not like it when a new student joined the WhyTry? group in the middle of the semester. This was a threat to trust built up within a small group. Trust among the group may have decreased when another student was added at mid-semester. This information is important to remember for future groups. Keeping the group consistent with regard to membership increases trust and cohesion for these students.

Educator Reflections

School social workers and school psychologists who participated in the PDU recorded their reflections on the WhyTry? intervention and the implementation process. Many of them reported that they enjoyed the multimodal interactive instruction model. The incorporation of the posters, journaling, music, and group activities captured and maintained the interest level of the students as well as the facilitators. There were comments on individual analogies. Regarding the use of the Reality Ride analogy in the classroom, one school psychologist said, "It is far less confrontational, challenging and emotionally provocative to ask a student, 'What track do you think you are on right now?' than to issue a direct prompt such as 'sit down, raise your hand, etc.' This question fosters the student's development of insight into his/her behavior, facilitates self-monitoring, and increases that chance of generalization of skills into the 'outside' world." A school social worker stated that he appreciated that fact that the WhyTry? curriculum "fearlessly addresses the difficulty and challenges inherent in doing the right thing." He continued, "WhyTry? does not 'sugar coat' the realities of peer pressure, anger, or difficult life circumstances; instead it challenges students to use that energy in a productive way. The program also attempts to instill a sense of internal motivation in students." Finally, PDU participants noted another important component of the WhyTry? curriculum regarding the concepts of freedom, opportunity, and self-respect. It was stated by one of the educators participating in the PDU that through the WhyTry? lessons "freedom, opportunity, and self-respect become more than abstract concepts or things that adults describe to young people. They become things that kids can define for themselves, which is far more meaningful." Overall, educators participating in the PDU related positive experiences with the intervention.

Challenges to Implementation

The school social workers and school psychologists who participated in the PDU reflected on the challenges of implementing the WhyTry? intervention. These observations steer future implementation and application of WhyTry? in the school setting. Two themes arose from the reflections about these challenges to implementation. Those themes were time and space. One of the biggest challenges to implementing WhyTry? in groups was time. Many of the school social workers and school psychologists using this intervention said that they had difficulty having a consistent time for group each week. There were conflicts with classroom time, required meetings, and standardized testing. These conflicts required rescheduling group time and restructuring the delivery of certain lessons. For example, they would combine groups to cover two topics or hold a group meeting twice in one week. This does not appear to affect fidelity of the intervention because the group facilitator covered all aspects of the WhyTry? intervention during those times, including teaching the visual metaphor, using music, and the body/kinesthetic activities. Another challenge for the group meeting was finding space to meet. One group solved this problem by holding meetings before school. However, attendance at the group did decrease throughout the semester. Another challenge that was mentioned when implementing with small groups was the size of the groups. The facilitator said that she had "very small groups" of three to five children. She believes that larger groups that included peer models would have had more impact and improved the delivery of all aspects of the lessons. Her plan for next year includes partnering with other mental health professionals to increase referrals for group. She is also planning to include students who participated in the group this school year so as to provide leadership opportunities.

Case Study Summary

Overall this model for implementing the WhyTry? intervention proved successful. Student services personnel participated in a professional development course that provided the opportunity to implement the skills learned in training with the support of colleagues and a WhyTry? coach. These professionals then implemented WhyTry? in small group settings for students needing Tier 2 intervention. Students were chosen for this intervention based on their inadequate response to the Tier 1 universal supports. Indicators that these students were not adequately responding to Tier 1 intervention included number of office referrals, observation data, and rating scale data. Once students were in the intervention, mental health professionals used data from the Level System and observations to monitor progress related to behavioral goals. As a result of this intervention, on average, students' negative behaviors in the classroom decreased. Those who did not improve were referred for more intensive intervention. Furthermore, student interviews showed that students gained information from the intervention and enjoyed "WhyTry? class." Also, the social workers and other educators implementing WhyTry? were able to collaborate throughout the year and worked together to develop ideas for overcoming obstacles to implementation and created plans for implementing the intervention during the next academic year.

KEY CONSIDERATIONS FOR IMPLEMENTATION

The research base for WhyTry? is showing promising results. A standard method of program delivery and an instrument to measure the fidelity of implementation have been developed. A clear understanding of which students are most likely to respond to WhyTry? is available in program outcome anecdotes but will need to be further researched. Methods of tracking individual student progress as a result of the program implementation are included and outcomes should be graphed to monitor student progress. As with any targeted group intervention at the Tier 2 level, challenges of scheduling a group at a time when students can attend and have the least impact on academics must be considered.

Implementation of WhyTry? requires attending the training and adhering to guidelines put forth in the manual to implement the program. The training includes instruments that measure the fidelity of implementation increasing the likelihood that the intervention will produce good outcomes for students. Program training and materials are very reasonably priced compared to other evidence-based programs.

Knowledge and Skills Needed by School Social Workers

The knowledge and skills needed by school social workers to implement WhyTry? include an understanding of the theories that are the underpinning of the program and very familiar to school social workers, a philosophical and working understanding of Tier 2 interventions in the RtI process, and understanding how to implement an evidence-based program in a school setting with fidelity.

Skills needed for implementing a Tier 2 intervention include working with the school to set criteria that indicate the need for a Tier 2 intervention and matching that need with the intervention. Also required are understanding the measurement and interpretation of individual student outcomes resulting from a targeted group intervention, and the ability to determine the need for Tier 3 intervention based on Tier 2 outcomes.

CONCLUSION

Although WhyTry? can be implemented in other tiers, this chapter provided an example of its implementation as a Tier 2 targeted group intervention within the context of an RtI model. It is utilized as an early intervention strategy to address the needs of students not met by a Tier 1 intervention. Despite the need for more research, this program has proven to be successful with students and is a cost-effective intervention. Anticipating barriers to implementation is a key to the process of protecting the fidelity of a program. The case study reminds the practitioner that time and space can impact the effectiveness of Tier 2 targeted group interventions. Anticipating barriers to implementation is a key to the process of protecting the fidelity of a program.

APPENDIX 7.A: FIDELITY CHECKLIST

Fidelity Checklist

The purpose of this fidelity measure is to see how implementation of *WhyTry* aligns with theory underlying the *WhyTry* program. This measure also provides feedback to educators on what is working with the *WhyTry* program and what is not working. This feedback is valuable information used to understand the implementation of *WhyTry* in schools.

Section One: Demographic Information
Today's date_____   Observer _____
Type of intervention: Individual   Small Group   Classroom
Number of adult facilitators: _____
Group size (# *children*) minimum: _____ maximum_____
Length of intervention (*minutes*): _____

Section Two: Tracking WhyTry Intervention Style (some of these items will be implemented in separate sessions).

	Intervention STYLE (*check every item below*)	Yes	No
Item 1	Adult uses "**attention getter**"		
Item 2	Adult teaches **visual metaphor**		
Item 3	Adult uses **poster set** to teach visual metaphors		
Item 4	Adult uses **8 × 10 picture** to teach visual metaphors		
Item 5	Adult uses **powerpoint** to teach visual metaphors		
Item 6	Adult uses **music**		
Item 7	Adult uses **body/kinesthetic** activities		
Item 8	Adult processes **body/kinesthetic** activities		
Item 9	Adult uses **journal** activities		
Item 10	Adult **praises** or affirms student's contributions		
Item 11	Adult **follows student's interest** through the lesson		

Section Three: Tracking Student Response

	Student Response STYLE (*check every item below*)	Yes	No	N/A
Item 1	Student is **actively listening** during lesson			
Item 2	Student **responds to questions** from teacher			
Item 3	Student can explain **basic concept** of visual analogy at end of lesson			
Item 4	Student engages in **body/kinesthetic** activities			
Item 5	Student completes **journal** activities			

Check this box if over 50% of the observation was of an activity unrelated to the WhyTry Intervention □

Comments:
Section Four: Definitions and Tips for Coding

ADULT USES "ATTENTION GETTER": An "attention getter" is used when the adult facilitator begins the lesson with a short video clip, icebreaker, music, or other group activity. This can include any other quick activity that will grab students' attention and build relationships among the students and between student and adult. For example, have a "show and tell" where students and teacher take time to tell each other about hobbies, family, background, recent vacations.

ADULT TEACHES VISUAL METAPHOR: Adult teaches visual metaphor to students by introducing the core concept and walking the students through analogy step-by-step following the numbers on the poster or in the PowerPoint.

ADULT USES POSTER SET/8X10/POWERPOINT: This question asks about the presentation of the material. The visual metaphor is the same in all three mediums. This is asked to gain a sense of what teachers/instructors are using and the combination they are using. Adult facilitator can use all three of these in one lesson, but it is not necessary to use all three.

ADULT USES MUSIC: Adult facilitator uses music during the lesson to reinforce content student is learning. This could be music provided on *WhyTry* CD, music adult provides, and/or music student(s) provide.

ADULT USES BODY/KINESTHETIC ACTIVITIES: Adult facilitator leads students through body/kinesthetic or experiential activity reinforcing the concept taught in core visual analogy. Adult may spend entire lesson on this activity and not teach visual analogy. S/he reviews core concepts through body/kinesthetic learning using multi-sensory learning.

ADULT PROCESSES BODY/KINESTHETIC ACTIVITIES: Adult processes the relevance of the kinesthetic activity to the core concept of the visual metaphor. There are a series of suggested questions to follow in the *WhyTry* curriculum manual to guide facilitator through discussion. This discussion connects visual analogy and kinesthetic activity together.

ADULT USES JOURNAL ACTIVITIES: The *WhyTry* journal is provided as a supplemental text book for the curriculum. To answer yes on this question, the adult will use activities from the journal in and/or outside of class to reinforce the core concepts.

ADULT PRAISES OR AFFIRMS STUDENT'S CONTRIBUTIONS: Adult acknowledges student's contribution to class through verbal and/or written expression. A student's contribution to the class is not defined by successes or failures but by the student's presence.

ADULT FOLLOWS STUDENT'S INTEREST THROUGH THE LESSON: Student points to something or starts talking about something related to the core concept and the adult follows the student's lead and starts talks about this too.

STUDENT IS ACTIVELY LISTENING DURING LESSON: Student makes eye contact with the adult. S/he nods his or her head in agreement or shakes head in disagreement. This student answers the adult's questions and may even ask some of his/her own.

STUDENT RESPONDS TO QUESTIONS FROM THE TEACHER: Student answers when teacher asks question.

STUDENT CAN EXPLAIN BASIC CONCEPT OF VISUAL METAPHOR AT END OF LESSON: The student discusses the basic concepts of a visual metaphor after the lesson. For example, after learning the Reality Ride, student explains that decisions have consequences.

STUDENT ENGAGES IN BODY/KINESTHETIC ACTIVITIES: The student engages in activity. Do not evaluate the student's participation. Only mark whether or not the student was present and participated.

STUDENT COMPLETES JOURNAL ACTIVITIES: Student completes journal activities either inside or outside the classroom. Again, do not evaluate the student's work.

REFERENCES

Acuna, A., Vega, L., Meza, J., Marquez, M., & Vera, D. (2008, April 5). *Outcome evaluations methods and results for the South Los Angeles Resiliency (SOLAR) project.* Presentation at the 2008 School Social Work Association of America Conference. **Los Angeles, CA.**

Baker, D. (2008). *Examining the effectiveness of the WhyTry? program for children receiving residentially based services and attending a non-public school.* Unpublished doctoral dissertation, University of Southern California.

Bushnell B., & Card, K. (2003). *Alpine School District longitudinal study.* Unpublished evaluation for the Alpine School District. **Provo, UT.**

Denver Public Schools. (2006). The Denver plan. Retrieved January 9, 2009, from http://thedenverplan.dpsk12.org/.

Denver Public Schools. (2008). Facts and figures. Retrieved January 26, 2009, from http://communications.dpsk12.org/newsroom/facts-and-figures/about-denver-public-schools/.

Eggett, G. D. (2003). *An intervention to remediate motivational shortcomings.* Unpublished doctoral dissertation, Nova Southeastern University. **Los Angeles, CA.**

Froh, J. J., Seffick, W. J., & Emmons, R. A. (2008). Counting blessings in adolescents: An experimental study of gratitude and subjective well-being. *Journal of School Psychology, 46*(2), 213–233.

Hennessey, M. L., & Rumrill, P. D., Jr. (2003). Treatment fidelity in rehabilitation research. *Journal of Vocational Rehabilitation, 19,* 123–126.

Heward, W. L. (2003). *Exceptional children: An introduction to special education.* Upper Saddle River, NJ: Pearson Education.

Kamphaus, R. W. & Reynolds, C. R. (2008). *BASC-II Behavioral and Emotional Screening System (BASC II BESS),* Upper Saddle River, NJ, Pearson Education, Inc.

Lakoff, George. (1989). A figure of thought. *Metaphor & Symbolic Activity, 1*(3), 215–226.

Moncher F. J., & Prinz R. J. (1991). Treatment fidelity in outcome studies. *Clinical Psychology Review, 11*, 247–266.

Moreno, R., & Mayer, R. (2007). Interactive multimodal learning environments. *Educational Psychology Review, 19*, 309–326.

Mortenson, B. P., & Rush, K. S. (2007, October 25). *PRIDE: 28-day summer program for at-risk students*. Presentation at Towson University. **Orlando, FL.**

Noell, G. H., Witt, J. C., Slider, N. J., Connell, J. E., Gatti, S. L., Williams, K. L., Koenig, J. L., Resetar, J. L., & Duhon, G. J. (2005). Treatment implementation following behavioral consultaiton in schools: A comparsion of three follow-up strategies. *School Psychology Review, 34(1), 87–106.*

O'Donnell, C. L. (2008). Research and its relationship to outcomes in K12 curriculum: Defining, conceptualizing, and measuring fidelity of. *Review of Educational Research, 78*(1), 33–84.

Vanderheyden, A. M., Witt, J. C., & Gilbertson, D. (2007). A multi-year evaluation of the effects of a response to intervention (RtI) model on identification of children for special education. *Journal of School Psychology, 45*(2), 225–256.

Vinogradov, S., & Yalom, I. D. (1989). *Group psychotherapy*. American Psychiatric Association. Washington, D.C.

8

TIER 2
CASE EXAMPLE:
RECONNECTING YOUTH

VALERIE BOSTICK, DANIEL DIEHL, & KATE M. SCATES

This chapter is an introduction to the Reconnecting Youth (RY) program, explaining how it fits within the school context in a Response to
Intervention (RtI) framework, and providing a case example from a
Reconnecting Youth program in Evansville, Indiana. By identifying key
components such as program implementation and evaluation, as well as
maintaining fidelity and understanding of the knowledge and skills
required for school social workers, this chapter highlights Reconnecting
Youth and its effective use in the classroom setting.

OVERVIEW OF RECONNECTING YOUTH

Reconnecting Youth is a school-based program designed to reengage
students into the school environment (Reconnecting Youth Company,
2008). Recognized as a model program by the Substance Abuse and
Mental Health Services Administration (SAMHSA, 2008), Reconnecting
Youth (RY) utilizes a collaborative model involving school personnel, peers,
and parents working together to address substance use, aggression, depression, and other emotional stressors impacting school performance. The
semester-long program is designed for students in grades 9 through 12.
Typically, students take a daily (or every other day) class covering topics
such as decision making, self-esteem, communication, and personal control
(www.reconnectingyouth.com, retrieved 8/28/2008). School and

community activities are utilized to promote bonding to the school and to encourage healthy lifestyle choices. Program staff members maintain contact with parents throughout the program to encourage support of the student's new skills at home. The program addresses multiple risks and encourages and builds school bonding, a protective factor against substance use and poor school performance. The RY program includes four components:

1. *Reconnecting Youth Class*—a semester-long class designed to enhance self-esteem, decision making, personal control, and interpersonal communication.
2. *School Bonding Activities*—strategies for establishing drug-free activities and friendships and for improving a teenager's relationship to school.
3. *Parent Involvement*—the school enlists parental support at home for the day-to-day life skills learned in RY and provides progress reports.
4. *School System Crisis Response Plan*—a plan for suicide prevention and post-suicide intervention (www.modelprograms.samhsa.gov, 2008, p. 5).

As an "indicated" program, RY is open only to those who have been invited to participate based on individual risk factors that are affecting school attendance or performance. SAMHSA defines "at risk of school dropout" as "having fewer than the average number of credits earned for the grade level, high absenteeism, a significant drop in grades, or a history of dropping out of school" (www.modelprograms.samhsa.gov, 2008, p. 2). Additionally, the RY program defines the following criteria to help identify students who may benefit from participating:

1. Is behind in credits for grade level AND is in the top 25th percentile for absences and has a GPA less than 2.3 (or a sharp drop in grades).
2. Has a prior dropout status.
3. Is referred by school personnel and meets one or more of the criteria in point 1 (www.reconnectingyouth.com, retrieved 8/28/2008).

Characteristically, students are identified under these categories by the RY coordinator, with support from the school principal, school counselors, school social worker, or other school personnel. Once a student is invited to participate, the recruitment process is continued by presenting identified students with information about the program and then having an individual meeting with each student outlining the main components of the class. It is imperative that students understand the components of the program, as RY is designed for students who are ready to make positive changes in their lives.

Unlike a Tier 1 universal approach, this Tier 2 program is intended to help schools reach out to those students who are on the cusp of disengaging themselves from the school setting as a whole. Reconnecting Youth provides schools with a tool to reengage these students by promoting and embracing group bonding with positive peer influences, encouraging leadership and responsibility, and developing self-awareness skills that support academic achievement.

The RY class is designed to meet daily (or on a block schedule every other day) for an entire semester. Once incorporated into the schedule, the class becomes part of the high school curriculum, with students ideally receiving credit(s) applied toward their graduation requirements. RY developers recommend having 10–12 students per class led by a teacher who has experience and interest in working with high-risk youth and has successfully completed the RY training. The curriculum itself is delivered in five modules:

1. Getting Started
2. Self-Esteem Enhancement
3. Decision Making
4. Personal Control
5. Interpersonal Communication (www.reconnectingyouth.com, retrieved 8/28/2008).

With 80 sessions in the program, the Reconnecting Youth teacher should implement one 50 minute lesson daily or two 50 minute lessons during a block schedule period every other day. The first 10 sessions of RY focus on familiarizing the students with the workbook format, giving a pre-test to gather baseline data, orienting students to the purpose and structure of the class, and assisting students with setting goals for the class.

The premise of the program is to achieve three program goals: increased school achievement, decreased drug involvement, and decreased suicide-risk behaviors (Reconnecting Youth Company, 2008). Accomplishing these goals requires skills and strategies that are addressed in four different areas: at school, with peers, with self, and with family.

Program Outcomes

Prior research and multiple program evaluations demonstrate that Reconnecting Youth is effective in helping high-risk youth increase their school achievement, reduce their alcohol/drug involvement, and decrease their depression, aggression, and suicidal behaviors. Specifically, RY has been shown to address the problem of youth drug/alcohol use as a multidimensional construct including (1) access to drugs and alcohol, (2) frequency of alcohol use, (3) frequency of other drug use, (4) drug use control problems, and (5) adverse drug use consequences (Eggert, Thompson, Herting, & Randell, 2001). Due to the broad scope of the

RY program, outcomes are evident in several aspects of participants' lives. Studies indicate promising results in various areas of academic and social functioning domains.

Documented academic outcomes include increased grade point average (GPA) for all classes; decreased dropout rates; more positive, connected relationships with teachers; increased credits earned per semester; and increased school bonding (Eggert & Kumpfer, 1997; Eggert & Nicholas, 2004; Eggert, Thompson, Herting, Nicholas, & Dicker, 1994; Thompson, Horn, Herting, & Eggert, 1997). Research has also highlighted decreases in substance abuse and associated risk factors including decreased hard drug use (e.g., cocaine, hallucinogens, tranquilizers, depressants, stimulants, opiates); decreased drug use control problems; and decreased adverse drug use consequences (Eggert & Kumpfer, 1997; Eggert & Nicholas, 2004; Eggert et al., 1994; Thompson et al., 1997). Finally, studies have documented program impacts on social and emotional adjustment including decreased depression and hopelessness; decreased anger control problems and aggression; decreased anxiety and perceived stress; stronger self-confidence and ability to handle stress; decreased suicidal behaviors and risk; and increased personal control (Eggert & Nicholas, 2004; Eggert, Thompson, Herting, & Nicholas, 1995; Thompson et al., 1997).

CASE STUDY: RECONNECTING YOUTH AS A TIER 2 INTERVENTION IN EVANSVILLE, INDIANA

Through the School Community Council, the Evansville Vanderburgh School Corporation (EVSC) is implementing a unique community-school approach that involves partnerships with over 70 community organizations (Diehl, Gray, & O'Connor, 2005). The Council's mission is to establish school sites as places of community to enhance youth and family development (EVSC School Community Council, 2008). These partnerships have allowed the EVSC and its partners to leverage local, state, and federal funding sources to implement programs and services designed to address the many issues facing students, families, and the local community. Over several years, the Reconnecting Youth program has been implemented in EVSC largely as a result of a partnership with Youth First, Inc., a key community partner and "the leading provider of research proven prevention and early intervention programs and services in Evansville, Indiana and surrounding communities" (Youth First, Inc. 2008). Youth First, Inc. is credited for bringing this unique program to the school district and surrounding communities. The following case study illustrates how the Reconnecting Youth program can be implemented as a Tier 2 intervention within the school setting. This study also highlights the benefits of school-community partnerships as an approach to implementing a program of this nature. Toward this aim, a description of program implementation is provided, followed by key local evaluation findings. Next, a discussion of RY as it relates to the Response to Intervention (RtI) framework follows. Through this case study, challenges of implementation and potential solutions to overcoming these obstacles highlight how this program can be incorporated into the school environment.

Program Implementation

Implementation should begin with not only a thorough understanding of all components of the program, but with an understanding of how Reconnecting Youth will fit within the context of each individual school. Evansville is the third largest city in the state of Indiana and the largest city in southern Indiana. Though Evansville is the core city of the county, the school corporation encompasses the entire county, known as the Evansville Vanderburgh School Corporation (EVSC). The Vanderburgh County 2000 Census reported the total population to be 171,922. In the EVSC, there are five high schools and two alternative high schools divided among 6,888 students, along with 10 middle schools, one alternative middle school, and 20 elementary schools. There are also a number of private and parochial schools as well as two charter schools. In all, the public school sector includes approximately 22,350 students.

Reconnecting Youth was offered to all five EVSC high schools at the start of the 2006/2007 school year with the support of two federal grants: the Safe Schools/Healthy Students grant and the Grant to Reduce Alcohol Abuse. These grants supported full-time social workers (through Youth First, Inc.) to deliver evidence-based prevention programs to the high schools as well as funds for RY training, materials, and program supplies. Although offering RY for credit whenever possible is recommended, there was initial challenge in finding times to position RY classes in the schools' previously full schedule of classes. Furthermore, some schools did not have a classroom or teacher available during these preferred school schedules. However, a prominent early theme of participant focus groups continued to be students' desire to offer the program for credit (Diehl, Chadwell, Crecelius, & Vote, 2008).

As a result, the EVSC decided to offer the RY course under the code of a health elective, which required the RY facilitator (the school social worker in this case) to co-teach with an RY-trained licensed health teacher. To transition RY into the schedule more easily, two of the five EVSC high schools opted to offer RY initially as a noncredit course during the resource/enrichment period of their block schedule. Block scheduling allows for a 90 minute resource/enrichment period every other day, which provides time for a program like RY to be implemented without impacting the academic schedule. This strategy proved successful because in the following year of implementation, the number of schools offering RY increased to three, with two of them offering the class for credit. By the final year of the grants, only one of the five high schools had yet to offer RY; the reason was that the only health teacher in the building was fully booked. However, after observing the benefits that could be gained by their students through RY, this school is continuing to pursue creative approaches to providing the program, such as exploring hiring an itinerant health teacher or volunteer with the appropriate credentials.

Student Recruitment, Retention, and Program Fidelity

Before Reconnecting Youth can be taught, a recruitment process occurs with students being identified and interviewed to be considered for the class. Again, it is important to note that RY should be offered as a choice to those students invited to participate because of the themes of self-work and personal commitment to change involved in the course. Students are typically identified by the school counselors, social workers, and/or principals as fitting the criteria for RY and are then interviewed by the school social worker, at which time they are introduced to the components of the program. If RY is being offered for credit, it is critical to ensure that students are able to fit the course into their academic schedules and still maintain the required credits needed to graduate. When RY is offered during the resource block, students should be able to attend without its interfering with other classes. One important recruitment challenge that was noted for EVSC should be emphasized. Many of the students referred to RY faced difficulties with school attendance and credit retention. Therefore, although RY may be offered for credit, the student may lack other specific credits required to graduate, and a health elective credit from RY may not count toward these requirements. Conversely, this type of program works specifically to address attendance and school achievement issues by helping motivate students to successfully reengage in their school experience. Through the psycho-educational support of RY, students can increase their chances to graduate from high school and pursue their goals. Therefore, assisting students and school personnel in understanding these benefits of the program is an important recruitment strategy.

Recruitment efforts at each school differ according to the school climate, administration, and personnel. As Reconnecting Youth has become a more recognized program within the EVSC, implementation has increasingly become less complicated. Initially, ample time should be given to meet with administrators and school personnel to explain the RY concept, gather insight as to the readiness level of the school for RY, and build buy-in. Each school has its own strengths and limitations, which play an important role when deciding to add a new program—especially one as intensive as RY. For EVSC, it is estimated that RY takes up to 40 hours of preparatory work before the first day of class. Offering encouragement and support to school personnel and RY facilitators along the way is imperative in implementing a successful RY curriculum. The EVSC has addressed ways to employ a more uniform recruitment process, thereby reducing the amount of school personnel time needed to manage the program. Collaboration between the RY facilitator (Youth First School Social

Worker), the social worker's clinical supervisor (employed through Youth First), the project coordinator of the grant overseeing the program, and program coordinators overseeing the programs themselves has allowed for a much smoother and more timely recruitment process.

Inevitably, changes occur that are out of the facilitator's control when working with this indicated population. Sometimes students move to another school or are suspended, or students' schedules do not ultimately work out when the semester begins. It should be expected that enrollment numbers could drop somewhat from implementation to graduation for a variety of reasons. For example, of the three EVSC high schools offering RY during spring 2008, the retention statistics were as follows: 20 students enrolled, 16 graduated; 14 students enrolled, 11 graduated; and 12 students enrolled, 8 graduated. In these cases, nongraduating students either dropped the course due to schedule conflicts early on, transitioned to another school, were suspended or expelled, or in rare cases were asked to leave the class due to noncompliance with group norms. These are challenges from which to continually learn and to address. Though each year and each group dynamic is different, various barriers can still exist.

A challenge that has been successfully addressed in EVSC relates to program fidelity. Of the three high schools offering RY during the spring 2008 semester, one was not able to offer the program for credit due to limited time in the academic schedule, which did not allow for the provision of a certified health teacher. The school was still supportive of the program, however, and encouraged the school social worker to offer the program during the resource/study hall period. While this solution addressed the issue, students were consistently being pulled out of RY by teachers and counselors to make up exams, complete late work, or meet other classroom requirements in which they were falling behind. The success of RY depends on fidelity to the program and attendance is a key piece of meeting this requirement. After meeting with the head academic counselor to discuss alternatives to pull-out, an agreement was reached to continue offering RY during the resource period for noncredit, but the class itself would be considered a required element of the participating students' school day, therefore restricting their availability to be pulled out by teachers to meet other academic needs during that time. This action helped to ensure the fidelity and effective delivery of the program. This solution also highlights the importance of school personnel buy-in and ongoing collaboration.

Local Evaluation Findings

A pre-experimental time series pre-, mid-, and post-test design was used to measure the evaluation questions. The Student Outcomes Inventory (SOI) was administered to youth before, during, and after the program, and a Reconnecting Youth Completion Survey (RYCS) was administered at the end of the program. Evaluation questions were developed based on previous research supporting key outcome domains: (1) increased school adjustment,

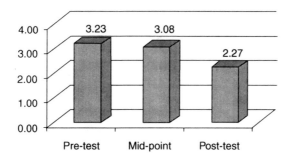

Figure 8.1 Drug use pervasiveness.

(2) decreased drug involvement, and (3) increased mood management (Eggert & Kumpfer, 1997; Eggert & Nicholas, 2004; Eggert et al., 1994; Thompson et al., 1997). A final evaluation domain examined participant perceptions with regard to program implementation. This study was part of a three-year evaluation of several federal grants used to support the program implementation (Diehl, Chadwell, Crecelius, & Vote, 2008). Since a complete review of this study is beyond the scope of this chapter, only a brief summary of key findings from the third year of implementation follow.

A total of 30 of 41 students completed both pre- and post-test data. Of the 41 students who started in the program, the majority reported previous drug and/or alcohol use, with 88% reporting alcohol use within the last year, 68% marijuana, 41% other drugs, 12% methamphetamines, and 49% prescription drugs. Further, 49% reported being in a physical fight, and 57% reported having an unexcused absence. Based on results of pre- and post-test evaluations, positive differences in drug involvement, mood management, and school adjustment were noted.

DECREASED DRUG INVOLVEMENT   Significant decreases in the pervasiveness of use were noted across evaluation periods suggesting less of a presence of drugs and alcohol within a participant's life. Figure 8.1 presents a comparison of the mean scores for the Drug Use Pervasiveness scale across evaluation periods. Higher scores on this scale indicate increased drug and alcohol use pervasiveness or a stronger presence of drugs and alcohol in an individual's life. A significant decrease ($p < .05$) was noted across all evaluation periods. As for drug use frequency, decreased mean scores from pre-test to post-test were evident for total use, alcohol use, and marijuana use. However, findings were not statistically significant.

Finally, drug use progression showed a statistically significant decline from pre-test to post-test. Figure 8.2 presents a comparison of pre-, mid-, and post-test scores on the Drug Use Progression Subscale. Higher scores indicate the use of "harder drugs" as a result of progress through the gateway drug use pattern. Significant decreases in mean scores were noted from pre-test to post-test, indicating less progress in drug use ($p < .05$).

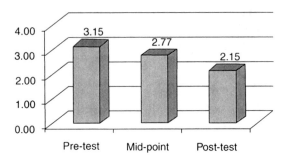

Figure 8.2 Drug use progression.

INCREASED MOOD MANAGEMENT Significant decreases in perceived stress were found across evaluation periods. While no other effects were found, generally, mean changes were favorable in most cases. For example, scores for Anxiety and Hopelessness decreased across all time periods. Scores for Depressed Affect, Anger/Aggression, and Perceived Stress decreased from pre-test to post-test. Scores for the Family Distress Subscale decreased from pre-test to mid-point, but increased from pre-test to post-test. Finally, Self-esteem/Personal Control and Family Support scores increased from pre-test to post-test.

IMPACT ON SCHOOL ADJUSTMENT The impact on school adjustment outcomes was mixed. Students did report an overall increase in grades and school bonding from pre-test to post-test, but results were not statistically significant. Due to the manner in which data were available, these data were not examined in the context of educational records.

In addition to the findings above, participants reported a number of positive benefits of the program. Specifically, since completing Reconnecting Youth, 65% of youth reported decreasing substance use, 91% reported making better decisions, 89% reported doing better in school, 60% reported better attendance in school, and 92% reported that they would recommend the program to other students.

Focus groups conducted with students were used to further examine perceived program outcomes and aspects of program fidelity. When asked how participation in RY helped students succeed in school, the following themes emerged: (1) improved grades, (2) improved attendance, (3) increased communication with teachers, (4) decreased disruptive behavior, and (5) improved accountability. Students reported significant improvement in their grades. A student who had been failing all of his classes had all passing grades at the end of RY. One student reported that he was not going to graduate before RY, but now he would finish with his class. Several students improved their attendance by coming to school on time and not skipping class. Communication skills learned in the program led to improved social relationships and support. For example, one student who used to argue with his teachers said, "I have stopped being so angry and I can communicate with my teachers now." Another student said that he had managed to avoid getting into a fight since participating in the program. Again, these changes may be attributed to a sense of accountability resulting from the program facilitator's monitoring. As one student stated, "I don't get credit for this class and I still want to take it." Additional questions identified other key themes in the areas of decreased drug involvement and improved mood management. For example, one student stated, "I was always in a bad mood before this class; this year I am happy and looking forward to things." Several students also reported quitting drug use during the course of the program. For example, one student stated that this class had helped her stay clean for longer than she ever has before. Another student stated, "I think before I do things now, I think about the instructor and others in the class." This reduction seemed to be attributed to a level of accountability within the group. For instance, one participant stated, "We have all become really close friends and we care what happens to everyone."

Though there were many positive outcomes, the most rewarding of all were the success stories and testimonials from RY students. Each school had a special graduation ceremony for those who successfully completed the class, recognizing both the challenges and achievements of each student. This is an important part of the RY process for teachers and administrators to be a part of as it provides insight to the ultimate goals of the program. The coordinators were fortunate to have tremendous buy-in from the teachers and social workers trained to lead RY. Feedback from teachers in particular indicated a desire to continue to co-teach RY in the future.

RECONNECTING YOUTH AND THE RtI PROCESS

Assessing Student Progress

Outcome evaluation data can aid in informing the RY leader of the progress or lack of progress of each student. These measures provide critical information for differentiation and instructional decision making within the RtI process by highlighting factors that may indicate a student needs a more intensive individualized intervention (Tier 3). Outcome evaluation points provide data in two areas: Extent to which students are achieving goals, and results of immediate intervention. Program goals may be measured in the following areas:

> *Measures to assess school achievement.* School Records—last semester, middle of present semester, at exit, and at follow-up (end of next semester); Student Outcomes Inventory (SOI) or High School Questionnaire (HSQ)—pre-intervention at invitation, weeks 3, 9, 13, end of RY semester, and end of following semester

Measures to assess drug involvement. Drug Involvement Scale for
   Adolescents in the SOI or HSQ—pre-intervention at invitation,
   weeks 3, 9, 13, end of RY semester, and end of following semester

Measures to assess mood management. SOI—Moods and Experience
   scale score or single items OR HSQ—Individual Scales for anger
   control problems, depression, hopelessness, perceived stress,
   suicide-risk behaviors, and other moods and life experiences
   (pre-intervention at invitation, weeks 8, 9, 13, end of RY
   semester, and end of following semester)

Immediate intervention outcomes are evaluated in the following ways.
Personal competencies (skills) are assessed with the Personal and Social Skills
Inventory (PSSI): pre-intervention, at invitation, at weeks 3, 9, 13, end of
semester, and end of following semester. Social support resources are
assessed with the Group Social Support Checklist, Leader Social Support
Checklist, or HSQ—Individual Scales for school bonding, support for
school from multiple sources, family support, along with other scales measuring the amount and perceived sense of support in the RY High School
Questionnaire (measured at the same times as the PSSI above).

HOW DOES RECONNECTING YOUTH FIT IN THE STRUCTURE OF RtI?

In the Response to Intervention Tier 2 structure, Reconnecting Youth
addresses students' needs in a manner that can determine the need for
further Tier 3 intervention or may designate a level of success that places
the student back at the Tier 1 level. Throughout the program, not only are
students monitoring their own work, but the school social worker and
teaching instructor are also observing and working directly with each
individual student. This type of direction allows for the constant assessment of student progress throughout the RY semester.

KEY CONSIDERATIONS FOR IMPLEMENTATION

As each school environment is unique, the basis for determining whether
Reconnecting Youth is the appropriate program for a particular student
population would depend on the Tier 1 screening data being examined.
For example, a school might form a group to investigate the specific needs
of their school, and if those needs include addressing attendance issues;
dropout rates; overall attitude about school; and documented cases of
depression, anxiety, or other disorders affecting school attachment and
achievement, then it may be determined that a program like Reconnecting
Youth would be a good fit for addressing these concerns as a targeted
group intervention.

Likewise, a school might already have data dictating a need for this
type of approach through school surveys or questionnaires previously

administered, or school officials may look into administering these instruments. Reconnecting Youth is designed to address specific issues relative to achievement in both the school and outside environments and, like all programs, must be investigated and matched to the needs of each individual school.

Program Costs

Monetary costs for the program can be separated into three categories. First, qualified personnel must be hired to teach the class. Reconnecting Youth developers also recommend one-full time program coordinator for every five to six classes to offer support and consultation to the classroom teachers. Additionally, training must be obtained by all key players, which is offered in several ways: 5 days in length, for 5 to 7 people, 1 trainer—$750/day plus expenses; 5 days in length, 8 to 14 people, 2 trainers—$1,500/day plus expenses; follow up consultation days for 5 to 70 people—$750/day. Program materials are offered in the form of a curriculum book—Reconnecting Youth: A Peer Group Approach to Building Life Skills—with student handouts for photocopying at $179; teacher manuals and reproducible forms book—$69; a parent training video—$49.95; and sets of support materials sold separately in sets of five and more (stickers, pencils, T-shirts, etc.)—$15 - $22.50. Classroom materials, in sets of five, are sold separately and include the student workbooks. The average cost for a Reconnecting Youth program is estimated to be between $5, 001 and $10, 000 (SAMHSA, 2008, p. 8). Evaluation cost could range from 7% to 15% depending on the level of evaluation warranted.

Required Training

The RY program maintains that training is essential for leaders and coordinators, while training for support personnel and site administrators is recommended. The training experience includes presentations and modeling by the trainer, practice teaching with structured feedback for the participants, learning how to use critical process and outcome data-gathering tools, learning how to build a supportive infrastructure for the RY program, and developing an RY School Support Team (Reconnecting Youth Company, 2008). To maintain and sustain fidelity to the program, proper training is a fundamental part of implementing an RY class.

KNOWLEDGE AND SKILLS REQUIRED BY SOCIAL WORKERS

Understanding of Tier 2 Interventions in the RtI Process

A successful RY program requires a working understanding of all three tiers of the RtI framework and how RY fits within the second tier. School social workers must be able to identify and evaluate student needs in order to match the appropriate supports/interventions to these needs. While all students will have access to interventions at the universal (Tier 1) level, as social workers and school personnel become more familiar with students exhibiting a greater need for support, it will be easier for them to discern which students might benefit from a targeted, Tier 2 intervention such as RY.

Perhaps more important, the school social worker must continually assess a student's progress or lack of progress throughout the use of a Tier 2 intervention. Thorough assessment of students' response to this particular intervention helps determine which students may need Tier 3 intensive, individualized interventions. As in most situations, it is better to make such decisions based on group consensus and data rather than just one's own opinion. Having input from people who know the student best will help to ensure the successful transition from a Tier 1 to a Tier 2 approach, and likewise, from a Tier 2 approach to a Tier 3 level of intervention. Though different in each case, examples of people collaborating for the benefit of the student may include parents/guardians; a particular teacher or other school personnel who know the student well or with whom the student has a trusting relationship; the principal; and perhaps other community figures involved in the student's life. The school social worker can be a key figure in this process and often is responsible for organizing and maintaining this entire transition.

Understanding How to Implement an Evidence-based Program within a School Setting

Schools have been in the practice of implementing programs in classrooms, with small groups, or even school-wide for years. Some work very well and evoke positive change in the school environment. For others, there is a lot more trial and error involved. Different programs will yield different results depending on how they are used and, specifically, how they acclimate to each unique school environment. As money for programs has become increasingly obtained from grants, formal evaluation processes are more frequently required. When a program has a history of positive outcomes and shows trends in the intended direction, it is more likely to be considered for use in other venues. When an administrator or teacher is searching for such programs for implementation at a particular school, a program showing results backed with research will gain more attention and support than a program that has never been evaluated.

Evidence-based programs have a history of showing promising and successful results. Well-researched programs also identify potential barriers to successful implementation and/or case examples of what has worked well and what has not from other school sites. The advantages of choosing an evidence-based program are many, especially when presenting the program for use in a school. School staff and faculty are already limited in their time to teach what is academically required during the school day, and while many schools are interested in addressing other student needs, such as social, emotional, and behavioral, they simply do not have the time to extensively research the costs and benefits of the multitude of programs available.

Implementing an evidence-based program often means a school will become a part of the research as well. Because evidence-based programs often have evaluation tools already available, there is an opportunity to gather data relative to the target population, hence providing important information for the positive development of both student success and overall school environment. Of course, being a part of an evidence-based curriculum requires strong commitment to the fidelity of the program. Achieving the intended results is dependent on this commitment and thus must be thoroughly communicated to all key partners and throughout the school.

Recognizing the accountability that an evidence-based program can bring to one's school is an asset in itself. Achieving buy-in from key players sometimes is a difficult task, but it can be made easier with the use of data and positive outcomes from programs under consideration. Incorporating evidence-based programs into the school curriculum can be beneficial for students, families, and the school community at large.

The Importance of Measuring Program Fidelity

Program fidelity or implementation integrity is an integral part of Reconnecting Youth. From the RY facilitator delivering the curriculum to the structure of the implementation, the overall assessment of the program is based on these characteristics. Components of assessing program fidelity include evaluating these factors using materials included in the RY curriculum. Process evaluation includes measuring the leadership delivery of the class as designed through measures such as the weekly Group Building Behaviors Checklist; the weekly Life Skills Training Behaviors Checklist; and the Group and Leader Social Support Checklists at two weeks into the program and monthly at the end of each unit (National Center for Mental Health Promotion and Youth Violence, 2008).

In the EVSC, program fidelity is always a key focus for effective program delivery. Fidelity is maintained through monthly supervision meetings for the school social workers, monthly observations of each class by the clinical supervisor, daily availability of support from clinical supervisor and program coordinators through the use of e-mails, phone or face-to-face meetings, consultation with RY developers when warranted, and at least one roundtable meeting per semester with all RY facilitators, program coordinators, clinical supervisors, and grant project coordinators in attendance.

Like universal interventions, targeted interventions, when carried out with fidelity, should support the school social worker in identifying students who are in need of additional support. The school social worker must recognize the significance of delivering a program to the utmost level of fidelity, for analyzing a student's response to an intervention delivered without fidelity to the program is not a fair assessment of that student's behavioral needs (Sandomierski, Kincaid, & Algozzine, 2007).

Understanding Student Outcomes from a Targeted Group Intervention

Appropriate determination of the need for Tier 3 interventions should be based on a student's response or lack of response to the Tier 2 level of intervention already in place. Likewise, if the current response to intervention is insufficient, factors such as program fidelity must be addressed to ensure that the student's needs warrant further intervention or were perhaps not adequate due to failure of effective delivery rather than failure of student response to the intervention. As previously noted, the process for determining the need for different levels of intervention should consider the inclusion of various people invested in the student's academic and social/emotional well-being.

SUMMARY

In the context of a Response to Intervention (RtI) model, Reconnecting Youth is a Tier 2 targeted group early intervention strategy that addresses the needs of students not met by Tier 1 universal supports. This chapter has illustrated the benefits of this program for students and schools, along with potential challenges and solutions in implementing the program in the school setting. As a SAMHSA model program, RY has a substantial research base and fits well within the RtI framework. Process and outcome evaluation measures provide continuous tracking of student progress, which allows decisions to be made throughout implementation. However, to implement this program within an RtI framework, school social workers must have an understanding of Tier 2 interventions, knowledge of implementing such programs within the school setting, an understanding of basic concepts of program fidelity, and an understanding of how to track outcomes from a targeted group intervention. Collectively, the use of Reconnecting Youth as an early intervention strategy within Tier 2 provides school social workers with further support in addressing the diversity of issues facing students and schools.

REFERENCES

Diehl, D., Chadwell, J., Crecelius, S., & Vote, A. (2008). *Year three: Grant to reduce alcohol abuse.* Evaluation Report submitted August 8, 2008, to Evansville Vanderburgh School Corporation and Youth First, Inc, Evansville, IN.
Diehl, D., Gray, C., & O'Connor, G. (2005, fall). The school community council: Creating an environment for student success, *New Directions for Youth Development, 107,* 65–72.
Eggert, L., & Kumpfer, K. L. (1997). *Drug abuse prevention for at-risk individuals.* Rockville, MD: National Institute on Drug Abuse.

Eggert, L., & Nicholas, L. (2004). *Reconnecting Youth: A peer group approach to building life skills.* Bloomington, IN: National Educational Service.

Eggert, L. L., Thompson, E. A., Herting, J. R., & Nicholas, L. J. (1995). Reducing suicide potential among high risk youth: Tests of a school based prevention program. *Suicide and Life-Threatening Behavior, 25*(2), 276–296.

Eggert, L. L., Thompson, E. A., Herting, J. R., Nicholas, L. J., & Dicker, B. G. (1994). Preventing adolescent drug abuse and high school dropout through an intensive school-based social network development program. *American Journal of Health Promotion, 8*, 202–215.

Eggert, L. L., Thompson, E. A., Herting, J. R., & Randell, B. P. (2001). Reconnecting youth to prevent drug abuse, school dropout, and suicidal behaviors among high-risk youth. In E. F. Wagner & H. B. Waldron (Eds.), *Innovations in adolescent substance abuse intervention* (pp. 51–84). Oxford: Elsevier Science.

Evansville Vanderburgh School Corporation (EVSC) School Community Council. (2008). School Community Council. Retrieved November 12, 2008, from http://www.schoolcommunitycouncil.com.

National Center for Mental Health Promotion and Youth Violence. (2008). *Reconnecting Youth: A peer group approach to building life skills.* Retrieved November 12, 2008, from http://www.promoteprevent.org.

Reconnecting Youth Company. (2008). *Reconnecting Youth prevention program.* Retrieved November 12, 2008, from http://www.reconnectingyouth.com/RY/.

Sandomierski, T., Kincaid, D., & Algozzine, B. (2007). Response to intervention and positive behavior support: Brothers from different mothers or sisters with different misters? *Positive Behavioral Interventions and Supports Newsletter, 4*(2), 1–4. Retrieved August 25, 2008, from http://www.pbis.org.

Substance Abuse and Mental Health Services Administration (SAMHSA). *SAMHSA model programs: Reconnecting Youth.* Retrieved November 12, 2008, from http://modelprograms.samhsa.gov.

Thompson, E. A., Horn, M., Herting, J. H., & Eggert, L. L. (1997). Enhancing outcomes in an indicated drug prevention program for high-risk youth. *Journal of Drug Education, 27*, 19–41.

Youth First, Inc. (2008). *Youth First!* Retrieved November 12, 2008, from http://www.youthfirstinc.org/.

SECTION III

Tier 3 Intensive Individual Interventions

Figure III.1[a]

Typically about 1% to 5% of any school's population will have needs that are best met with intensive individual interventions in Tier 3. Many of these students have not adequately benefited from universal supports provided in Tier 1 or targeted group interventions in Tier 2. Chapters in this section describe the essential features of intensive individualized interventions along with two examples that illustrate the application of intensive individualized interventions.

In Chapter 9, Clark and Gilmore described the key features of designing and implementing intensive individualized interventions including specific procedures for conducting a functional behavioral assessment; defining and identifying the problem; establishing a pre-intervention baseline of performance; doing problem validation and analysis; designing the intervention including goal setting, progress monitoring, and evaluation; and ensuring implementation integrity. Timm and Marckmann illustrate the application of these procedures with a kindergarten student in Chapter 10. In Chapter 11 Eber, Lindsey, and White provide an example of the use of intensive individualized interventions in a family-centered wraparound process implemented across home, school, and community settings.

9

TIER 3 INTENSIVE INDIVIDUALIZED INTERVENTIONS

JAMES P. CLARK & JENNIFER GILMORE

It is expected that most but not all students will adequately benefit from universal supports provided in Tier 1 and targeted interventions in Tier 2, but typically about 1% to 5% of any school's population will have needs that are best met with intensive individualized interventions in Tier 3. In this chapter we describe the essential components of a process for developing intensive individualized interventions for these students. This includes specific procedures for conducting a functional behavioral assessment; defining and identifying the problem; establishing a pre-intervention baseline of performance; doing problem validation and analysis; designing the intervention including goal setting, progress monitoring, and evaluation; and ensuring implementation integrity. We also discuss the acutely individualized assessment and data based decision-making skills that are required to appropriately design and evaluate intensive individualized behavior interventions and the higher level of specialized support and services that are necessary to ensure adequate implementation. The placement of intensive individualized interventions in a Response to Intervention (RtI) system are proposed along with key considerations for implementing these interventions. Finally, knowledge

131

and skills that school social workers will need to provide intensive individual interventions are identified.

FUNCTIONAL BEHAVIORAL ASSESSMENT

As stated in Chapter 1 the four basic steps of problem solving are applied in Tier 3 as they are throughout the RtI system. These steps include (1) problem identification and definition, (2) problem analysis, (3) intervention plan development and implementation, and (4) evaluation, that is, evaluating the effectiveness of the plan (Clark, 1998; Tilly, 2002). However, implementation of this process in Tier 3 requires higher levels of rigor and precision in assessment, intervention design, monitoring, and evaluation as these procedures are used with students who need more intensive and individualized interventions.

Crucial to the successful design, implementation, and evaluation of intensive individualized interventions in Tier 3 is proficiency in conducting a functional behavioral assessment (FBA). Data from the FBA are essential to obtaining a clear and concise problem identification and definition. A functional behavioral assessment is "the *process* of coming to an understanding of why a student engages in challenging behavior and how student behavior relates to the environment" (Tilly et al., 1998, p. 1). Further, this approach to assessment "enhances understanding of the purpose and effect of the behaviors of concern" (Clark, 1998, p. 6) and is also functional in that it provides data useful in designing interventions (Clark et al., 2006).

Thus, functional behavioral assessment data facilitate an understanding of the purpose or function of a student's behavior. This not only helps to craft a clear identification and definition of the problem behavior but it also is critical in helping to design an intervention that is appropriately matched to the function of the behavior. As stated in Chapter 12 the effectiveness of interventions that have been based on functional assessments has been demonstrated in recent studies (Ingram, Lewis-Palmer, & Sugai, 2005). The durability of interventions that are based on functional behavioral assessments has also been documented (Kern et al., 2006).

The evidence base for the approach to functional behavioral assessment and intervention design presented here draws from the long and rich applied behavior analysis research literature. Understanding the cause and effect relationship between environment and behavior has long been the pursuit of this research. Skinner (1953) first used the term *functional analysis* to describe the systematic examination of the interactions of problem behavior and the environment. Research over the following decades focused on the effects of environmental consequences, such as attention or escape from demands, on problem behavior. Iwata, Dorsey, Slifer, Bauman, and Richman (1994) developed the first comprehensive functional analysis of problem behavior through the use of a methodology to study the multiple effects of positive, negative, and automatic reinforcement on self-injurious behavior. More recently, in a quantitative review of 277 empirical studies Hanley, Iwata, and McCord (2003) found that 86% of problem behaviors were maintained by positive social reinforcement, 89% were maintained by negative social reinforcement, and 60% maintained by automatic reinforcement (nonsocial behaviors that are reinforced by stimulation directly produced by the response).

Coupled with the studies cited above that demonstrate the efficacy and durability of interventions that are based on functional behavior assessments, applied behavior analysis research has identified the set of intervention procedures that are most likely to impact problem behaviors, primarily positive and negative social reinforcement. In addition, *gain* (attention or tangibles) and *escape from demands or nonpreferred tasks* are the most frequent functions that maintain problem behavior. Hanley, Iwata, and McCord (2003) have proposed that an ABC (Antecedent-Behavior-Consequence) model for conducting a functional analysis "provides a more rigorous demonstration of causation" (p. 168) and have recommended this model as a best practice. The ABC model provides greater precision in understanding the relationships between conditions of the environment that occur prior to the problem behavior, the problem behavior, and consequences of the problem behavior that either maintain or decrease its presence. As is evident in the following discussion, successful intervention outcomes will be highly dependent on the precise match of functional assessment data and specific procedures selected for inclusion in intervention plans. Thus, the close alignment of assessment data demonstrating the function of problem behaviors and specific intervention procedures selected for intervention is critical in ensuring successful intervention outcomes.

PROBLEM IDENTIFICATION AND DEFINITION

A clear and concise understanding of what constitutes a problem is critical to problem identification and definition, the first step of the problem-solving process. A behavior problem is defined as "the difference between what is expected and the actual student behavior or performance" (Upah, 2008, p. 210). This definition sets the expectation that diminishing or eliminating the discrepancy between the student's behavior and what is expected will be the focus of the intervention.

Functional behavioral assessment data will document the existence and magnitude of the discrepancy and will provide information needed to define the problem behavior in operational terms. First, however, it must be determined that the behavior is educationally relevant and that it is alterable. There are many behaviors that can be categorized as different, odd, or even unusual. The key is whether they are educationally relevant. This must be determined situationally. A certain behavior may be educationally relevant for one student and not relevant for another depending on the situation in which the behavior occurs. Consider the behavior of rocking and flapping. In one situation a child may be rocking and flapping to a degree and intensity that it truly impedes the ability of the student (or the student's classmates) to engage in learning and to benefit from the core curriculum. Another student may be rocking and flapping to even the same degree and intensity but may be successfully benefiting from the core curriculum without impeding the ability of classmates to do likewise. For a behavior to be considered educationally relevant it must be significantly and directly interfering with the student's ability, or the ability of classmates, to meet school-wide behavior expectations or to access and benefit from the core behavior curriculum.

It is also obviously essential that a behavior be alterable if it will be the focus of an intervention. Alterable behaviors are those that can be changed by actions that are within the span of control of school personnel. Examples of alterable behaviors include physical or verbal aggression, and inattention or off-task behaviors. Behaviors or conditions that are not alterable include student characteristics such as general intelligence, physical or medical conditions, and socio-economic status.

Once it has been determined that a behavior is educationally relevant and alterable, an operational definition of that behavior can be developed. An operational definition of the problem ensures that everyone involved with developing interventions has a shared understanding of what needs to change and how success of interventions might be measured. The operational definition of behavior must be "objective (observable and measurable), clear (so unambiguous that it could be read, repeated, and paraphrased by observers), and complete (delineates examples and non-examples of the behavior)" (Heartland Area Education Agency 11, 2002, p. 38).

Consider the following nonexample of problem identification: "The student is aggressive at school." This statement does not provide a clear and complete description of what *aggressive* looks like or does not look like. Also not apparent are the particular conditions in which the student is aggressive. Therefore, this statement does not meet the criteria of being objective, clear, and complete. As a result, the statement, "the student is aggressive at school, " could actually look like any of the following three problem identification examples.

Example 1: The student engages in physically aggressive behavior, aimed at adults, when given a nonpreferred task or demand. Examples include but are not limited to spitting, hitting with force potential of leaving a mark, kicking with force potential of leaving a mark, and scratching aimed at adults. Nonexamples include but are not limited to spitting outside while playing, lightly slapping at an adult, kicking the garbage can on the way to sharpen his pencil, scratching an itch.

Example 2: The student engages in physically aggressive behavior aimed at peers when engaged in a large group activity or unstructured setting. Examples include but are not limited to pinching, slapping, poking, kicking, or choking aimed at peers. Nonexamples include but are not limited to reciprocal "roughhousing" with peers, such as poking, tickling, and shoving.

Example 3: The student is aggressive toward himself when given a nonpreferred task or demand to complete independently. Examples include biting the back of his hand with enough force to leave a mark and/or slapping the side of his head with enough force to be heard by others when two arm-lengths away. Nonexamples include sucking or lightly biting on fingertips and/or lightly slapping the side of his head, inaudible by others from two arm-lengths away.

It is striking how the statement "aggressive at school" can actually look like three distinctly different sets of behaviors if the problem identification and definition is not objective, clear, and complete. Clarity at this step of the problem-solving process is critical to ensuring a common understanding of the problem and in providing the specificity that is needed to design interventions and measure their results.

ESTABLISHING A PRE-INTERVENTION BASELINE

Once there is a validated and operationally defined problem identification, establishing a baseline, or pre-intervention level of performance, is critical. The first step in gathering baseline data is selecting a method for measuring the behavior that will be most conducive to data analysis and that will capture true behavioral change. Common dimensions of behavior that may need to be measured are frequency, intensity, and duration. Consider the problem identification above. Aggression may be measured by how often it occurs during the day (frequency), how much physical damage or instructional disruption it causes (intensity), or the amount of time that passes from the onset of the event to its conclusion (duration). Dimensions of behavior that are most likely to yield valid and reliable data for decision making are those that should be selected for measurement. What might be the most appropriate dimension of behavior to measure for a student with aggressive behavior that occurs three times per day, with a marginal level of physical damage, and lasts an average of 85 minutes during each act? A team may document a decrease in the frequency of incidents and even in the intensity of incidents but if the duration is maintaining or even increasing, one set of data may be indicating progress while other data suggest a need for changing the instruction/intervention. Practitioners must determine what exactly about the behavior is most problematic.

Through the process of reviewing existing data—for example, incident documentation and school records—interviewing adults who know the child best, and interviewing the student if appropriate, a practitioner may be able to gather sufficient information to establish a baseline level of performance. In the aggression example, adequate and valid documentation may exist on the duration of each incident and there may be several incidents to analyze. However, in many cases additional convergent information will need to be gathered with structured interviews and direct observations.

Results of the review of existing data and interviews can help identify the most critical periods of time in which to conduct observations. To establish an accurate baseline, direct observation of a minimum of three observations of the identified problem behavior must be conducted. The median data point is the preferred value for representing baseline performance. The median is the middle value of the distribution of scores/measures—that is, the value above and below which an equal number of scores/measures fall. The mean, or arithmetic average, of data points is not considered to be an accurate indication of baseline performance. To illustrate the rationale for using the median data point, consider this duration example. The durations of physical aggression incidents measured in minutes are 16, 75, 85, 93, and 102. If the mean were selected, the baseline point would be 56 minutes. If the median were selected it would be 85 minutes. It may be that the value 16 is an outlier that is significantly skewing the data. It is critically important to establish an accurate measure of pre-intervention baseline performance since determinations of progress and the success of interventions will be measured against this baseline.

PROBLEM VALIDATION AND ANALYSIS

Though not the most time-consuming or complex procedure, problem validation is a critical step in the problem-solving process. As stated earlier, a problem is defined as "the difference between what is expected and the actual student behavior or performance" (Upah, 2008, p. 210). Problem validation is the process of determining that a difference between the student's behavior and the expectations of the setting does in fact exist and then measuring the exact magnitude of this difference. As Upah (2008) points out, this is important because "validating the existence of the discrepancy provides information as to the intensity of the problem to determine whether it is best addressed through targeted or intensive supports, or possibly even through improving the core instruction if significant numbers of students are exhibiting similar levels of performance" (p. 212). If it is determined that there is little or no difference between set expectations and the student's behavior, the problem definition and the stated severity of the problem will need to be reexamined. If the difference is moderate and other students have similar discrepancies, Tier 2 targeted group interventions may be appropriate. To warrant intensive individualized interventions in Tier 3 the discrepancy must be significantly different from that of peers or expectations/standards of the setting.

After the problem behavior has been validated, problem analysis is conducted to determine why the problem is occurring. This is a critically important component of a functional behavior assessment. The purpose of problem analysis is " to understand the salient characteristics of a problem and to use that understanding to identify potential problem solutions" (Christ, 2008, pp.159–160).

Multimethod problem-analysis data collection procedures are used. These include reviewing, interviewing, observing, and testing (RIOT). Relevant educational records, reports, samples of work completed by the student, and other information may be *reviewed*. The student's parents, teacher, paraprofessional, and others may be *interviewed*. Systematic *observations* of the student may be conducted to validate and analyze the problem behavior. In some cases *tests*, or structured checklists or standardized assessments, may be used to corroborate other findings. An ecological assessment approach should be followed in which these procedures are used to collect data from multiple sources or domains. These domains are often referred to as ICEL, i.e. instruction (how skills are taught), curriculum (what skills are taught), environment (the setting in which skills are taught), and the learner (the student to whom skills are taught) (Christ, 2008). RIOT procedures used to assess ICEL domains ensure that multiple sources of data are used to analyze the problem and that these data are converged to optimize a complete understanding of why the problem is occurring. Data generated from these procedures will also be useful in determining the function of the problem behavior and in designing interventions.

Understanding why a behavior problem exists and is maintained requires an understanding of the function of the behavior. Most often behaviors function either to gain or escape attention or demands. Examining antecedents (what happens before the behavior occurs) and consequences (what happens after the behavior occurs) can provide some clues about what function or purpose the behavior serves for the student. Assessing ICEL domains with RIOT procedures can also assist in determining behavior functions.

Critical to the success of an intervention plan is the appropriate identification of the function of the behavior and matching that function to the instructional strategies included in the intervention plan. If the function of the identified problem behavior is not adequately matched to the intervention, the behavior is likely to continue and in some cases get worse. Consider again the aggression example. If the function of the student's aggression is properly identified as *escape demands* but the antecedent strategies, instructional replacement behavior, reinforcement, and/or consequences are geared toward that of *gain attention*, the mismatch of behavior function and the intervention plan will not likely ensure successful results.

DESIGNING AN INTERVENTION PLAN

Intensive individualized interventions designed in Tier 3 must be clearly and specifically described in a written plan. A step-by-step description of the procedures that will be used to accomplish goals ensures that everyone involved in implementing these procedures has a common understanding of what is expected. A written plan also enhances the likelihood that intervention strategies will be implemented as intended, thereby increasing the level of implementation integrity.

Designing interventions begins with the identification of ambitious goals that typically aim for peer comparable performance. In most cases it is desirable for the discrepancy between the student's pre-intervention behavior and the typical behavior of same age peers to be mostly diminished or totally eliminated. Pre-intervention performance is represented by the baseline. The desired level of performance is defined by the goal statement. Problem validation data are used to establish the pre-intervention baseline and to identify ambitious goals that are stated in complete, precise, meaningful, and measurable terms.

Consider again the "aggression" example described earlier. The pre-intervention baseline is an average of three daily incidents with a duration average of 85 minutes. The desired performance level is zero daily incidents with a duration average of zero minutes. The goal might be stated as follows:

> Example: Within eight weeks, with an intervention plan in place,
> [student] will engage in an average of less than one aggressive
> incident (including but not limited to spitting, hitting with force
> potential of leaving a mark, kicking with force potential of leaving a
> mark, and scratching aimed at adults aimed at an adult) lasting less
> than 10 minutes in duration.

After a goal has been identified intervention strategies must be designed. Strategies are selected that will have the greatest chance of accomplishing the goal and that are matched to the magnitude of the performance discrepancy. Antecedent strategies are often used in an intervention plan to decrease the likelihood that the behavior will occur. These strategies are implemented before the undesirable behavior is anticipated to occur and may include warm-ups, schedules, prompting, strategic arrangement of the room, and other strategies. The function of the behavior should be considered when selecting antecedent strategies. For example, if the function of the identified problem behavior is escape from nonpreferred tasks or demands, highly preferred activities such as warm-up activities could be used. However, if the function of the identified problem behavior is gaining the attention of adults, warm-up activities might be used in conjunction with unconditional high rates of adult attention.

Because the problem analysis has led to an explanation of why the problem behavior is occurring, a replacement behavior can be identified and an intervention can be designed to teach that replacement behavior. A replacement behavior is a more socially acceptable or appropriate behavior that accomplishes the same outcome or function of the problem behavior. For some students the desired level of performance or desired behavior is the replacement behavior that needs to be immediately taught and reinforced. In some instances an approximation of the desired behavior may first need to be taught and reinforced and then systematically shaped into the desired behavior. This is often the case when there is a large discrepancy that requires a series of instructional steps and reinforcements to reduce or eliminate the behavior. Consider the student who is aggressive as a means to escape nonpreferred tasks or demands. The desired level of performance may be that the student completes all work requested by an adult. However, to reduce the discrepancy it may be necessary to initially teach the child how to temporarily and appropriately escape nonpreferred tasks and demands. This behavior can then be shaped into the desired behavior.

Replacement behaviors must be as easy to perform and as effective as the problem behavior. They must also serve the same function as the problem behavior. This ensures that the student will be able to actually acquire, perform fluently, and effectively generalize the replacement behaviors. If replacement behaviors do not meet these criteria, it is likely that the child will resort to the same problem behavior that has served the same function in the past. If the function of aggression in this example is to escape from demands and the replacement behavior that is being taught is asking for teacher assistance, which serves the function of gaining adult attention, it may appear that a valuable and crucial student skill is being taught. However, in this case it is not the skill or replacement behavior best matched to the function of the problem behavior. The child may learn an appropriate way to gain adult attention, but if the aggression was initially effective in escaping demands, it is highly likely that without being taught an appropriate replacement behavior, the child will resort to the problem behavior, that is, aggression.

When a replacement behavior is being taught, it is essential that the reinforcement schedule allow adequate opportunities for reinforcement and that the reinforcement is matched to the function of the behavior. For the problem behavior that serves the function of escape from demands, a powerful reinforcement may be for the student to earn additional opportunities to escape nonpreferred tasks or demands. For example, a student who has exhibited appropriate use of the replacement behavior during math class may be permitted to earn the ability to cross out three math problems on a test or to leave math class 10 minutes early. If gaining adult attention is not the function served by the problem behavior, earning token reinforcement to purchase items from the school store may not be as effective.

Consequence strategies are actions that follow the occurrence of a problem behavior and that increase the likelihood that the behavior will not occur again. It is particularly important to consider the function of the problem behavior when using consequence strategies in an intervention plan. Failure to do so can inadvertently result in further reinforcement and strengthening of the problem behavior. For example, if the function of aggression is to escape from nonpreferred tasks or demands and the consequence strategy put in place is time-out, the problem behavior will be reinforced. A more appropriate consequence strategy in this case might be escape extinction. With this strategy the nonpreferred task or demand is not removed when the problem behavior occurs (see Appendix 9.A for an example of how the components of an intervention plan can be organized).

PROGRESS MONITORING AND EVALUATION

Progress monitoring is the ongoing evaluation of relevant and accurate intervention data for the purpose of determining whether an intervention is working. Progress monitoring data are used throughout the implementation of an intervention plan to inform educational decision making. Direct and frequent measures of the student's response to the intervention plan must be reviewed to determine whether interventions are having the desired effect.

A decision-making plan is an effective procedure for assuring that these data are used systematically and in a data-based manner. A key element of this plan is a decision-making rule—a procedure that is established before the intervention is implemented that defines specifically how progress monitoring data will be used to evaluate the effectiveness of the intervention. It describes what action the intervention team will take when the rule is applied to progress monitoring data.

A four-point decision rule is commonly used in decision plans. The baseline median point and the point that represents attainment of the student's goal should be plotted on a graph and connected with a *goal line* (see Figure 9.1). A typical application of a four-point decision rule stipulates that if four consecutive data points fall below or above the goal line the intervention team will reconvene to consider what changes in the intervention may be needed. It is important to consider the amount of time the intervention has been implemented along with the application of a four-point decision rule. To have reasonable confidence that the data are reflecting performance that is a direct result of the intervention, the student must have been exposed to the intervention for an adequate amount of time. The amount of time will vary according to a variety of factors such as the type of intervention being implemented, the severity of the problem behavior, the rate of progress expected, and the discrepancy of the student's performance. A common, minimum amount of time that an intervention must have been implemented before a four-point decision rule is applied is approximately four to six weeks.

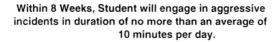

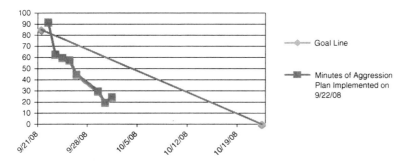

Figure 9.1   Student performance graph—favorable trend.

A number of decisions might result from the application of a four-point decision rule. If four consecutive data points fall below a goal line with a downward slope, an intervention team might decide that the intervention is having desirable effects and will continue to be implemented as written. An example is provided in Figure 9.1. Because the data indicate a decreasing trend, the intervention team agreed to continue the intervention plan as written.

If four consecutive data points fall above the goal line with a downward slope, the intervention team may decide that the intervention needs to be modified by increasing specialized instruction, supports, and/or reinforcement. An example is provided in Figure 9.2. In this case, because the data

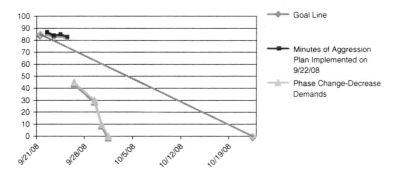

Figure 9.2   Student performance graph—flatline trend.

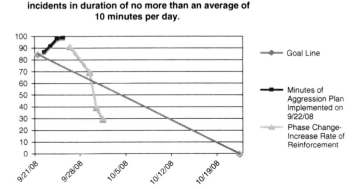

Figure 9.3   Student performance graph—increasing trend.

showed a flat-line trend, the team agreed to decrease the level of current academic demands. This modification of the intervention design is called a *phase change* and is usually identified on a graph with a *phase line* or with data points of a different color so that data from the two different interventions can be clearly distinguished.

In some cases when four consecutive data points show a marked trend in a direction opposite the desired direction of the goal, the intervention team will reconvene to review whether the intervention is being correctly implemented. An example is provided in Figure 9.3. After an increasing trend in the data appeared, the team reconvened to review implementation information and agreed that the reinforcement schedule was not being implemented as written. The team agreed to implement the reinforcement as written providing a higher level of reinforcement than what had actually been delivered. This is also an example of a phase change.

The application of decision-making rules is a method of formative evaluation that occurs throughout the implementation of the intervention. As Upah (2008) explains, "The purpose of formative evaluation to determine the likely success of an intervention during its implementation so that it can be modified or changed to increase the likelihood that intended results will be achieved" (p. 218). Summative evaluation occurs after the intervention has been fully implemented and is intended to determine whether the intervention was effective in accomplishing the goal. Valid formative and summative evaluations of intervention effects cannot be achieved without progress monitoring data generated from direct and frequent measures of the student's response to the intervention, the application of decision-making rules to these data, and the ongoing scrutiny of the data by the intervention team that is dedicated to discovering what enables learning for the student.

ENSURING IMPLEMENTATION INTEGRITY

Decisions regarding the effectiveness of any intervention plan cannot be made with confidence if the interventions are not actually implemented as designed. Direct and systematic attention to implementation integrity, sometimes referred to as treatment integrity, is essential to data-based decision making. Implementation integrity refers to the degree to which an intervention has been implemented as designed. Without high levels of implementation integrity, it is not possible to know whether changes in a student's performance are the result of the intervention or if other factors have contributed.

For an intensive individualized intervention to have adequate implementation integrity, at least 80% of the plan components must be implemented as designed at least 80% of the time. An implementation checklist is a tool that can be used to ensure high levels of integrity (see Appendix 9.B for an example). Key procedures described in the intervention plan are selected to be included in the checklist, such as procedures for antecedent strategies and teaching replacement behavior. Completion of these procedures are logged by individuals who are responsible for their implementation—for example, a teacher or paraprofessional. Other members of the intervention team may also conduct periodic observations of these procedures being implemented in order to corroborate the data collected in the checklist. Levels of implementation integrity can then be calculated from these data.

Assuring acceptable levels of implementation integrity is essential to ensuring that effective interventions can be verified. Decisions about what supports are needed by a student to be successful are critically dependent upon implementation integrity. In RtI systems that rely on intervention data to make high stakes decisions such as special education eligibility determination, implementation integrity is particularly important (see Chapter 12).

CONTEXT: HOW DO INTENSIVE INDIVIDUALIZED INTERVENTIONS FIT IN THE STRUCTURE OF RtI?

Intensive individualized interventions in Tier 3 typically require the use of intervention procedures that are significantly restrictive or intrusive. These interventions are used when student needs are not met with universal supports in Tier 1 or targeted group interventions in Tier 2. There are two situations when this might occur.

First, the intensity of a student's behavior may indicate the need for immediate consideration of the need for an intensive individualized intervention. If the student's behavior is significantly discrepant from peers and is potentially dangerous, the extent of specialized instruction, support, and procedures that are needed may warrant an intensive individualized intervention. Behaviors that may fall into this category could include self-injurious behavior or significantly aggressive behavior toward peers and/or adults. For example, if a student is averaging 40 episodes of self-injurious behavior per day resulting in significant tissue damage, it is unlikely that universal supports in Tier 1 or targeted group interventions in Tier 2 would be adequate for quickly addressing this need while ensuring the safety of the student. In this case it would not be appropriate to provide universal supports in Tier 1 or targeted group interventions in Tier 2 for a period of four to six weeks with little or no improvement before moving to an intensive individualized intervention.

A second situation that may justify moving to an intensive individualized intervention is when universal supports in Tier 1 and targeted group interventions in Tier 2 have resulted in little or no change in the behavior, the behavior has actually become worse, or the student's rate of progress is significantly slower than acceptable. Establishing a data-based decision-making rule before implementing these interventions is crucial in these situations.

As emphasized in Chapter 1 differential support and interventions provided to students across the tiers is continuously driven by screening and progress monitoring data. Changes in needed supports and interventions require that this not be considered a linear process. In this sense an intensive individualized intervention should be viewed as simply a highly differentiated strategy for teaching the same behavior expectations articulated in the school's behavioral curriculum or school-wide behavioral expectations.

KEY CONSIDERATIONS FOR IMPLEMENTATION

School social workers have a unique opportunity to use their behavioral assessment and intervention development skills in providing intensive individualized interventions to students in Tier 3. In some schools, efficient implementation of these interventions may require that the school social worker function in a consultative role designing behavior implementation plans and guiding others in their implementation. In other school settings, the school social worker may more appropriately serve in a direct service role conducting FBAs and implementing behavior intervention plans. Combinations of these roles will be needed in many situations.

Teaming with other providers such as school psychologists, school counselors, school nurses, and educational consultants is an ideal opportunity to build multidisciplinary teams that can ensure comprehensive services to students with significant behavioral needs. The involvement of parents throughout the implementation of intensive individualized interventions is critical and will ensure that the unique knowledge of parents can be tapped in designing, implementing, and evaluating intensive individualized interventions.

KNOWLEDGE AND SKILLS NEEDED BY SCHOOL SOCIAL WORKERS

School social workers will need skills in functional behavioral assessment, intervention design, progress monitoring, and formative and summative evaluation to provide intensive individualized interventions in Tier 3. Skills in using software for managing and displaying progress data are needed to ensure accurate analysis of progress data and to assess the effectiveness of interventions. Proficiency in using data-based decision making when designing, implementing, and evaluating intensive individualized interventions is vital for school social workers seeking an active leadership role in this process. Since a functional approach to assessment and intervention development is not a common feature of school social work practice, most practitioners will need to engage in a variety of professional development activities to acquire and maintain these essential skills and knowledge (see Chapter 14).

CHAPTER SUMMARY AND CONCLUSIONS

The process of providing intensive individualized interventions in Tier 3 includes specific procedures for conducting a functional behavioral assessment; defining and identifying the problem; establishing a pre-intervention baseline of performance; doing problem validation and analysis; designing the intervention including goal setting, progress monitoring, and evaluation; and ensuring implementation integrity. These components of the process require ongoing data-based decision making including the need to collect, display, and analyze specific student performance data. The high level of rigor required in conducting functional behavioral assessments and designing and evaluating interventions in this process requires advanced skills in these areas. Many school social workers will need to seek out professional development activities to acquire and maintain the skills essential to practicing in this manner. School social workers should play a leadership role with teams that are providing intensive individualized interventions by becoming proficient with this process and by advocating these practices.

APPENDIX 9.A INTERVENTION PLAN

INTERVENTION PLAN: STRATEGIES

Name: Student_____ DOB: 1-3-2002_____ Date: 03-30-2008_____

Problem Behavior: Student will refuse to comply with adult requests in multiple settings, including small group, independent seatwork, recess, center time, snack, and large group time. His non-compliance and aggressive behaviors are directed at adults rather than peers. Examples of non-compliance include: hitting staff and himself, kicking, throwing objects, hitting his teeth/mouth with his hand, yelling, twisting as an attempt to not walk. Student will tantrum at times and is inconsolable. Tantrum behaviors are kicking, yelling or screaming, hitting or swatting at an adult, crying, lying on the ground. Non-examples include: choosing to play with the water table rather than another toy of choice during centers time, touching a staff member's hand as a sign he is wanting to hold hands, leaning towards a peer to touch them.

Hypothesized Function: Avoidance/escape of tasks.

Replacement Behavior: Student will be taught appropriate ways to temporarily escape non-preferred tasks and/or demands.

Antecedent/Setting Event Strategies: *What antecedent and setting event strategies will be used to decrease the problem behavior and/or increase the replacement behavior?*

Procedures/Strategies	Materials	Schedule (When/How Often)	Where	Person(s) Responsible
Student will have an object schedule in place to transition from activities throughout the day.	carpet square lunch tray	Throughout the day during each transition.	In all school settings.	Special Education Teacher, General Education Teacher, 1:1 Adult Assistant
All work activities will be modified to meet Student's pre-academic needs. i.e. If his peers are working on an art project that involves cutting, gluing multiple pieces, and coloring; the activity may be pre-cut so that he only cuts one side (or no cutting required), he may have only 3 pieces to glue, and as much independent coloring as appropriate.	Modified work activities as appropriate	Daily- throughout the day.	In all school settings/ throughout the building.	Special Education Teacher, General Education Teacher, 1:1 Adult Assistant

Alternative Skills to be Taught: *How will the replacement behavior be taught?*

Procedures/Strategies	Materials	Schedule (When/How Often)	Where	Person(s) Responsible
Student will be taught to appropriately escape demands by using an "All done" switch. Whenever Student uses this switch he will immediately have his break request honored.	Switch programmed with "All done."	During work sessions	In all school settings/throughout the building	Special Education Teacher, General Education Teacher, 1:1 Adult Assistant
Student will engage in a work : break routine during instructional time. During this time he will also be taught to use an "All done" switch to appropriately (temporarily) escape a non-preferred demand.			In the classroom setting.	Special Education Teacher, General Education Teacher, 1:1 Adult Assistant
Work : Break Protocol 1. Student will transition to a designated workspace. 2. Student's switch will be placed near him and pre-programmed to say, "All done." 3. Goal appropriate work will be broken down into short tasks. (Flip Chart will be on Green Work sign.)	Switch programmed to say "All done." Flip Chart with: 1) Work 2) Break 3) Smile 4) Get Ready			

4. If Student presses the switch, at any time, he will receive an immediate break.

Timer

A "Break" is defined as: 1 minute with the demand removed. Adult attention will be kept to a minimum and is very neutral. He will not have access to his preferred items during this time. (Flip Chart will be on Red Break sign.)

5. If Student completes the task, he will have "Student Time."

Work Tasks

"Student Time" is defined as: 2 minutes of access to preferred items. Adult interaction is very engaging and positive at this time. (Flip Chart will be on Blue Smiley Face sign.)

• 30 Seconds before Student transitions back from a break or Student time, the adult working with him will say "Get ready to work", Student. (Flip Chart will be turned to Yellow Get Ready sign.)

Skill Building Reinforcement Strategies: *How will the replacement behavior be reinforced?*

Procedures/Strategies	Materials	Schedule (When/How Often)	Where	Person(s) Responsible
When Student completes a work task, he will receive 2 minutes of "Student Time." During "Student Time" he will have access to highly preferred items and adult interaction will be highly engaging and positive. There will be no demands placed on him at this time. Student will not have demands/directives placed on him during times of use of highly preferred activities. (Ex. When Student has completed his time with coloring, timer goes off, verbal prompt of change, highly preferred activity introduced, no demands placed on him during that highly preferred activity time)	Basket with highly preferred objects/toys.	During work tasks.	In the classroom setting.	Special Education Teacher, General Education Teacher, 1:1 Adult Assistant

Reduction Oriented Consequence Strategies: *What consequence strategies will be used to decrease the problem behavior?*

Procedures/Strategies	Materials	Schedule (When/How Often)	Where	Person(s) Responsible
If Student tantrums, the space around him will be made as safe as possible. (i.e materials that he may hurt himself on will be moved.)	Safe space in classroom	As Needed	In all school environments	Special Education Teacher, General Education Teacher, 1:1 Adult Assistant
• An adult will be present at all times. • During this time, he will **not** have use of highly preferred activities, music, etc. • Adults will not interact with Student. • Prompts to transition/comply will be delivered in 1-minute increments in a neutral, consistent, and concise manner. "Sit in chair Student." • A transitional object (i.e. highly preferred toy) will be used during transition. If Student is transitioning compliantly he will have access to the object, if he is not transitioning compliantly the adult working with him will have the object and play with it. • Once Student successfully transitions to his designation, he will receive a high rate of verbal praise from the adults and access to his preferred item for 2 minutes.	None	As tantrum behaviors occur		
During tantrum behavior (refusal to comply, refusal to transition, etc.) Student will not be physically moved or interacted with unless his behavior is such that he is in immediate danger (i.e. Student is displaying tantrum behaviors in a doorway that children are coming in and out of and there is no other option). If Student needs to be moved, it will be no more than what is needed to keep him and his peers safe.				

Intervention Plan: Strategies form developed by Heartland Area Education Agency 11, Johnston, Iowa. Used with permission.

APPENDIX 9.B IMPLEMENTATION CHECKLIST

Intervention Steps: Student A) Date:				Component Integrity %	Permanent Products/Objectives/ Tools	Adult Initials
Environmental Changes Student reviewed school rules and expectations at the beginning of the day one-on-one with an adult.						
Building and Reinforcing Alternative Skills and Replacement Behaviors Student had the ability to appropriately gain adult attention throughout the school day, i.e. a break card or an emergency card was in place.						
Student received a high rate of adult attention when she was complying with classroom expectations.						
Teacher/Parent/Caregiver Responses Student was on a 15-minute work, 5-minute break schedule in all school environments with the exception of general education.					Timer to run down from 15 minutes during work and 5 minutes during break.	
Break activities were highly reinforcing. i.e. art, free reading, game with adult/peer, etc.					Highly reinforcing break activities	
When Student was not working or engaged in inappropriate classroom behaviors, she received no attention from the adults, outside of her 30 second prompts.						
Safety Plan A room clear was implemented when Student's behavior became potentially dangerous or disruptive to her peers.						

Implementation Checklist developed by Heartland Area Education Agency 11, Johnston, Iowa. Used with permission.

REFERENCES

Christ, T. J. (2008). Best practices in problem analysis. In A. Thomas & J. Grimes (Eds.), *Best practices in school psychology—V* (pp. 209–224). Washington, DC: National Association of School Psychologists.

Clark, J. P. (1998). Functional behavioral assessment and behavioral intervention plans: Implementing the student discipline provisions of IDEA '07. *The Section Connection, 4*(1), 6–7. Washington, DC: National Association of Social Workers.

Clark, J. P., Timm, A., Gilmore, J., & Dedic, B. (2006, March 30). *Response to intervention: A problem-solving approach to enabling learning.* Paper presented at the 100th Anniversary of School Social Work Conference sponsored by the School Social Work Association of America, Boston, MA.

Hanley, G. P., Iwata, B. A., & McCord, B. E. (2003). Functional analysis of problem behavior: A review. *Journal of Applied Behavior Analysis, 36*(2), 147–185.

Heartland Area Education Agency 11. (2002). *Improving children's educational results through data-based decision-making.* Johnston, IA: Author.

Ingram, K., Lewis-Palmer, T., & Sugai, G. (2005). Function-based intervention planning: Comparing the effectiveness of FBA function-based and non-function based intervention plans. *Journal of Positive Behavior Interventions, 7*(4), 224–236.

Iwata, B. A., Dorsey, M. F., Slifer, K. J., Bauman, K. E. & Richman, G. S. (1994). Toward a functional analysis of self-injury. *Journal of Applied Behavior Analysis, 27*(2), 197–209.

Kern, L., Gallagher, P., Starosta, K., Hickman, W., & George, M. (2006). Longitudinal outcomes of functional behavioral assessment-based intervention. *Journal of Positive Behavior Interventions, 8*(2), 67–78.

Skinner, B. F. (1953). *Science and human behavior.* New York: Macmillan.

Tilly, W. D., III. (2002). School psychology as a problem solving enterprise. In A. Thomas & J. Grimes (Eds.), *Best practices in school psychology IV* (pp. 25–36). Bethesda, MD: National Association of School Psychologists.

Tilly, W. D., III. Knoster, T. P., Kolvaleski, J., Bambara, L., Dunlap, G., & Kincaid, D. (1998). *Functional behavioral assessment: Policy development in light of emerging research and practice.* Alexandra, VA: National Association of State Directors of Special Education.

Upah, K . R . F. (2008). Best practices in designing, implementing, and evaluating quality interventions. In A. Thomas & J. Grimes (Eds.), *Best practices in school psychology—V* (pp. 209–224). Washington, DC: National Association of School Psychologists.

10

TIER 3
CASE EXAMPLE:
FUNCTIONAL BEHAVIOR
ASSESSMENT DATA
COLLECTION AND
ANALYSIS

WENDY MARCKMANN & ANDREA TIMM

Data collection and analysis for intensive individual interventions in Tier 3 are critical for decision making and development of appropriate behavioral interventions. Intensive individual interventions begin with a thorough functional behavioral assessment (FBA). Through the FBA process data collection is determined by individual student needs and the behavior of concern. This results in data collection methods that are highly student specific. The procedures for analyzing data utilize both qualitative and quantitative methods. Practitioners use professional judgement, research-based practices, technology for data collection and analysis to determine behavioral interventions and modifications. Effectiveness of behavioral interventions is determined by analysis of data that document ongoing student performance, integrity of intervention implementation, and comparisons to set district behavioral standards or peer comparison data. This chapter illustrates the use of Tier 2 targeted group interventions and Tier 3

154

intensive individual interventions with Allyson, a kindergarten student who was enrolled in a public elementary school.

FBA CASE EXAMPLE: ALLYSON

At the beginning of the intervention process, Allyson was a kindergarten student who had attended a preschool program in a neighboring school district. The general education teacher, building principal, and guidance counselor received limited information on her success in preschool due to her sporadic attendance. Upon entering kindergarten, Allyson's family environment also changed. Allyson and her biological mother left the family home and moved into her maternal grandmother's home in a new school district. Allyson started the school year with behaviors that concerned the classroom teacher. These behaviors included refusing to respond to teacher comments, refusing to transition within the room and outside of the room, refusing to eat, crying and sucking on her fingers. The general education teacher gathered her complete educational record and made contact with Allyson's mother to start thinking about ways to get Allyson to engage in the general education instruction.

The general education teacher and Allyson's mother worked together to develop a plan for supporting her that included providing her with a safe spot in the classroom that would allow her to participate even when she refused to transition. The general education teacher also allowed Allyson to color when she was not engaging in work since that was a highly preferred activity. Individual attention and support was also provided through daily contact with the guidance counselor. The general education teacher made daily contact with Allyson's mother through use of a home/school note. Anecdotal data were collected by the general education teacher to determine whether the frequency of the behavior was decreasing. This was documented on the home/school note. The teacher and the parent did not write a formal goal to monitor progress. The teacher reported that based on an informal review of the home/school notes the original behavior of concern was resolved. This support was provided during the first six weeks of school.

The teacher noticed a new set of concerning behaviors approximately six weeks into the school year which included physically and verbally aggressive behaviors. The increase in intensity and frequency of the new behaviors prompted the general education teacher to refer Allyson to the school intervention team.

TARGETED GROUP INTERVENTION

The team determined that Tier 1 universal supports had not been sufficient to ensure Allyson's behavioral progress. A more intensive intervention was warranted based on the limited progress in response to Tier 1 interventions and an increase in intensity of Allyson's behavior. The team reviewed the home/school notes (anecdotal records) and held a meeting with Allyson's mother, grandmother, general education teacher, grade level representative, school social worker, and school administrator. The meeting resulted in the development of a low-rigor FBA (based on interviews and teacher observations) and a Tier 2 intervention based on the initial FBA hypothesis of *attention from peers and adults.*

Although Allyson had multiple behaviors of concern, the team prioritized the behaviors that were interfering with her participation in classroom instruction. The behavior selected for the intervention was defined as *physical aggression including open hand slapping, kicking, pinching peers or adults; nonexamples included attempting to slap (fake slap), bumping into others, holding hands, holding onto arms, grabbing clothing.* The problem was defined in objective, clear, and complete terms.

The team collaborated to determine the most appropriate goal that would focus on increasing positive behaviors throughout the school day. Data were collected on the percentage of intervals (sections of the day) that were free from physical aggression. The team agreed to collect and graph the data daily. The general education teacher would document Allyson's progress on a data collection sheet. The school social worker would collect the data collection sheets and graph the data for the team to review. Three days before initial implementation of the Tier 2 intervention, Allyson had a baseline of 20% of her day being free from physical aggression. Due to the intensity of the behaviors the team developed a six-week goal and set a meeting to follow up on her progress. The following goal was established: *In 10 weeks, given a daily reinforcement plan and daily behavioral instruction, Allyson will earn 97% of stickers for demonstrating behaviors that are free from physical aggression.*

The intervention plan for Allyson needed to include teaching of new skills, reinforcement of appropriate behaviors, and reduction-oriented consequences that were matched to the function of behavior as indicated on the FBA. The intervention included planned, frequent attention for demonstrating appropriate behavior that did not include physical aggression. Multiple adults including the general education teacher, school administrator, art and PE teachers in all settings throughout the school day provided the attention for appropriate behaviors. The team determined that Allyson needed to receive direct social skills instruction targeted at keeping her hands and feet to herself. This instruction was provided in a small supplemental skills group by the general education teacher with support from the guidance counselor. The small group consisted of students targeted for supplemental behavioral support as well as appropriate peer role models. The direct social skills training occurred twice a week for new learning. Generalization and maintenance instruction occurred throughout the day, including center activities, large group instruction, and transition.

The general education teacher implemented the targeted group intervention for three weeks. She then applied the four-point data-based decision-making rule to determine whether she needed to make changes to the intervention by visually analyzing the data to learn whether four points had fallen above or below the goal line. (See Chapter 9 for more specific information about the use of decision-making rules.) She noticed four weeks

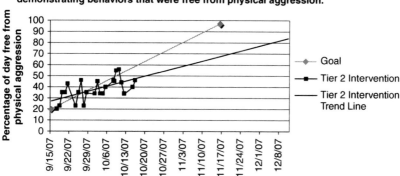

In 10 weeks, given a daily reinforcement plan and daily behavioral instruction, Allyson will earn 97% of stickers for demonstrating behaviors that were free from physical aggression.

Figure 10.1   Initial progress monitoring data.

into the intervention that Allyson was making progress but not at the rate that was needed for her to reach her goal in the defined time frame, and four consecutive data points had fallen below the goal line (see Figure 10.1).

The data prompted the teacher to consult with the school social worker. They analyzed the data and decided that it would be appropriate to increase the amount of positive adult attention when Allyson was demonstrating behaviors free from physical aggression. Positive adult attention was increased because it matched the hypothesized function of the behavior, that is, to gain attention from peers and adults. They decided to increase reinforcement because Allyson was responding to the intervention but her rate of progress was not as fast as the team had hoped. The general education teacher and the school social worker also knew that Allyson had been taught the appropriate social skills during the previous intervention and that she had been able to demonstrate them in multiple settings. Therefore they wanted Allyson to increase the frequency of demonstration of appropriate physical interactions with multiple practice opportunities and frequent feedback. Following best practices in social skill instruction, Allyson's performance deficit would require an intervention that consisted of prompting the use of skill(s), reinforcement of skills, and withholding reinforcement of the problem behavior (Rahn-Blakeslee, Rankin, & Volmer, 2008).

The team reconvened as planned 10 weeks after the start of the targeted group intervention to review the data as a large group. During the intervention, the general education teacher and school social worker consulted frequently about her data and used the four-point decision-making rule to determine whether she was making progress toward her goal. Allyson's peers in the previous intervention group had responded and did not require additional supports. The team determined that initially

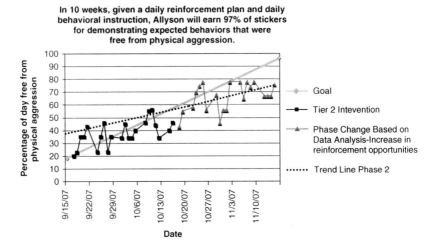

In 10 weeks, given a daily reinforcement plan and daily behavioral instruction, Allyson will earn 97% of stickers for demonstrating expected behaviors that were free from physical aggression.

Figure 10.2 Phase change progress monitoring data.

the increase of reinforcement and instruction had a positive impact on Allyson's behavior. However, they were concerned about Allyson's slow progress toward her behavioral goal (see Figure 10.2). This concern was supported by data. The last four data points were below the goal line, which indicated that the team needed to consider instructional changes or modification to the current intervention plan. However, the team determined they were not ready to make any modifications to the current intervention because three weeks of implementation was not sufficient to determine whether changes in performance could be attributed to the intervention.

INCREASING THE FUNCTIONAL BEHAVIORAL ASSESSMENT RIGOR

The team felt that more intensive problem analysis was required to validate the hypothesized function of *attention* and to confirm the hypothesized function with more in-depth data analysis. The school social worker led the process of collecting and analyzing data to conduct a more rigorous FBA. (See Chapter 9 for a description of the use of RIOT [Review, Interview, Observe and Test] and ICEL [Instruction, Curriculum, Environment, and Learner] procedures.) This FBA was expected to help the team develop positive behavior interventions that were matched to the function of the behavior. The team scheduled a follow-up meeting in two weeks to review the FBA summary. The current intervention would continue as written until the team reconvened. At that meeting the team would review the data on the current intervention that had been implemented over three weeks.

The school social worker next collected data needed to formulate a more rigorous FBA using RIOT/ICEL procedures. This assessment enhanced the understanding of undesirable behaviors as well the purpose and function of Allyson's behavior. The updated FBA summary would increase in rigor to match the intensity of Allyson's behavior.

The first step in this process was to validate the problem behavior. The school social worker decided to collect peer comparison data since the school Allyson was attending had not implemented school-wide positive behavior supports (PBS). If Allyson's school had been implementing PBS the school social worker would have compared Allyson's behavior to school-wide behavior expectation data. Data were collected on five of Allyson's typical peers using the same data collection methods used in her current intervention, (i.e., percentage of sections of the day that peers were free from physical aggression). Allyson's peers were free from physical aggression 100%, 100%, 95%, 95%, and 97% of the day, respectively. The median score of 97% free from physical aggression was used as the best measure of peer performance. The school social worker then compared Allyson's behavior, 46% free from physical aggression, with that of her peers, 97% free from physical aggression. She was able to determine that Allyson was more than two times discrepant from her peers and that this was a clear indication that an intensive individualized intervention was warranted.

Next, the school social worker wanted to know exactly what was happening before Allyson exhibited physical aggression and exactly what happened following the aggression. Multiple antecedent behavior consequence (ABC) observations were completed over several days in the general education classroom setting (see Figure 10.3). In this situation, five observations were required to obtain sufficient data to identify the function of her behavior. Structured interviews that focused on events that influence the problem behavior in the school setting were also completed with adults who knew Allyson well. The general education teacher, kindergarten classroom associate, and Allyson's mother were interviewed. Convergent data from these two assessments helped to identify potential setting events, antecedents, and maintaining consequences. These data were used to develop a hypothesis about the function of Allyson's behavior. The hypothesis was validated through ongoing data collection and analysis.

From an analysis of the results of the systematic observations, structured interviews, and ongoing intervention data, a pattern of antecedents emerged. Antecedents are events that trigger the occurrence of the problem behavior (e.g., getting an assignment, being given a direction). Data showed that 68% of Allyson's physical aggression occurred during independent work time or following a teacher direction (see Figure 10.4). These were categorized as nonpreferred activities for Allyson during the structured interview process.

The school social worker also wanted to know what was happening in the school environment immediately following the problem behavior that might be maintaining the behavior. She collected observation data on the consequences following the problem behavior, such as reprimands, peers laughing, being sent to the office and talking to secretary, having the

ABC Sheet

Directions: When a target behavior occurs, complete each
section briefly.
Target Behaviors to include: physical aggression

Date & Time, Clas	Antecedent Type of activity, Type of demand	Behavior	Consequence	Perceived Function
10/27 10 am	Teacher reading book	Slapped teacher's arm	Allyson removed from group to table	Escape
10/27 10:30	Playing with friend at kitchen center	Pinched peer	Sent to table to color independently	Escape
10/27 11:05	Small group reading instruction	Hit teacher	Corrected, teacher skipped Allyson and went onto next student	Escape
10/27 12:10	In line to transition to lunch	Kicked associate	Teacher pulled her out of line scolded her, Allyson walked with teacher to the lunchroom 2 min. after the class went to lunch	Attention
10/27 1:13	Independent work at table, Associate giving Allyson one on one assistance	Hit associate and screamed	Associate ignored behavior and continued to provide assistance	Escape
→		Crawled under desk and kicked at associate's feet	Associate prompted Allyson to return to chair (Allyson stayed under desk)	Escape

Figure 10.3 Antecedent behavior consequence observations.
Source: ABC Sheet developed by Heartland Area Education Agency 11, Johnston, Iowa.
Used with permission.

demand removed. A summary of the ABC observation data showed that 59% of the time Allyson was sent away from the group or the room. She was also given attention 35% of the time (see Figure 10.5).

The school social worker needed to know which of these consequences were maintaining the behavior. Thorough problem analysis indicated that if Allyson was sent away from the group the physical aggression stopped 91.4% of the time. If Allyson was sent out of the room the physical aggression stopped 86.6% of the time. Adult attention, such as interactions with a teacher or classroom associate, did not result in percentages this high (see Figure 10.6). Further interviews with teachers indicated that they were removing Allyson from the original demand/setting, then providing adult attention to intervene in her

Enter Problem Behavior 1 Here	Enter Total Occurrences of Behavior 1 Below	Antecedent Events (List Others Below If Not Present)	Enter Total Occurrences of Each Antecedent	What Antecedent Makes the Behavior More or Less Likely?
Physical aggression	85	Independent	28	33%
		Modeled	1	1%
		Visual Cue	2	2%
		Interruption		0%
		Told "No"	4	5%
		Told "Wait"		0%
		Alone		0%
		Free Time	20	24%
		In Line		0%
		Teacher Direction	30	35%
		Peer's Turn		0%

Figure 10.4   Antecedent events table.
Source: Developed by Heartland Area Education Agency 11, Johnston, Iowa. Used with permission.

Enter Problem Behavior 1 Here	Enter Total Occurrences of Behavior 1 Below	Actual Consequences (List Others Below If Not Present)	Enter Total Occurrences of Each Consequence	What Consequences Most Often Follow the Problem Behavior?
Physical aggression	85	Ignored	5	6%
		Adult Attention	30	35%
		Peer Attention	5	6%
		Sent Away from Group	35	41%
		Sent Out of Room	15	18%
		Threatened		0%
		Given Item		0%
		Other:		0%
		Other:		0%
		Other:		0%

Figure 10.5   Consequence events table.
Source: Developed by Heartland Area Education Agency 11, Johnston, Iowa. Used with permission.

CONSEQUENCE	Tally	STUDENT REACTION		% Effective (Total stopped/Total Tallies)
		Stopped	Continued	
Ignored	/////	/////	0	5/5 100%
Adult Attention	///// ///// ///// ///// ///// /////	///// ///// ///// /////	///// /////	20/30 67%
Peer Attention	/////		/////	0/5 0%
Sent Away from Group	///// ///// ///// ///// ///// ///// /////	///// ///// ///// ///// ///// ///// //	///	32/35 91.4%
Sent Out of Room	///// ///// /////	///// //// ///	//	13/15 86.6%
Threatened				
Given Item				
Other:				

Figure 10.6 FBA data tool.
Source: Developed by Heartland Area Education Agency 11, Johnston, Iowa. Used with permission.

physically aggressive incidents. If the teacher just provided adult attention and did not remove the original demand she would continue to be aggressive.

Therefore, the initial hypothesis of adult attention maintaining the problem was not accurate. Rather, data now supported a hypothesis that *escape from nonpreferred demands maintained by adult attention* was the function of the physical aggression. The school social worker was now able to develop the following summary statement of the behavior for the team that was based on convergent data: *When given a nonpreferred activity, Allyson will become physically aggressive to escape the activity. The physical aggression is maintained by adult attention.*

The team reconvened to discuss the new hypothesized function of Allyson's behavior. They concurred with the new hypothesized function and supporting data. Appropriate replacement behaviors were identified that would allow Allyson to escape nonpreferred activities as efficiently as being physically aggressive. A replacement behavior is a more socially acceptable or appropriate behavior that accomplishes the same outcome or function as the problem behavior. The team also increased Allyson's reinforcement for using the identified replacement behavior due to previous success with high frequency of reinforcement. The team decided to teach the replacement behavior of requesting a break. Requesting a break would allow Allyson to escape nonpreferred tasks quickly and easily. Therefore it was hypothesized that she would not need to resort to physically aggressive behaviors to escape demands. When Allyson appropriately requested a break it was agreed that it would be immediately honored so that the replacement behavior was as efficient and effective as the problem behavior. The team determined that they would collect data on Allyson's use of break requests so that they could eventually shape the new behavior into the desired behavior of sitting quietly at her desk when she needed a short break from work demands.

The team addressed the antecedents for the problem behavior in the intervention plan. Prior to transitioning into a nonpreferred task, the teacher would remind Allyson with verbal and visuals cues that she was allowed to ask for a break. If the teacher noticed that Allyson was becoming less engaged in an activity she would approach Allyson and nonverbally point to the break request visual cue on her desk. For nonpreferred tasks that had previously triggered high frequencies of physical aggression, the teacher would shorten the original demand prior to presenting the task for Allyson to complete. The shortened tasks would increase the likelihood of completion of the task by decreasing the intensity of the nonpreferred task.

The team developed an intervention with reduction-oriented consequence strategies that would not allow Allyson access to the function of her behavior when displaying inappropriate behaviors. Allyson would no longer be allowed to leave the classroom or escape assigned tasks by the use of physical aggression. If Allyson became physically aggressive, the teacher would say, "Allyson, you may request a break" and point to the break request visual cue every 30 seconds until Allyson made the appropriate request or continued with the original demand. If Allyson requested a break, she could remain in the break area for two minutes. This amount of time was chosen to allow Allyson sufficient time to leave the demand but also to allow her to maintain progress with the task. If Allyson wanted to remain in the break area she could do so as long as she requested this appropriately. When Allyson returned from a break she would have to return to the original pre-shortened demand. If Allyson's class had moved onto a new task, she would not move on until she completed the original task. This strategy was implemented so that Allyson would not request long breaks during a nonpreferred task to escape the demand. This would teach Allyson that she could break upon request but the demand would not be removed.

ENSURING IMPLEMENTATION (TREATMENT) INTEGRITY

The team needed to be able to draw conclusions about the extent to which the intervention worked. Treatment integrity needed to be monitored to ensure that the intervention was being implemented as designed. An implementation checklist including key intervention components was created to increase the fidelity of the intervention that was being implemented by multiple adults. The checklist would help remind the adults about the intervention components and serve as a procedure for monitoring implementation integrity (see Figure 10.7).

Implementation Checklist

Student: Allyson   Grade: K   Teacher: Mrs. Smith
Observer: _____

Directions: Put a checkmark in the column for *each step* for which there is evidence of a permanent product. At the end of each day, *calculate daily integrity* by dividing the *calculate component integrity* by dividing the number of checkmarks for each step by the total number of days per week.

Intervention Step Date	M	T	W	TH	F	Component Integrity %	Permanent Products
Visual cues available for break requests.							1. Visual cues are visible in the classroom
Tasks are shortened before they are presented.							2. Permanent products of shortened tasks are maintained.
Allyson is reminded that she can take a break before each transition with the use of a verbal or visual cue.							
Skill instruction on requesting a break appropriately is provided daily.							3. Skill instruction log maintained by teacher with time, date, and topic of instruction.
Break area is visible in the classroom.							
Breaks honored as requested.							
When Allyson is displaying negative behavior, she is prompted every 30 seconds with a reminder that she can request a break.							
Allyson is not allowed to leave the classroom or escape a demand by demonstrating negative behaviors (physical aggression).							
Daily Integrity %							

Figure 10.7   Implementation checklist.
Source: Developed by Heartland Area Education Agency 11, Johnston, Iowa. Used with permission.

To implement the intervention, the general education teacher asked for training from the school social worker. Prior to implementing the behavior plan, the school social worker modeled implementation of the intervention with all adults. The school social worker would also be present in Allyson's classroom periodically during the first three days of implementation, which was also expected to enhance implementation fidelity.

The team then implemented the plan with the support of the school social worker. The teacher and the school social worker reviewed the data after three weeks to allow for a sufficient length of time for instruction. The data were then analyzed using the four-point data-based decision-making rule. The teacher and school social worker continued to implement the plan as written because the data indicated that Allyson was making adequate progress toward her goal (see Figure 10.8).

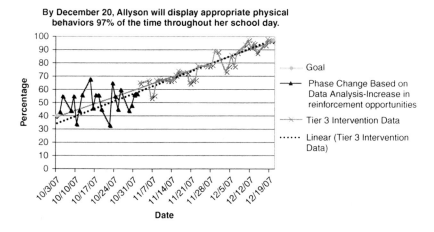

Figure 10.8   Tier 3 progress monitoring data.

CONTEXT: HOW DO FBAs FIT IN THE STRUCTURE OF RtI?

Intensive individualized intervention is the third tier in the response to intervention model. Only 1% to 5% of students will need these interventions. Students in this tier require highly individualized planning, access to extensive resources, and staff with high-level professional skills. Effective interventions are highly specific and are not transferable to multiple students even when problem behaviors are similar in nature.

In most cases, before designing and implementing a Tier 3 intensive individual intervention, practitioners should consider data from Tier 1 universal supports and Tier 2 targeted group interventions. This ensures efficiency by matching interventions to the type and intensity of problems, thereby avoiding the use of extensive resources when they are not needed. Previous intervention data, review of school records, and interviews of key team members help answer the question of when to begin more intensive interventions.

KEY CONSIDERATIONS FOR IMPLEMENTATION

In this case example the student benefited from a targeted group intervention to address her instructional needs for gaining new skills and an intensive individualized intervention to improve her ability to demonstrate learned skills across a variety of school settings on a consistent basis. The example illustrates how decision making about matching interventions to needs and in particular to the function of behavior is driven by the ongoing collection and analysis of student performance data. School staff, particularly classroom teachers, will need considerable support to ensure their full and meaningful participation in the design and implementation of these interventions. In many cases school social workers will need to become more comfortable with being in a consultative role with teachers as rigorous FBAs are conducted and interventions are designed and implemented. Checking for implementation (treatment) integrity when teachers are primary implementers of interventions can become contentious if trusting inter-professional relationships are not established and maintained. This will test the relationship skills of practitioners as objectivity and data-based decision making are put into action.

Involving parents throughout this process is critical. School social workers will often be in a position to engage parents and to communicate the data-based process to them in clear and understandable terms. Schools will need to initiate efforts to ensure that parents are provided with ample opportunity to participate in the process and that all parents understand the kinds of differentiated supports and interventions that are available to any students who need them.

KNOWLEDGE AND SKILLS NEEDED BY SCHOOL SOCIAL WORKERS

As indicated in Chapter 9, school social workers will need advanced skills in functional behavioral assessment and intervention development to provide intensive individualized interventions to students in Tier 3. Practitioners will need to become proficient in determining the function of behavior, as illustrated in this example, and in designing intervention plans that align with behavior function. Also, as indicated in Chapter 9, school social workers will need skills in using software for managing and displaying progress data. Most school social workers will need professional development supports for acquiring and maintaining such knowledge and skills (see Chapter 14).

CHAPTER SUMMARY AND CONCLUSIONS

Intensive individualized interventions in Tier 3 involve a small number of students but consume a large percentage of school resources. School social workers will need refined skills in functional behavioral assessment, problem analysis, intervention design, and data analysis to design and implement effective intensive individualized interventions. Effectively ensuring implementation integrity is a particularly critical feature in this process— one that requires data-based decision making and effective communication and relationship building with teachers and other school staff who are directly implementing these interventions.

REFERENCE

Rahn-Blakeslee, A., Rankin, B., & Volmer, S. (2008). *Applying effective strategies to social skills assessment and instruction.* Johnston, IA: Heartland Area Education Agency 11.

11

TIER 3
CASE EXAMPLE:
WRAPAROUND

LUCILLE EBER, BRENDA LINDSEY, & MARGARET WHITE

Response to Intervention (RtI) Tier 3 approaches are based on a fundamental belief that all children can learn and succeed in school if instruction and behavioral supports are adjusted to match the frequency and
intensity of student needs. Students identified in need of Tier 3 level
interventions display highly intensive academic and/or behavioral problems
across home, school, and community settings (Scott & Eber, 2003). They
require individualized intervention plans tailored to meet their unique needs.
Providing these can be a daunting task for schools, especially when addressing the needs of students who display challenging emotional-behavioral
issues (Brown & Michaels, 2006; Hawken & O'Neil, 2006). Although these
students may receive special education, they experience limited success
(National Center for Educational Statistics, 2008; Wagner, Newman,
Camento, Levine, & Garza, 2006). RtI intervention approaches aim to
improve educational outcomes for all students, including those with serious
emotional and behavioral problems, by incorporating data-based decision-
making processes and implementing evidence-based practice approaches.

Tier 3 behavioral interventions include family-centered wraparound.
Wraparound is an approach that entails the development of individualized
intervention plans based on unique student strengths and needs across
home, school, and community (Scott & Eber, 2003). School-wide
Positive Behavior Support estimates that 1% to 5% of students with complex emotional and behavioral needs will require Tier 3 level interventions,
and wraparound should be an essential component of an integrated

academic/behavioral approach (Freeman et al., 2006). Family-centered wraparound utilizes families (including the student) as key informants and decision makers in determining desired outcomes and strength-based intervention strategies. The process promotes person-family-centered values and practices that are carefully implemented with families and school staff in lead roles, thereby increasing the likelihood of success (Albin, Lucyshyn, Horner, & Flannery, 1996; Crone, Horner, & Hawken, 2004).

This chapter describes how wraparound processes and strategies can be integrated into Tier 3 RtI interventions. We define wraparound as well as the necessary steps for implementation. We also explain how to integrate data-based decision-making methods into the wraparound processes through the use of specially designed data collection tools. Finally, we provide a case example that illustrates data-based decision making with the wraparound process.

WHAT IS WRAPAROUND?

Wraparound is a problem-solving approach used to develop and implement intervention plans tailored to the unique individualized needs of students who exhibit chronic problem behaviors (Burns & Goldman, 1999; Scott & Eber, 2003). The process was originally used as part of a community-based system of mental health care for children with serious mental illness that required residential placements or extended periods of hospitalization. The approach utilizes team problem-solving strategies based upon a child-centered approach. Students and their families are supported through a combination of natural supports, interagency services, and academic/behavioral interventions. A comprehensive care plan is developed that addresses critical life domains including medical, legal, safety, cultural, spiritual, and social needs. The wraparound plan and strategies reflect the values and beliefs of the child's family, community, and cultural background (VanDenBerg, 1999). It is different from traditional special education and mental health service delivery with its focus on connecting families, schools, and community partners in effective problem-solving relationships. Prominent practices include (1) active participation of children and families in team planning, design, and implementation processes; (2) team membership and strategies tailored to strengths and needs across home, school and community; and (3) an unfailing commitment to design and implement a comprehensive plan over time despite setbacks or obstacles that arise during the process.

Wraparound relies on services that are identified and designed with the needs of the child and family in mind rather than what resources are traditionally available or what services are typically provided. The ultimate goal is for the youth to experience success within the context of their families and their home schools. This makes wraparound a genuine family and community-based approach that is unlike individualized educational programs (IEP) and traditional mental health treatment plans (Burchard, Bruns, &

Burchard, 2002). The essence of wraparound and its core elements are guided by 10 principles as described by Burns and Goldman (1999):

1. *Community-based.* Services incorporate local resources and are delivered within the child's community.
2. *Individualized, strength-based, needs-driven.* Interventions are tailored to the unique assets and desires of students with chronic problem behaviors.
3. *Culturally competent.* Strategies and methods employed respect the cultural background of the child's family and community.
4. *Families as full partners.* Parents play a critical role in assessing strengths and needs, designing relevant interventions, and evaluating outcomes.
5. *Team process.* Child and family team problem-solving approaches are a fundamental part of the wraparound process.
6. *Flexibility.* A combination of traditional and nontraditional intervention methods is encouraged.
7. *Balance of resources.* Adequate resources are required to ensure opportunities for success.
8. *Unconditional commitment.* Team members agree that they will continuously work toward success. Giving up is not an option.
9. *Collaborative process.* Teams rely upon consensus-building strategies and techniques to design and implement interventions.
10. *Measurable outcomes.* Wraparound incorporates ongoing data collection and analysis during assessment, intervention, and evaluation phases.

These tenets are the foundation upon which interventions are created during the wraparound process.

Eber (2003) described the wraparound approach as a defined process that begins with specific steps intended to engage key players, establish ownership, and secure sanction of those persons who spend the most time with the student (i.e., family, teacher). This creates an atmosphere in which interventions and supports are more likely to be implemented consistently. The process includes a comprehensive assessment of the needs of adults who support the youth and organizes assistance for them on behalf of the child. For example, a wraparound team may seek community resources to help a family find stable housing so the pressure associated with eviction is alleviated and parents can devote attention to a home-based behavior intervention plan for their child. Other possible strategies that wraparound teams can take include arranging transportation, recreation opportunities, and social supports. Teams can also organize additional supports for teachers who may be challenged by students with complex emotional and behavioral issues. For example, a plan to modify a problem behavior at school may be more likely to succeed if the teacher has a colleague who is able to model for them how to educate a student about a replacement behavior or how to logically reinforce the behavior in the classroom.

The wraparound process is different from traditional individualized educational programs (IEPs) and other school-based team approaches (Eber, 2003). Wraparound defines specific roles and tasks for various team members, especially natural support persons. It is crucial to have a designated team facilitator who will ensure that a strength-based person-family-centered focus is respected and that the wraparound planning process is followed faithfully. The facilitator is usually a school social worker, counselor, or school psychologist who leads the team until the goals of the plan have been achieved.

The chief difference between wraparound and typical special education and mental health treatment planning approaches is the emphasis placed on building productive relationships and support networks between the youth and his or her family (Burchard, Bruns, & Burchard, 2002; Eber, 2005). This is achieved by creating a unique team that is motivated to achieve agreed-upon quality-of-life indicators. Crucial questions asked of children and their families during the team development process include these: "What would a good school day for you (or for your child) look like to you?" "What would life at home look or feel like if it was better?" "How would you define success for your child five years from now?" These deliberate strategies for engaging families and creating team cohesiveness are necessary to ensure that a strong wraparound team and plan is developed.

Wraparound is distinguished by conscious and consistent efforts to focus on strengths and needs identified by the child and family (VanDenBerg, 1999). This calls for considerable effort and focused techniques by the team facilitator to ensure that team members refrain from emphasizing problem areas and predetermined ideas of "needs" that are presented as services (Eber et al., 2008). For example, "He needs an alternative placement," or "She needs counseling," or "She needs a one-on-one aide." These are examples of services rather than big needs. It is vital that assessments include the breadth and depth of strengths and needs across settings (home, school, and community) as well as life domains. Wraparound requires the identification of *big needs* such as those that cannot be met in a short period of time or can be met from a menu of possible interventions. For example, "John needs to feel respected at school" or "Juan needs to feel competent about his reading ability." *Big needs* highly engage family members in the team process and if met bring about a significant improvement in the quality of life for the child as well as those who spend the most time with them.

The wraparound approach creates a cohesive and collaborative team of family members, natural support providers, and professionals. Interventions are developed and implemented across settings and generate a sense of accomplishment by students, families, teachers, and others closely involved in the daily life of the child. This increases the probability that interventions will be implemented appropriately and effectively, thereby enhancing the chances of sustainable outcomes across home, school, and community.

IMPLEMENTING WRAPAROUND

The Facilitator

Wraparound team facilitators should be skilled at translating the stories of the family, child, and teacher(s) into strength and needs data that can be used to guide the team. Other critical skills include the ability to non-judgmentally communicate the family's vision to ensure the big needs are identified that will bring about an improved quality of life. Wraparound facilitators must also be able to assist the team in problem-solving and decision-making processes to achieve consensus. School social workers are logical choices to serve as wraparound facilitators because of their training and experience in strength-based assessments and person-in-environment perspectives.

Phase 1: Engaging the Family and other Key Players

The team facilitator begins the wraparound process by using individualized engagement strategies with the family and youth, teacher, and other potential team members (Miles et al., 2006; Walker & Schutte, 2004). Families may be hesitant to participate due to prior negative experiences with schools, so special efforts can be needed to ensure that families do not feel judged or blamed. The facilitator must emphasize that families are not expected to change the problem behavior of their child at school. A facilitator may say "We are not being successful enough or positive enough with your child, so we are going to change our approach to make sure he is going to have success." This is a different message from what the parent may have received from school in the past and is a subtle way to set the stage for a different type of process to take place.

The initial conversations with the family must establish family trust, buy-in, and voice to ensure the integrity of the wraparound process. While engaging and developing rapport, the family should be asked to help select team members and meeting locations (Eber, 2003). Then, initial meetings are held at which time the team comes to consensus about the strengths of the child and family as well as prioritizes the big needs. After this is accomplished, the team brainstorms strategies that will bring about an improved quality of life. Progress toward achievement of these goals is continually assessed in subsequent meetings as interventions based on strength and need are implemented across home, school, and community settings. A focus on using natural supports (e.g., people, settings, and resources) ensures a cultural and contextual fit (Albin et al., 1996) and increases the capacity of the child and family and teacher to sustain improvements over time.

Phase 1: Beginning the Process

The facilitator works closely with the family, student, and teacher to build trust and ownership of the wraparound process (Eber et al., 2009). The first step is for the facilitator to reach out to the family and arrange a time and place to meet with them. During this meeting, the facilitator should focus on gaining a better understanding of the family's perceptions of the situation and begin the process of building relationships. The facilitator must explain the wraparound process and identify strengths and big needs as well as potential team members. It is helpful for the family to suggest the meeting location (local restaurant, church, etc.) as this can make them more comfortable and begin to gain trust in the wraparound process. The family must also be asked to identify the natural supports or persons who are connected to the family by relationship (e.g., relatives, friends, coach, pastor) and could be potential team members. These should be people who can support the family and provide information about the big needs.

Once potential team members have been identified and the family has given permission for the team facilitator to contact them on the family's behalf, the facilitator should have individual conversations with those persons to explain the wraparound process. The facilitator must give them an opportunity to share their perceptions of the situation, including any frustrations. By using reflective listening and a nonjudgmental approach, the facilitator will ensure that the team members make positive contributions to the process. The facilitator's role is to reframe the family and other team members' stories into data that can be used to ensure efficient and effective team meetings. Necessary information that must be collected during the beginning phase of wraparound includes identification of potential team members, a comprehensive strength assessment, a list of two to four big needs, and baseline data gathered from the wraparound data tools (discussed in another section of this chapter).

Phase II: Initial Plan Development

The initial phase of the wraparound process requires that the facilitator help the team transition from engagement and assessment of strengths and needs to initial plan development (Eber et al., 2008). This needs to occur as quickly as possible, typically within two weeks from the time that initial contacts are made. Baseline data regarding child, family, and teacher perceptions of strengths and needs are shared and used to guide team consensus about the big needs. The facilitator shares the data then assists the team in brainstorming strategies that will capitalize on the identified strengths and address unmet needs. The team comes to consensus about appropriate strategies to be implemented and delineates tasks and roles of members. A safety plan should be developed if team members believe this is an imminent need. As time goes on, the facilitator continues to gather and review data across settings from multiple sources to assist the team in monitoring progress on an ongoing basis. By focusing on collecting and analyzing meaningful data, team members are less likely to judge and blame one another or resort to reactive, punitive intervention strategies.

Phase III: Putting the Plan into Action

This phase of the wraparound process requires the team to review and revise the initial plan in response to ongoing progress (Eber et al., 2008). The facilitator should schedule regular meetings for the team and ensure that data are continuously collected and analyzed to guide implementation of the plan across home, school, and community. During these meetings, teams should review the data to identify areas of success and concern. This information can be used to revise the wraparound plan as needed. It is important for the facilitator to keep the team focused on the big needs and achievement of long-term goals.

TRANSITION FROM WRAPAROUND

The time will come when regular meetings are no longer needed. This is the final phase of wraparound and requires that a transition plan be developed to sustain the gains that have been made. The facilitator helps the team review and celebrates their accomplishments. Some families may want to share their experiences with other families that have children with challenging behavioral and emotional issues (Eber et al., 2008).

CONNECTING RESPONSE TO INTERVENTION AND WRAPAROUND

The RtI model is a continuum of interventions that provides a graduated system of support. Tier 1 interventions are school-wide and are effective for most students. Tier 2 interventions target students at risk of school failure and typically include small group behavior change approaches. Tier 3 interventions are more complex and intended for students who require the highest level of support. All three tiers must be in place for wraparound to have the greatest impact (Carr, 2006). Wraparound offers a way for schools to assist students who display the most challenging problem behaviors and have the greatest needs. These students experience difficulties across multiple settings and frequently have a history of failed interventions. The situation demands a more comprehensive process that matches the intensity of problematic issues. Wraparound enables schools to partner with families and community partners to create an inclusive and practical plan for assistance.

USING DATA-BASED DECISION MAKING WITH WRAPAROUND

Response to Intervention requires the use of data collection and analysis to inform decision making in schools about curricula and behavioral approaches (Lewis-Palmer, Sugai, & Larson, 1999; Nakasato, 2000; Sugai & Horner, 1999). Tier 3 approaches also entail the use of data by individual child and family teams to make decisions about effective interventions. Schools can also utilize the data to make changes that will support and sustain successful practices as demonstrated by positive student outcomes.

Data-Based Decision-Making Tools for Wraparound

The Illinois Positive Behavior Interventions and Supports Network promotes the use of wraparound data tools. These assessments were created based on information gained from focus groups of wraparound facilitators associated with interagency community-based local area networks (LANs) from 2000 to 2002 (Eber et al., 2008). The tools were piloted in schools for three years from 2004 to 2007. They were developed for the purpose of helping child and family teams collect and utilize critical data for decision making on behalf of youth with serious emotional and behavioral issues. Under the guidance of wraparound facilitators, these data tools are distributed and the findings disseminated to team members at 30- to 90-day intervals through the wraparound team process.

There are four wraparound data tools, which are designed to guide the process by gathering and organizing information from multiple sources and settings (Eber et al., 2008). They include the Student Disposition Tool, the Home School Community Tool (HSC-T), Educational Information Tool (EI-T), and the Wraparound Integrity Tool (WIT). The Home School Community Tool (HSC-T) is the primary data assessment that is used throughout all phases of the wraparound process. It measures student strengths and needs relative to five life domains: health/safety, social, emotional, behavioral, and cultural. The assessment tool also measures outcomes across different settings (home, school, and community) and collects data from multiple sources (teacher, family, and student). Figure 11.1 illustrates sample questions from the HSC-T.

Another assessment that is used at all phases of wraparound implementation is the Educational Information Tool (EI-T). This data collection tool provides a teacher rating of the student's classroom functioning in academic and social/emotional domains. As can be seen in Figure 11.2, sample items are rated by the teacher on a Likert-type scale (1 = Never, 4 = Always). Items include prompts such as "passes quizzes and tests," "engages in appropriate classroom discussions/activities," "has friends,"

Needs/Strengths	COMMUNITY				HOME				SCHOOL			
	need		strength		need		strength		need		strength	
	high 1	some what 2	some what 3	high 4	high 1	some what 2	some what 3	high 4	high 1	some what 2	some what 3	high 4
Safety/Medical/Basic Needs												
7) Health does not limit child's activity												
8) Sees a doctor or nurse when needed												
9) Is safe from violence/crime												
10) Has adequate/safe physical environment												

Figure 11.1   Sample item from the Home School Community Tool (HSC-T).
Source: Illinois Positive Behavior Interventions and Supports Network. Retrieved from www.pbisillinois.org.

SECTION I: (ALL ISTAC PROGRAMS) Based on your expectations of children in your classroom, please indicate the extent to which the above student...	Never	Sometimes	Frequently	Always	Not Applicable
11) Attends school	1	2	3	4	N/A
12) Completes class assignments on time	1	2	3	4	N/A
13) Works independently	1	2	3	4	N/A
14) Completes homework on time	1	2	3	4	N/A
17) Participates in classroom discussions and activities	1	2	3	4	N/A
18) Pays attention in class	1	2	3	4	N/A
19) Participates in extracurricular activities	1	2	3	4	N/A
20) Has friends	1	2	3	4	N/A
21) Engages in socially appropriate behavior with peers	1	2	3	4	N/A

Figure 11.2   Sample items from the Education Information Tool (EI-T).
Source: Illinois Positive Behavior Interventions and Supports Network. Retrieved from www.pbisillinois.org.

and "engages in appropriate classroom behavior with adults." By collecting information from multiple informants across settings, wraparound team members can examine situation- and setting-specific data to gain a better understanding of how the child is truly functioning on a daily basis (De Los Reyes & Kazdin, 2005; Offord et al., 1996; Renck, 2005). When using wraparound data tools, team members need to consider the contributions of different informants, even if their reports are different from those of other informants. The wraparound process embraces unique and diverse perspectives offered by team members, which provides opportunities for learning about different ways that others deal with a student with complex needs.

The facilitator completes the initial strength and needs assessment by using the HSC-T and EI-T during the initial conversation phase about the wraparound process (Eber et al., 2008). The data are entered in a user-friendly, immediately accessible, online database known as SIMEO (Systematic Information Management of Educational Outcomes). This system provides immediate feedback through creation of single-student graphs that can be used by the team to guide decision making at wraparound team meetings. Team facilitators are trained and supported by technical assistance provided by the Illinois SW-PBS Network on how to enter and organize data so it can be meaningfully used at meetings.

Other recommended data assessments are the Wraparound Fidelity Index-4 (WIFI4) and the Wraparound Integrity Tool (WIT). The WIFI4 measures reliability of the wraparound process from the perspectives of the child, the caregiver, and team members. Evaluation takes place after the wraparound process has concluded and does not allow for self-assessment of wraparound during the active team process (Bruns et al., 2004). In an effort to provide wraparound teams with continuous assessment, the Illinois SW-PBS Network has been developing the Wraparound Integrity Tool (WIT). The WIT is designed to offer wraparound teams the opportunity

Current Status					
In Place (5)	Mostly In Place (4)	Somewhat In Place (3)	Minimally In Place (2)	Not In Place (1)	Phase I: Engagement & Team Preparation
					9) Met with family to gather their perspective & position
					10) Met with key team members to gather various perspectives
					11) Generated a strengths list (multiple settings & perspectives)
					12) Generated a Team member list with the family
					13) Team member list includes natural supports
					14) Scheduled an initial Child/Youth & Family Team meeting with the family

Figure 11.3 Sample items from the Wraparound Integrity Tool (WIT).
Source: Illinois Positive Behavior Interventions and Supports Network. Retrieved from www.pbisillinois.org.

to self-assess wraparound fidelity on a regular basis (at the start of the team process and every one to three team meetings thereafter). Teams can use the findings to evaluate their progress and self-correct to ensure that they faithfully follow wraparound principles (Eber et al.2009). Figure 11.3 includes sample items from the WIT. A measure of fidelity is crucial to achieving effective outcomes for interventions, such as wraparound. Dobson and Cook (1980) noted that if intervention plans are vague and delivered in an inconsistent manner, the likelihood of achieving successful outcomes is greatly reduced. The measurement of wraparound fidelity using the WIT is ongoing and three-year tracking of students within the SIMEO system are positive and significant (Eber & Hyde, 2006). Wraparound data tools and detailed information about SIMEO are available from the Illinois Positive Behavior Interventions and Supports Network www.pbisillinois.org.

CASE EXAMPLE: WRAPAROUND PROCESS FOR SIERRA

A middle school student from a school district located in a suburb of a large city in the Midwestern part of the United States was chosen as a case example to illustrate how data-based decision-making processes can be used to guide implementation of Wraparound and RtI Tier 3 interventions. Lincoln Middle School implemented an RtI plan that includes a continuum of proactive school-wide discipline approaches at all three tiers. Tier 1 interventions are guided by a leadership team that meets on a regular basis. School staff regularly teach behavioral expectations to students and acknowledge them for exhibiting desired behaviors. The leadership team collects and analyzes school-wide data on an ongoing basis. It is used to inform team decision making about Tier 1 intervention efforts. At Tier 2, interventions include a mentoring program for at-risk students, a check and connect program, and small group social skills counseling groups provided by the school social worker, school social work interns, and school psychologist. Tier 2 interventions are coordinated by an additional leadership team that is charged with the responsibility of overseeing interventions at this level. They collect and analyze data on a regular basis and use the results to identify areas of success and concern. The responsibility of leading a Tier 3 intervention team is a natural fit for school social workers.

The following case study illustrates how a Tier 3 highly intensive and individualized wraparound process was successfully implemented.

Sierra is a seventh grade student at Lincoln Middle who was referred to the school social worker due to extremely poor attendance and chronic health issues. The school social worker collected baseline attendance data, which revealed that Sierra's daily school attendance was 39% at the time of referral at the end of the second quarter. Sierra recently moved to the area and began attending Lincoln Middle School at the beginning of the school year. The school social worker noted that she was isolated from her peers and did not have any friends at school. Sierra and her family lived at a local homeless shelter and struggled to meet their basic needs of food and clothing. Based on school attendance data, she was already receiving Tier 2 interventions. These interventions were not successful and Sierra was referred to the Tier 3 intervention team. The team recommended that the school social worker contact Sierra's mother to see if she would be interested in a wraparound team process. Her mother agreed to participate and the school social worker served as the wraparound team facilitator.

The initial phase required the school social worker to meet with Sierra and her mother to explain the wraparound process, determine strengths and big needs, and identify potential team members. Based on information from the initial interview, the school social worker completed the Home School Community Tool (HSC-T). Sierra's teachers completed the Education Information Tool (EIT). These baseline data were entered into the SIMEO online database. Sierra and her mother chose wraparound team members that included their minister, stepdad, neighbor, language arts teacher, science teacher, social worker intern, and a technical assistance coordinator with the Illinois SW-PBS Network.

Each person was assigned a distinct role. Sierra's strengths included reading and creative writing. She believed her language arts teacher was very interested in her success at school and played a key role in implementing the wraparound plan at school. The social work intern began counseling Sierra on an individual basis during the second quarter of school but had developed a limited rapport with her. However, the intern had a great relationship with Sierra's mom and worked actively to assist in locating critical medical and social services to address Sierra's chronic health problems. The minister served as Sierra's spiritual leader. Since he was well acquainted with the family, he encouraged Sierra to attend school on a regular basis and participate in a local church youth group. He played a key role in reducing Sierra's peer isolation. The Illinois SW-PBS technical assistance coordinator provided guidance and support to the school social worker throughout as she gained experience in utilizing data in the wraparound process.

Other school staff and community members joined as team members as the wraparound process progressed. Based on the best times available for the family and their minister, Friday after school was chosen as the scheduled time for team meetings. The teachers on the wraparound team demonstrated their commitment to Sierra by attending meetings consistently. Although some team members were unable to attend meetings due to work commitments, they fulfilled valuable roles in the implementation and refinement process.

During the initial phase of the wraparound process, the team reviewed a list of Sierra's identified strengths and needs across home, school, and community settings. Her strengths at school were that she "loves reading, was smart, worked hard, was respectful to staff and worked independently and had very positive relationships with teachers and the school social worker." At home, Sierra's strengths were that she was "street smart, " a skill necessary for living in a homeless shelter; she had excellent life skills in caring for herself and others, and was very helpful. In addition, her mother noted that Sierra was a great big sister. In the community, Sierra regularly attended religious services, was respectful, and followed rules.

Data were collected by the school social worker to monitor and evaluate the effectiveness of the wraparound process. The results from the Home School Community Tool (HSC-T) were entered into the Systematic Information Management for Educational Outcomes (SIMEO) online database system. Data in Figures 11.4–11.6 illustrate Sierra's baseline strengths across home, school, and community settings while Figures 11.7–11.9 depict her needs across all settings. The graphs identified a concern related to Sierra's health. This was a contributing factor for her poor school attendance. The big need was determined to

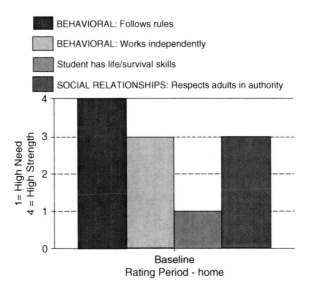

Figure 11.4   Sierra's baseline strength data in home setting identified during initial phase of wraparound.

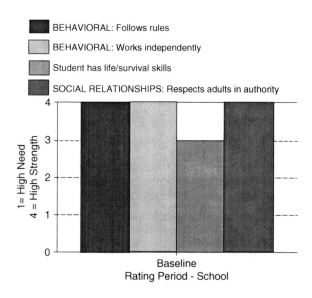

Figure 11.5 Sierra's baseline strength data in school setting identified during initial phase of wraparound.

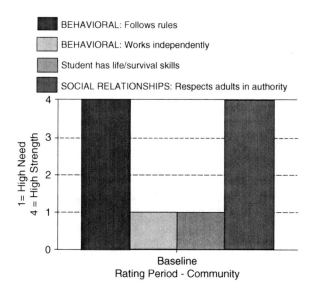

Figure 11.6 Sierra's baseline strength data in community setting identified during initial phase of wraparound.

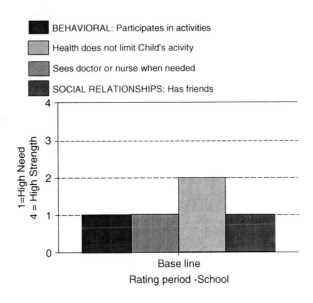

Figure 11.7 Home School Community Tool (HSC-T) data identified Sierra's big needs at home.

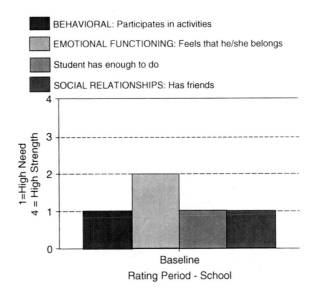

Figure 11.8 Home School Community Tool (HSC-T) data identified Sierra's big needs at school.

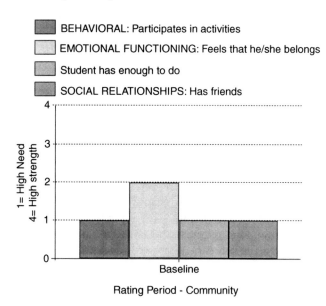

Figure 11.9 Home School Community Tool (HSC-T) data identified Sierra's big needs within the community.

be that Sierra needed to feel well enough to attend school regularly. By focusing on the big need throughout the wraparound process, the team was able to brainstorm potential strategies and develop consensus toward a comprehensive plan.

A key strategy of the wraparound plan was to address Sierra's unmet medical needs. Sierra was turned away from her traditional medical services at the local clinic due to trouble with Sierra's medical card. The computer system listed the family's previous address. Although Sierra's mother notified officials of the family's change of address, they were denied medical care. In order to get health services for Sierra's chronic health issues, her mother was forced to take her to the emergency room. Sierra experienced serious stomach pain almost nightly and her mother took her to the emergency room (usually around 2 A.M.) to obtain medication for severe pain. These visits caused Sierra a lack of sleep, which was also a contributing factor to her poor school attendance.

A local medical social worker joined the wraparound team and was instrumental in helping Sierra get adequate medical care. The medical social worker resolved the computer system problem and arranged for an appointment for Sierra to see a pediatric gastroenterologist. It was later learned that Sierra had an intestinal parasite, which was causing the severe abdominal pain, so addressing her unmet medical needs proved to be a top priority. Another medical issue that was identified was that Sierra needed eyeglasses. The school social worker arranged for Sierra to have an eye exam and get eyeglasses through a program offered by the local WalMart store. The school social work intern provided transportation to optometrist appointments. Once these issues were addressed, her health care issues were resolved.

At school, a primary strategy was that Sierra check in with her language arts teacher each morning before school. This gave her a place to go at the beginning of school when other students gathered with their friends. Because Sierra had not yet been able to make friends, she did not have anyone to "hang out" with at the beginning of the day when students congregated. This informal "check and connect" was a beginning in Sierra's forming relationships with people at school. The role of the teacher was to make sure that Sierra had her school supplies as well as to greet her and make her feel welcome in the building. Other teachers joined the wraparound team as time progressed and invited Sierra to visit them in their classrooms during lunch in an effort to increase her comfort level at school. Eventually, they encouraged Sierra to involve her peers by inviting them to join her in their classrooms during lunch.

The next need addressed was Sierra's physical needs. Because she and her family were living in a homeless shelter, the family brought very few items with them. Sierra had two sets of clothing, including two pairs of sweat pants. The school social worker understood that it is important to most middle school students that they fit in by dressing like their peers. Sierra felt her clothing set her apart. The school social work intern approached the local area network to secure funding to purchase clothing for Sierra. The new clothes also helped meet the big need of helping Sierra feel as though she belonged. The school social work intern enlisted a friend to donate her services and provide Sierra with a new hairstyle that boosted her self-image.

The team continued to review and revise the wraparound plan. One of Sierra's strengths was her reading skills. She loved to read but did not have transportation or access to books through the local library. A team member took Sierra to the library and helped her get a library card. The team member explained how to use the bus system and helped Sierra map out a route to the library so Sierra could continue to check out books.

To increase peer friendships, with the help of her minister, Sierra became very active in a weekly church youth group. The friendships she made eventually carried over into school. The minister helped Sierra secure funds so she could participate in a mission trip with the local group. This experience added to her sense of independence, increased her involvement in other activities, and strengthened peer relationships. It is important to note that Sierra even received additional financial support for the trip through donations from teachers, school staff, and her mother's friends.

As the implementation of the wraparound plan progressed, the team focused on the following: (1) using data for decision making, (2) discussing with Sierra and her family how they felt the plan was working, and (3) addressing other needs that were not part of the initial plan or that needed to be revised or strengthened. During this phase, Sierra was encouraged to participate in the AVID (Advancement Via Individual Determination) program at her school. The AVID program targets economically disadvantaged students who have the potential to be successful college students and who would be the first one in their family to go to college. The team believed that the program would provide an excellent academic opportunity as well as help expand opportunities for Sierra to develop more peer relationships.

Sierra demonstrated tremendous improvement in attendance over the school year. Her daily attendance rate increased from 39% to 85 %. The data shared at team meetings is depicted in Figures 11.10–11.12. The graphs illustrate substantial gains in Sierra's participation in activities. Whereas she had no participation across home, school, and community settings at the beginning of the wraparound process, her growing participation in activities during the program became a strength. Sierra's social relationships changed over time with the assistance of wraparound. She and her family noted significant increases in the number of friends she had at school and within the community. Gains were made by resolving Sierra's serious health care issues. These achievements were celebrated by the team during their meetings. As the team moved into the final phase of the wraparound process, members worked diligently to create a transition plan for Sierra. This included planned recreational and social activities during the summer months as well as reliance on natural supports and services to ensure success in the following school year.

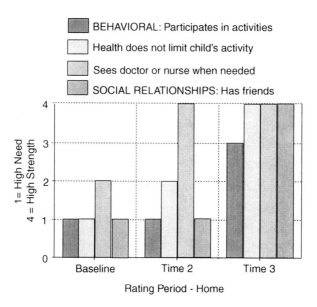

Figure 11.10   Results from Home School Community Tool (HSC-T) for Sierra administered at end of school year: Home.

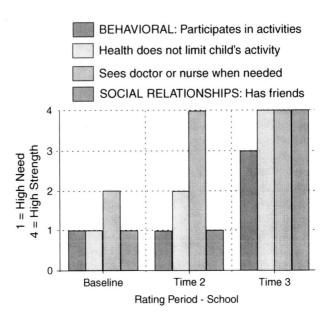

Figure 11.11 Results from Home School Community Tool (HSC-T) for Sierra administered at end of school year: School.

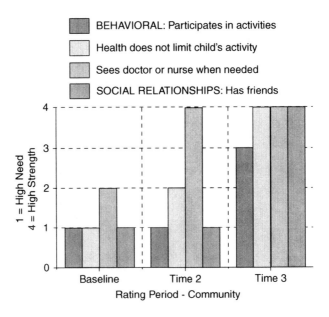

Figure 11.12 Results from Home School Community Tool (HSC-T) for Sierra administered at end of school year: Community.

CHAPTER SUMMARY AND CONCLUSIONS

Building the capacity for effective Tier 3 wraparound approaches in schools is challenging. School social workers should position themselves to assume key roles in facilitating wraparound teams. It is imperative that school social workers gain the specialized knowledge and skills needed to work effectively with students who require comprehensive behavior supports, not only at school but at home and in the community. Developing the essential skills to successfully engage families, students, and teachers who may be frustrated and experiencing stress requires systematic training and opportunities to practice over time.

A related issue is that the time required to facilitate wraparound planning teams is not always available. Schools do not allocate planning time commensurate with the level necessitated by Tier 3 students. This results in inadequate data, weak interventions, or faulty implementation. Students are often removed to restrictive settings before the wraparound process can be successfully carried out. Specialized personnel are not positioned to guide teams of parents and teachers through the team development process so that highly individualized interventions can be provided, monitored, and refined over time. Instead, they spend the bulk of their time assessing students for special education eligibility or attempting to provide interventions listed on individualizad education programs that are often insufficient in intensity or dosage to effect change for a student. School social workers, school psychologists, and counselors may feel "locked into" providing the interventions written on IEPs even though these interventions may not have an adequate evidence base for the presenting problem.

As school social workers gain awareness of the critical elements associated with RtI implementation and the wraparound process, they are obligated to assess their job roles and responsibilities. The required changes are substantial and school social workers should assume leadership positions in RtI implementation efforts, especially at the Tier 3 level. Schools need to expedite efforts to build competency and capacity for supporting students with complex emotional and behavioral needs that require Tier 3 interventions. This includes full implementation of RtI approaches, especially Tier 1 and Tier 2 interventions that provide effective behavioral supports. The wraparound process should be an essential Tier 3 level approach due to its focus on linking families, schools, and community partners. To ensure the most favorable wraparound outcomes, schools must rely heavily upon data-based decision-making processes, ongoing self-assessment of fidelity, and rigorous progress monitoring.

REFERENCES

Albin, R., Lucyshyn, J., Horner, R., & Flannery, K. (1996). Contextual fit for behavioral support plans. In L. K. Koegel & G. Dunlap (Eds.), *Positive behavioral support: Including people with difficult behavior in the community.* Baltimore: Brookes.

Brown, F., & Michaels, C. (2006). School-wide positive behavior support initiatives and students with severe disabilities: A time for reflection. *Research and Practice for Persons with Severe Disabilities, 31*(1), 57–61.

Bruns, E., Burchard, J., Suter, J., Leverentz-Brady, K., & Force, M. (2004). Assessing fidelity to a community based treatment for youth: The wraparound fidelity index. *Journal of Emotional and Behavioral Disorders, 12*, 79–89.

Burchard, J., Bruns, E., & Burchard, S. (2002). The wraparound approach. In B. Burns & K. Hoagwood (Eds.), *Community treatment for youth: Evidence-based interventions for severe emotional disturbance and behavioral disorders.* New York: Oxford University Press.

Burns, B., & Goldman, S. (1999). *Promising practices in wraparound for children with serious emotional disturbances and their families.* Systems of care: Promising practices in children's mental health, 1998 Series (Vol 4). Washington, DC: Center for Effective Collaboration and Practice, American Institutes for Research.

Carr, E. (2006). SWPBS: The greatest good for the greatest number, or the needs of the majority trump the needs of the minority?. *Research and Practice for Persons with Severe Disabilities, 31*, 54–56.

Crone, D., Horner, R., & Hawken, L. (2004). *Responding to problem behavior in schools: The behavior education program.* New York: Guilford Press.

De Los Reyes, A., & Kazdin, A. (2005). Informant discrepancies in the assessment of childhood psychopathology: A critical review, theoretical framework, and recommendations for further study. *Psychological Bulletin, 131*, 483–509.

Dobson, D., & Cook, T. (1980). Avoiding Type III error in program evaluation: Results from a field experiment. *Evaluation and Program Planning, 3*, 269–276.

Eber, L. (2003). *The art and science of wraparound: Completing the continuum of schoolwide behavioral support.* Bloomington: Forum on Education at Indiana University.

Eber, L. (2005). Wraparound: Description and case example. In G. Sugai & R. Horner (Eds.), *Encyclopedia of behavior modification and cognitive behavior therapy: Educational applications.* Thousand Oaks, CA: Sage.

Eber, L., & Hyde, K. (2006). *Integrating data-based decision into the wraparound process within a system of school-wide positive behavior supports (PBS).* Summary of conference proceedings for the 18th Annual Research Conference for Children's Mental Health, Tampa, FL.

Eber, L., Hyde, K., Rose, J., Breen, K., Mcdonald, D., & Lewandowski, H. (2009). Completing the continuum of schoolwide positive behavior support: Wraparound as a tertiary-level intervention. In W. Sailor, G. Dunlap, G. Sugai, & R. Horner (Eds.), *Handbook of positive behavior supports: Issues in clinical child psychology.* New York: Springer.

Freeman, R., Eber, L., Anderson, C., Irvin, L., Horner, R., Bounds, M., et al. (2006). Building inclusive school cultures using school-wide positive behavior support: Designing effective individual support systems for students with significant disabilities. *Research and Practice for Persons with Severe Disabilities, 31*, 4–17.

Hawken, L., & O'Neil, R. (2006). Including students with severe disabilities in all levels of school-wide positive behavior support. *Research and Practice for Persons with Severe Disabilities, 31*(1), 46–53.

Lewis-Palmer, T., Sugai, G., & Larson, S. (1999). Using data to guide decisions about program implementation and effectiveness. *Effective School Practices, 17*, 47–53.

Miles, P., Bruns, E., Osher, T., Walker, J., & National Wraparound Initiative Advisory Group. (2006). *The wraparound process user's guide: A handbook for families*. Portland, OR: Portland State University, National Wraparound Initiative, Research and Training Center on Family Support and Children's Mental Health.

Nakasato, J. (2000). Data-based decision making in Hawaii's behavior support effort. *Journal of Positive Behavior Interventions, 2*, 247–251.

National Center for Educational Statistics. (2008). *Digest of Education Statistics*. Retrieved December 1, 2008, from http://nces.ed./gov/.

Offord, D., Boyle, M., Racine, Y., Szatmari, P., Fleming, J., Sanford, M., et al. (1996). Integrating assessment data from multiple informants. *Journal of the American Academy of Child and Adolescent Psychiatry, 35*, 1078–1086.

Renck, K. (2005). Cross informant ratings of behavior of children and adolescents: The "gold standard.". *Journal of Child and Family Studies, 14*, 457–468.

Scott, T., & Eber, L. (2003). Functional assessment and wraparound as systemic school processes: Primary, secondary and tertiary systems examples. *Journal of Positive Behavior Interventions, 5*(3), 131–143.

Sugai, G., & Horner, R. (1999). Discipline and behavioral support: Preferred processes and practices. *Effective School Practices, 17*, 10–22.

VanDenBerg, J. (1999). History of the wraparound process. In B. J. Burns & S. K. Goldman (Eds.), *Promising practices in wraparound for children with serious emotional disturbance and their families* (Vol 4). Washington, DC: Center for Effective Collaboration and Practice, American Institute for Research.

Wagner, M., Newman, L., Cameto, R., Levine, P., & Garza, N. (2006). *An overview of findings from wave 2 of the National Longitudinal Study-2 (NLTS2)* (NCSER 2006-3004). Menlo Park, CA: SRI International.

Walker, J., & Schutte, K. (2004). Practice and process in wraparound teamwork. *Journal of Emotional and Behavioral Disorders, 12*, 182–192.

SECTION IV

Implementing and Sustaining Response to Intervention (RtI) Systems

This final section of the book includes chapters that discuss the use of RtI procedures and practices in making special education eligibility decisions, the identification and selection of evidence based programs and practices, strategies for addressing the daunting challenge of adopting, implementing and sustaining RtI systems, and the challenges the profession needs to address in order to ensure that school social workers play active leadership roles in RtI development and implementation.

In Chapter 12 Clark and Timm describe the process of using data generated from RtI supports and interventions to make special education eligibility decisions for individual students. Procedures for using functional assessment and intervention data to document eligibility and the need for special education are presented along with a case example illustrating the application of these procedures. In Chapter 13 Raines describes strategies school social workers can use to identify and select programs and practices that are evidenced based. In Chapter 14 Alvarez, Clark, Marckmann, and Timm propose a role for school social workers in the adoption, implementation and sustainability of RtI systems. A detailed illustration of a case review professional development process designed to provide continuous practice feedback to school social workers practicing in RtI systems is also provided. In the concluding chapter Clark and Alvarez summarize the challenges to which school social workers will need to respond in order to ensure their active role in developing, adopting, implementing, and sustaining RtI systems. A call to action is issued challenging school social workers to become more active agents of change in this process.

12

SPECIAL EDUCATION ELIGIBILITY DETERMINATION IN RESPONSE TO INTERVENTION SYSTEMS

JAMES P. CLARK & ANDREA TIMM

This chapter describes how special education eligibility decision making should take place in Response to Intervention (RtI) systems. The Individuals with Disabilities Education Act (IDEA) policy foundations for evaluation and eligibility determination are reviewed. Procedures and practices are proposed that use student performance and intervention response data generated in RtI tiers to make special education eligibility determinations. A rationale for using response to intervention data in a problem-solving process instead of more traditional assessment battery results in a refer-test-place process are presented along with criteria to be used for eligibility determination. A case example illustrating a noncategorical eligibility determination process in an RtI system is also presented. The placement of special education in the context of an RtI system is described along with key considerations in making eligibility determination decisions. Noncategorical identification of students in the eligibility process is proposed as an essential and preferred practice in implementing RtI systems. Finally, knowledge and skills essential for school social workers to meaningfully contribute to this process are identified.

IDEA POLICY FOUNDATIONS FOR SPECIAL EDUCATION
ELIGIBILITY DETERMINATION

Anyone who is considering how special education eligibility determination can be accomplished in RtI systems must start with a clear understanding of the requirements of IDEA that are most relevant to this decision-making process. Since special education eligibility decisions are based on information generated by the full and individual evaluation, this is arguably one of the most salient IDEA provisions to consider. If designed and implemented with integrity, and clearly documented, response to intervention data will meet these requirements. IDEA regulations include these provisions for the full and individual evaluation (34CFR§300.305):

(a) *Review of existing evaluation data.* As part of an initial evaluation (if appropriate) and as part of any reevaluations under this part, the IEP Team and other qualified professionals, as appropriate, must—

(1) Review existing evaluation data on the child, including—

   (i) Evaluations and information provided by the parents of the child;
  (ii) Current classroom-based, local, or State assessments, and classroom-based observations; and
 (iii) Observations by teachers and related services providers; and

(2) On the basis of that review, and input from the child's parents, identify what additional data, if any, are needed to determine—

   (i) (A) Whether the child is a child with a disability, as defined in §300.8, and the educational needs of the child; or
     (B) In case of a reevaluation of a child, whether the child continues to have such a disability, and the educational needs of the child;
  (ii) The present levels of academic achievement and related developmental needs of the child;
 (iii) (A) Whether the child needs special education and related services; or
     (B) In the case of a reevaluation of a child, whether the child continues to need special education and related services; and
 (iv) Whether any additions or modifications to the special education and related services are needed to enable the child to meet the measurable annual goals set out in the

> IEP of the child and to participate, as appropriate, in the
> general education curriculum.

Two important features of these requirements deserve emphasis. First is the matter of what evaluation information must be considered in determining whether a child is eligible for special education. Evaluations and information provided by parents must be included along with direct assessments of the child's performance in the classroom through the use of classroom-based, state, or local assessments, and classroom-based observations of the child by teachers and related services personnel, such as a school social worker or school psychologist. For a student with significant behavioral needs, data needed to make a special education eligibility decisions are generated in the process of implementing an RtI three-tiered system. These data can provide all, or nearly all, of the evaluation information needed to fulfill the statutory requirements for a full and individual evaluation. These data might include the following:

1. Tier 1 screening data describing the student's behavioral
   performance in comparison to peers and school-wide behavioral
   expectations or performance levels expected in the core behavioral
   curriculum and that include the results of classroom-based
   assessments and observations.
2. Tier 2 progress monitoring data measuring the student's
   performance in response to targeted group interventions that might
   include additional classroom-based assessments and observations.
3. Tier 3 progress monitoring data measuring the student's response
   to intensive individualized interventions.

Additionally, for some students as per the specific regulatory requirements for evaluation procedures it may be necessary to screen the student's performance in other areas that may be relevant such as vision, hearing, or health:

> The child is assessed in all areas related to the suspected disability,
> including, if appropriate, health, vision, hearing, social and
> emotional status, general intelligence, academic performance,
> communication status, and motor abilities.
> (34CFR§300.304 (b) (4))

However, the regulation states that assessments in any of these areas are to be conducted if it is considered to be an area related to the suspected disability, and *if appropriate*. Batsche et al. (2005) emphasize that this means "in-depth assessment in all domains is not required. Such practices divert attention from important tasks where performance problems have been identified" (p. 28). Ensuring efficiency in RtI systems requires that deliberate attention be directed to making assessment and decision making germane to problem solving. In-depth assessment is appropriate only if screening indicates this need. For example, if the area of concern for a student is his or her behavior (an "area related to the suspected disability") and classroom academic assessments and teacher observations indicate no concerns with the student's cognitive ability or ability to meet academic performance expectations (screening), an in-depth assessment of general intelligence, such as an I.Q. test, would not be *appropriate* and therefore would not be a required component of the full and individual evaluation for this student.

With the need to ensure efficiency and appropriateness of assessments, and the emphasis on the use of functional assessments that directly inform the development of high quality interventions, school social workers will need to reconsider the relevance and utility of the social history or social development study in eligibility evaluations. While these assessments can be used for collecting information from parents, their use in an RtI system that relies on functional assessments may not always be appropriate. Moreover, the routine use of a standard social history protocol in a battery of assessments is not consistent with the tenets of RtI. School social work assessments must be relevant to the problem or behavior of concern and tailored in a manner that collects relevant and functional data, that is, data that assist in understanding the function of the behavior of concern and that can be used to design interventions (Clark, 2002).

A second feature of the full and individual evaluation requirements that is worthy of emphasis is often referred to as the *two-pronged test*. Two conditions must be present to determine that a student is eligible for special education. The first condition/test is whether the child has a disability, that is, "Whether the child is a child with a disability, as defined in §300.8" (34CFR300.305(a)(2)(i)(A). The reference here is to §300.8 of the IDEA regulations that lists and defines 13 disability categories in describing who is considered to be a "child with a disability."

The second condition/test is whether the student *needs* special education. Clearly the assumption is that not all students with disabilities will need special education to access and receive benefit from their educational program. So, to meet the two-pronged test for special education eligibility a student must not only have a disability but must also need special education to sufficiently benefit from the educational program. Special education is defined in the IDEA regulations as "specially designed instruction, at no cost to the parents, to meet the unique needs of a child with a disability" (34CFR300.39(a)(1)).

As pointed out in Chapter 1, the reauthorization of IDEA in 1997 shifted the focus of special education from ensuring access (child find) to an imperative for results. Past refer-test-place processes met the challenge of child find by giving heavy emphasis to evaluation procedures that efficiently identified and categorized students by using disability labels, thereby meeting the requirement to demonstrate that these students had disabilities. However, little if any attention was given to the need prong—whether these students had needs that were most appropriately met by providing special education. As a result of the focus on matching interventions to student performance needs and documenting the effects of interventions, problem-solving processes in RtI systems hold the greatest promise of meeting the challenge to achieve results by shifting the focus to the need prong.

Rich data documenting the actual effects of well-designed and implemented evidence-based interventions built on the results of functional assessments provide much more relevant information to educators striving to discover what works for struggling learners than do the scores on standardized assessments generated in standard assessment batteries (Clark, 2002). Indeed, considerable evidence has accrued documenting the value of functional behavioral assessment in designing effective interventions (e.g., Kern et al., 1994; Romaniuk et al., 2002; Umbreit, 1995). The relative effectiveness of interventions based on functional assessments has also been demonstrated in recent studies (Ingram, Lewis-Palmer, & Sugai, 2005) as well as the durability of functional assessment-based interventions (Kern et al., 2006).

In addition to requiring the full and individual evaluation, the IDEA regulations for evaluation procedures are also very relevant to eligibility determination. These include provisions such as these:

> Use a variety of assessment tools and strategies to gather relevant, functional, developmental, and academic information. (34CFR§300.304(b)(1))

> [Do] not use any single measure or assessment as the sole criterion for determining whether a child is a child with a disability and for determining an appropriate educational program for the child. (34CFR§300.304(b)(2))

> Assessments and other evaluation materials include those tailored to assess specific areas of educational need and not merely those that are designed to provide a single general intelligence quotient. (34CFR§300.304(c)(2))

> Assessment tools and strategies that provide relevant information that directly assists persons in determining the educational needs of the child are provided. (34CFR§300.304(c)(7))

The regulatory expectation of IDEA is clear that evaluation procedures used in a full and individual evaluation must include a variety of tools and strategies that are tailored to assess specific concerns about educational performance, and that these assessments are expected to generate information that is relevant in identifying specific needs. For students with behavioral needs these features are in keeping with the characteristics of functional assessments, that is, assessments providing information that enhances the understanding of the purpose and function of the behavior of concern and directly useful in developing the student's individualizad education program (IEP) or behavior intervention plan (Clark, 1998).

Note also that the IDEA does not require the full and individual evaluation to be multidisciplinary. The regulations specify that assessments are to be conducted by "trained and knowledgeable personnel" (34CFR§300.304(c)(iv)) but there is no requirement that these personnel represent multiple professional disciplines. Rather, the focus is on the relevance and functional nature of assessments.

USING A PROBLEM-SOLVING PROCESS FOR ELIGIBILITY DETERMINATION

The problem-solving process proposed here consists of four basic steps: (1) problem identification and definition, (2) problem analysis, (3) intervention plan development and implementation, and (4) evaluation, that is, evaluating the effectiveness of the plan (Clark, 1998; Tilly, 2002). These steps are applied at varied levels of rigor across all three tiers of the RtI system as supports and interventions are differentiated and matched to student needs. Typically, students who are considered for special education eligibility have had the problem-solving steps applied in Tier 1 screening when it was determined that the universal supports (behavioral curriculum or school-wide behavioral expectations) in the school's program were not sufficiently ensuring acceptable levels of behavioral performance. In these circumstances, screening results have identified and specifically defined the student's behavioral problem, an analysis of the problem has enhanced an understanding of its underlying causes, and the results of this analysis have helped to select a targeted group intervention matched to the problem. Progress monitoring data were then used for formative assessment, that is, to determine whether the intervention was working or needed to be modified, and for determining whether the intervention had been successful—a summative evaluation. Though this progression may be somewhat typical, as emphasized in Chapter 1, this is not always a linear process. Decision making about differentiating the nature and intensity of interventions and supports needed by students is continually informed by screening or progress monitoring data.

In most cases when special education eligibility is considered, it is expected that data from rigorous assessments and intensive individualized interventions will be available. Functional assessment procedures such as RIOT (review, interview, observe, test) have been used to provide convergent data in the areas of curriculum, instruction, environment, and the learner (ICEL) (Clark et al., 2006; Hosp, 2006). The function of the student's behavior has been determined and replacement behaviors have been identified. Functional assessment data have been used to design and implement evidenced-based interventions that have a high probability of success. The integrity of intervention implementation has been carefully monitored to ensure that interventions have been implemented as specified. Interventions are designed to accomplish ambitious goals. In most cases, this means attaining a level of behavioral performance that is comparable with peers of the same age. Progress monitoring data have been used to make decisions about needed changes in interventions and to determine whether interventions are working. (See the detailed description of intensive individualized interventions in Chapter 9.)

ELIGIBILITY DECISION MAKING

To satisfy the first condition of the two-pronged test it must be determined that the student has a disability. In an RtI system, disability is functionally defined as

> a skills deficit, a health or physical condition, a functional limitation, or a pattern of behavior that adversely affects educational performance. A disability 1) results in educational performance that is significantly and consistently different, diminished, or inappropriate when compared to the expectations for peers, and 2) significantly interferes with:
> a) access to general education settings and opportunites,
> b) developmental progress,
> c) involvement and progress in the general curriculum, or
> d) interpersonal relationships or personal adjustments.
>   (Iowa Department of Education, 2006, p. 7)

Note how this functional definition focuses on critical aspects of educational performance, that is, behaviors that are essential to be successful in school. Also note that the definition is concerned with how discrepant the student's performance is from what is expected of all students. This definition is also contextual and situational and as such is highly congruent with social work's focus on the person in the situation. Disability is viewed as a discrepancy between the expectations of a particular educational setting and the student's actual performance in that setting. Ultimately the concern is with the adverse effects this discrepancy has on educational success including social and emotional functioning. Thus, in this definition, disability is truly a difference that makes a difference.

To determine that a student has a disability as defined here, two critical elements must be considered. The first is the student's rate of progress in response to interventions that have been implemented. The rate of progress is compared to pre-intervention progress rates as well as to expectations and rates of progress for peers. Four essential questions must be addressed:

1. How does this individual's actual rate of skill acquisition compare to the expected rate of skill acquisition?
2. What is the frequency, intensity, and duration of the behavior?

3. Have the intervention(s) been developed, implemented, and monitored with integrity?
4. Under what conditions did the individual experience the most growth? (Iowa Department of Education, 2006, p. 10)

The second critical element that must be considered to determine that the student has a disability is discrepancy—whether the student's behavior differs from that of peers and the expectations of the particular educational setting. The analysis of discrepancy requires that a standard be established for what is considered to be appropriate expectation(s). This might include classroom expectations of the teacher, school-wide behavioral expectations that have been established and communicated to students and teachers, developmental norms, or school policy. The student's behavior is then examined to determine if it is above or below what is expected, or if it is within the range of what is expected. Four essential questions must be addressed to determine discrepancy:

1. What are the multiple sources of data that demonstrate the individual's performance is significantly discrepant from that of peers or expected standards?
2. How does the individual's current level of performance compare to that of typical peers or expected standards?
3. What is the magnitude of the discrepancy?
4. How important and significant is this discrepancy? (Iowa Department of Education, 2006, p. 12)

To satisfy the second condition of the two-pronged test, the student must be determined to need special education. Specifically, it must be established that progress made with well-designed, well-implemented interventions requires special education services to be sustained. It is not assumed that special education is the sole source of the intensive individualized interventions that may be needed to ensure progress. In some cases general education resources may be sufficient to ensure continued and acceptable progress. Six essential questions must be addressed to establish instructional need:

1. What are the individual's needs in the areas of instruction, curriculum, and environment?
2. What are the instructional strategies, accommodations, and modifications that will enable the individual's learning performance to improve?
3. What accommodations and modifications were provided which enhanced the individual's performance and allowed opportunity to acquire educationally relevant skills?

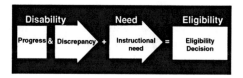

Figure 12.1   Essential components of special education eligibility determination.
Source: Adapted from the Iowa Department of Education, *Special Education Eligibility Standards*, January 2006, p. 7.

4. What, if any, ecological variables contribute to the interventions/accommodations/modifications not enhancing the individual's performance? Explain.
5. What is the pervasiveness of the area of concern across settings and time?
6. What ongoing, substantial, additional services are needed that cannot be provided by general education? (Iowa Department of Education, 2006, p. 13)

An integrated consideration of progress, discrepancy, and instructional need is essential to making defensible special education eligibility decisions in RtI systems that rely heavily on the use of response to intervention data. Figure 12.1 depicts the relationship of these considerations to the disability and need eligibility requirements. This decision making is data driven and requires the use of professional judgment. In this context professional judgment means "the reasoned application of clear guidelines to the specific data and circumstances related to each unique individual. Professional judgment adheres to high standards based on research and informed practice that are established by professional organizations or agencies" (Iowa Department of Education, 2006, p. 17).

Because special education eligibility determination is a high-stakes decision, it is critical that those involved in the decision clearly document that response to intervention data have demonstrated what specific services are needed to enable the student's learning. This means that knowing specifically what enables learning is a prerequisite to determining that a child is eligible for special education. Those making this decision must know what sustains acceptable rates of progress, reduces the discrepancy between the student's performance and that of peers and established expectation standards, and what specific instructional needs are essential for sustaining progress and reducing the discrepancy. This is the only way to determine whether specially designed instruction is actually needed. What enables learning must be known—that is, demonstrated with intervention data—so it can be determined whether these interventions require specially designed instruction. This is distinctly different from decisions often made in refer-test-place processes where the assumption is that after general education resources have been unable to determine what enables learning for the student, special education providers will somehow discover what is effective when the student begins receiving special education.

ELIGIBILITY DETERMINATION IN ACTION—A CASE ILLUSTRATION

Allyson has been provided multiple behavior interventions in recent years. Although her behavior has improved, she is continuing to require a number of interventions to provide instruction in targeted behavioral areas. Previous interventions have targeted inappropriate behaviors toward adults. Recently, a new behavior concern has emerged, that is, responding to adult directions with one individual reminder. More specifically, the problematic behavior has been defined as saying "no," refusing to complete assigned tasks, and attempting to leave the area or classroom. Nonexamples of the targeted behavior have been defined as asking for help, sitting quietly at her desk while waiting, and asking to leave the classroom. At times, her behavior has escalated to the level of requiring individual adult support to complete required activities. These behaviors have occurred multiple times daily and have required individualized adult attention to ensure the safety of Allyson and other students.

The school social worker has followed Allyson throughout the process of differentiating these behavioral supports. This has included data analysis, fading of intervention supports by decreasing the frequency of instruction and reinforcement, ongoing fidelity checks, and student observations. Ongoing involvement matched to the intensity of the problem enabled the school social worker to identify when further support was needed.

Progress monitoring data were collected as this current intervention targeted at responding to adult directions was being implemented (see Figure 12.2). The goal of this intervention was to increase Allyson's ability to follow directions with one reminder 90% of the time. The school social worker reviewed these data with the general education teacher and applied a four-point decision-making rule. As a result, two phase changes were made during initial implementation of the intervention. (See Chapter 9 for a more detailed description of the use of decision rules.) These phase changes included an increase in instructional time during her school day and additional reinforcement opportunities to improve her overall success with following directions. During consultation with the general education teacher the data were reviewed and it was determined that an updated functional behavioral assessment was needed to address her needs in her current classroom setting because of her slow progress. A team meeting was held to discuss the current concerns and what actions would be needed to increase her rate of progress, that is, to increase the slope of the trend line.

The school social worker conducted an in-depth review of the data, completed multiple systematic observations, and interviewed current

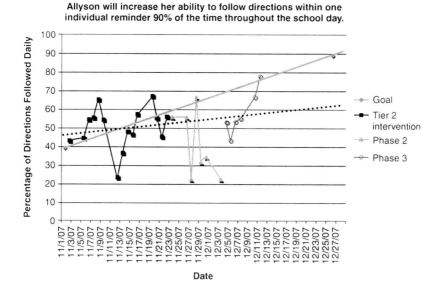

Figure 12.2   Allyson's progress monitoring data for Tier 2 intervention.

teachers. Previous data were also analyzed to determine what intervention strategies had been most effective in addressing problematic behaviors. The data documented that daily instruction paired with a high-frequency rein-forcement schedule was the most effective. These data were summarized and the team reconvened to consider what changes were needed to the current intervention addressing difficulties with following directions. It was deter-mined that although the function of the current problematic behavior had not changed, the intensity had greatly increased. The function of the beha-vior continued to be hypothesized as *escape from classroom demands to obtain attention from peers.* The intervention was modified to include an appro-priate procedure by which Allyson could escape from demands. The rein-forcement schedule for performing expected tasks was also modified. Additionally, daily instruction for how to follow teacher directions was provided to the whole class with individual sessions of practice and role-playing provided for Allyson. In response to Allyson's current needs for seeking peer attention and developing friendships, the team also added reinforcement that focused on earning time with peers. The team continued to collect data for decision making and a follow-up date was scheduled to determine the effectiveness of this modified intervention.

The team reconvened and discussed the intervention data (see Figure 12.3). Allyson's behavior had greatly improved with intensive instruction and reinforcement throughout her school day. A review of Allyson's progress in response to interventions, discrepancy from peers, and educational needs was facilitated by the school social worker and the general education teacher. The team determined that because of the high

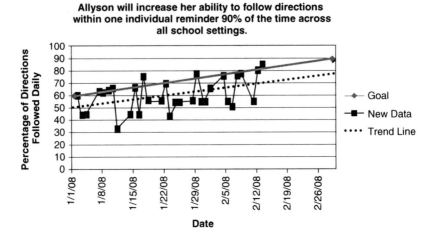

Figure 12.3   Allyson's progress monitoring data for successful intervention.

rates of reinforcement and time required for daily instruction, the maintenance of the current intervention was not sustainable in the general
education environment with the resources available.

Multiple factors assisted the team in this decision. First, although
Allyson was continuing to make progress in the general education environment, she was requiring a significant amount of daily support to learn and
generalize new skills. This instruction was becoming more specialized and
specific to her individual needs. Second, Allyson's behavior continued to be
significantly discrepant from that of her peers. Data documenting this
discrepancy were obtained through ongoing progress monitoring, class-
wide data samples, and systematic classroom observations. Last, specific
environmental supports, direct instruction, and resources were required to
maintain her current rate of progress.

These conclusions led the team to consider whether Allyson might
have a disability and whether special education services might be essential to ensuring her continued progress and benefit from her educational experience. The team decided that a full and individual
evaluation was needed to determine her eligibility for special education.
Allyson's parents provided their written consent for this evaluation to
be conducted.

The current intervention was continued and provided the data needed
for the full and individual evaluation. The school social worker summarized
progress monitoring data pertaining to progress, discrepancy, and educational needs. The current intervention was documented as well as her
progress on previous interventions. Critical components of this analysis
included her rate of progress over time, specific components of interventions, and implementation integrity. Allyson was making an average weekly

growth of 1.2% in the area of following directions over the last eight weeks of the intervention with a mean score over the last three weeks of 75%. Peers were demonstrating the ability to follow directions within one reminder 90% of the time without additional intervention. Therefore, Allyson was 1.5 times discrepant in the area of following directions compared to peers. She was also requiring fifteen minutes of instruction daily to maintain her performance, with reinforcers occurring every five to ten minutes. Allyson continued to require additional levels of reinforcement that focused on structured support with peers, frequent one-on-one verbal reinforcement, access to tangibles, and ongoing communication with parents. She had shown an overall increase in her performance but had not yet attained her goal of following directions 90% of the time.

Although she had made significant progress, Allyson was still 1.5 times discrepant from peers in the area of following directions. This discrepancy was documented by using peer comparison data and teacher expectations for same grade level peers. Convergent discrepancy data were also gathered through systematic classroom observations; interviews with her parents, teachers, and guidance counselor; and a norm-referenced assessment that allowed for comparison to same-age peers. Class-wide behavior management data were also reviewed. These data documented Allyson's current needs, her discrepancy from the performance of typical peers, and growth still needed.

As a result of the analysis of functional behavioral assessment data and data generated from implementing the behavioral intervention plan, the school social worker was able to identify the specific curriculum and instruction that Allyson required to make progress in the general education setting. The instruction targeted skill acquisition across multiple settings and the curriculum targeted Allyson's difficulties with the skills of following directions and seeking peer attention appropriately. Due to Allyson's current instructional needs, rate of progress, and the amount and nature of resources required to sustain the current intervention, the team determined that Allyson was eligible for special education services. The development of the individualized education program (IEP) utilized the intervention data to identify the specific specially designed instruction that was effective in addressing Allyson's current difficulties and that was essential to ensuring her access to a free, appropriate public education.

WHERE DOES SPECIAL EDUCATION FIT IN THE STRUCTURE OF RESPONSE TO INTERVENTION (RtI)?

Some proponents of three-tiered RtI models have contended that intensive individualized interventions in Tier 3 are synonymous with special education (e.g., Mellard & Johnson, 2008). This would suggest that special education is the sole source of intensive individualized interventions and therefore all intensive individualized interventions require the specially designed instruction provided by special education. This also suggests that general education resources are not capable of, nor responsible for, providing these services.

Special education is intentionally not specifically identified as a discrete tier in the model presented in this book. This is because, much like other highly specialized services and supports such as wraparound (see Chapter 11), special education is a particular set of specially designed services needed by relatively few students in Tier 3. For those students determined to be eligible for special education, intensive individualized interventions in Tier 3 will take the form of specially designed instruction described in an IEP. It is expected that the needs of other students requiring intensive individualized interventions will be met through the provision of other supports and services provided in Tier 3.

KEY CONSIDERATIONS FOR IMPLEMENTATION

Because special education eligibility determination in RtI systems relies heavily on the use of intervention data generated from all three tiers, it is essential that schools have data collection systems in place that will capture these data and make them efficiently available for use. Data systems for collecting school-wide behavior screening data in Tier 1 and data documenting the results of targeted group interventions in Tier 2 are needed to demonstrate the general education supports that have been provided for students with behavioral needs. Systems that enable the collection and display of progress monitoring data for students receiving intensive individualized interventions, such as charts and graphs, are also critical to this high-stakes decision-making process. School social workers may need to advocate for the computer software, hardware, and technical support needed to establish and maintain effective and efficient data systems.

Since special education eligibility decisions in RtI systems rely on data generated from monitoring the effects of well-designed, well-implemented behavioral interventions, it is essential that these data are valid and reliable representations of student performance. The reason is the same that requires standardized tests used in test batteries in refer-test-place systems to be administered according to standard test protocols so that they yield valid and reliable results. Procedures for ensuring treatment integrity throughout the implementation of interventions are the mechanism for ensuring that they have been implemented as designed and that improvements in student performance are actually the direct result of these interventions. (See Chapter 9 for a more detailed description of intervention integrity procedures.)

Though noncategorical identification of students who are eligible for special education is not a primary purpose or goal of RtI systems, it is a natural by-product of a decision-making process that utilizes functional assessment and intervention data. Functional behavioral assessments invariably do not generate the descriptive data that are needed to categorize students into specific disability categories, such as intelligence test results, scores on norm-referenced behavior scales, or academic screening assessments. Since school social workers in many states will need to advocate for this practice, it is important that they understand there is no federal requirement to use categorical designations for individual students. IDEA regulations state, "Nothing in the Act requires that children be classified by their disability so long as each child who has a disability that is listed in §300.8 and who, by reason of that disability, needs special education and related services is regarded as a child with a disability under Part B of the Act" (34CFR §300.111(d)). This provision is often confused with the federal requirement that states annually report the number of students receiving special education by disability category. Tilly, Reschly, and Grimes (1999) have explained this reporting requirement by clarifying that "in cases where children are identified with disabilities without a specific disability label, states can apportion these children across the disability categories based on historical averages" (p. 295). Some states indeed have satisfactorily met the reporting requirement in this manner.

KNOWLEDGE AND SKILLS NEEDED BY SCHOOL SOCIAL WORKERS

In order to make special education eligibility decisions in RtI systems, school social workers will need to be familiar with IDEA provisions for evaluation procedures as well as state and local requirements. School social workers will also need to understand the principles and practices of functional behavioral assessment identified in Chapter 9 and to seek out professional development opportunities to develop applied skills in behavior analysis. This is not typically a significant component of graduate social work programs. Skills in collecting, displaying, and making decisions with progress monitoring data will also be essential to determining student eligibility for special education. Proficiency with computer software that can efficiently sort data and generate visual displays of the data such as charts and graphs will be absolutely essential.

CHAPTER SUMMARY AND CONCLUSIONS

Special education eligibility determination is a high-stakes data-based decision that can be made in RtI systems using intervention data. This decision making is in accord with the provisions of IDEA and must rely on a rich set of information about how best to enable learning for students with disabilities. Data regarding a student's progress and response to interventions along with how effective such interventions have been in reducing the discrepancy between a student's performance and what is expected are critical in making these eligibility decisions. Intervention-based decision making also provides valuable information for targeting specially designed instruction for students with disabilities, ensuring that instruction will result in continued progress.

School social workers can play a significant role in advocating policies and procedures that support intervention-based decision making in the special education eligibility determination process. This advocacy will need to be targeted at the state and local levels. These policies and procedures can support the systematic use of intervention data in informing high-stakes special education eligibility decisions and in assuring that services are matched to student needs and are effective in enabling student learning.

REFERENCES

Batsche, G., Elliott, J., Graden, J. L., Grimes, J., Kovaleski, J. F., Prasse, D., Reschly, D. J., Schrag, J., & Tilly, W. D. (2005). *Response to intervention: Policy considerations and implementation*. Alexandria, VA: National Association of State Directors of Special Education.

Clark, J. P. (1998). Functional behavioral assessment and behavioral intervention plans: Implementing the student discipline provisions of IDEA '97. *The Section Connection, 4*(2), 6–7.

Clark, J. P. (2002). School social work assessment: Battery versus functional approaches. *The Section Connection, 8*(1), 4–5.

Clark, J. P., Timm, A., Gilmore, J., & Dedic, B. (2006, March 30). Response to Intervention: A Problem-solving Approach to Enabling Learning. Paper presented at the 100th Anniversary of School Social Work Conference sponsored by the School Social Work Association of America, Boston, MA.

Hosp, J. L. (2006). Assessment practices and response to intervention. *Communique, 34*(7), National Association of School Psychologists; www.nasponline.org/publications/cq/cq347rti.aspx.

Ingram, K., Lewis-Palmer, T., & Sugai, G. (2005). Function-based intervention planning: Comparing the effectiveness of FBA function-based and non-function-based intervention plans. *Journal of Positive Behavior Interventions, 7*(4), 224–236.

Iowa Department of Education. (2006). *Special education eligibility standards*. Des Moines: Author.

Kern, L., Childs, K. E., Dunlap, G., Clarke, S., & Falk, G. D. (1994). Using assessment-based curriculuar intervention to improve the classroom behavior of a student with emotional and behavioral challenges. *Journal of Applied Behavior Analysis, 27*, 7–19.

Kern, L., Gallagher, P., Starosta, K., Hickman, W., & George, M. (2006). Longitudinal outcomes of functional behavioral assessment-based intervention. *Journal of Positive Behavior Interventions, 8*(2), 67–78.

Mellard, D. E., & Johnson, E. (2008). *RTI: A practitioner's guide to implementing response to intervention*. Thousand Oaks, CA: Corwin Press.

Romaniuk, C., Miltenberger, R., Conyers, C., Jenner, N., Jurgens, M., & Ringenberg, C. (2002). The influence of activity choice on problem behaviors maintained by escape versus attention. *Journal of Applied Behavior Analysis, 35*, 349–362.

Tilly W. D., III. (2002). School psychology as a problem solving enterprise. In A. Thomas & J. Grimes (Eds.), *Best practices in school psychology IV*, 25–36. Bethesda, MD: National Association of School Psychologists.

Tilly W. D., III, Reschly, D. J., & Grimes, J. (1999). Disability determination in problem solving systems: Conceptual foundations and critical components. In D. J. Reschly, W. D. Tilly, III, & J. P. Grimes (Eds.), *Special education in transition*. Longmont, CO: Sopris West.

Umbreit, J. (1995). Functional assessment and intervention in a regular classroom setting for the disruptive behavior of a student with attention deficit hyperactivity disorder. *Behavioral Disorders, 20,* 267–278.

Ysseldyke, J., & Marston, D. (1999). Origins of categorical special education services in schools and a rationale for changing them. In D. J. Reschly, W. D. Tilly, III & J. P. Grimes (Eds.), *Special education in transition*. Longmont, CO: Sopris West.

13

EVIDENCE-BASED SCHOOL SOCIAL WORK PRACTICE AND RESPONSE TO INTERVENTION

James C. Raines

The challenge for any school social worker is to establish empirically supported prevention and intervention programs that support schools, classrooms, and individuals with specific needs. This chapter describes a five-step process of evidence-based practice (EBP) for school social workers and applies this process to a Response to Intervention (RtI) model of service delivery. Most important, this chapter points practitioners to resources they can access for suitable interventions for use with children and adolescents in schools.

DEFINITION OF EVIDENCE-BASED PRACTICE

Practice is defined here as the process of helping people adapt to the demands of their environment or modifying the environment to meet the needs of the people who inhabit it, or both. This person-in-environment perspective has been central to social work (Germain, 1979; Saari, 1986; Winters & Easton, 1983). Research demonstrates that there is a strong reciprocal relationship between children's emotional-behavioral health and the instructional environment. This mutual influence between child and context can be seen in three types of research. First, interventions that are integrated into the curriculum achieve more positive results and last longer than interventions offered adjunctively away from classrooms (hoagwood et al., 2007). Second, social-emotional learning has been linked to school success (Welsh et al., 2001; Zins et al., 2004). Third, positive school and classroom climates have been shown to prevent behavioral problems and school violence (Adams, 2000; Gettinger & Kohler, 2006). Thus, practice must encompass the larger process of enabling a better "fit" between students and their instructional milieu. For this reason, the term *practice* does not denote a specific counseling technique, treatment, or intervention. The originators of EBP defined it as the "conscious, explicit and judicious use of current best evidence in making decisions about the care of individual patients" (Sackett et al., 1996, p. 71). It involves a process of integrating the "best research evidence with clinical expertise and patient values" (Sackett et al., 2000, p. 1). The American Psychological Association (2005) clarifies the goal of evidence-based practice as follows. The purpose of EBP is "to promote effective practice and enhance public health by applying empirically supported principles of assessment, case formulation, therapeutic relationship, and intervention" (p. 5).

Scientifically Based Research

What is the legal definition of scientifically based research? The federal regulations for the Individuals with Disabilities Education Act and No Child Left Behind share the same definition found below (U.S. Dept. of Education, 2006):

Scientifically based research—

a) means research that involves the application of rigorous, systematic, and objective procedures to obtain reliable and valid knowledge relevant to education activities and programs; and
b) includes research that—

1. Employs systematic, empirical methods that draw on observation or experiment;
2. Involves rigorous data analyses that are adequate to test the stated hypotheses and justify the general conclusions drawn;
3. Relies on measurements or observational methods that provide reliable and valid data across evaluators and observers, across multiple measurements and observations, and across studies by the same or different investigators;
4. Is evaluated using experimental or quasi-experimental designs in which individuals, entities, programs, or activities are assigned to different conditions and with appropriate controls to evaluate the effects of the condition of interest, with a preference for random assignment experiments, or other designs to the extent that those designs contain within-condition or across-condition controls;

5. Ensures that experimental studies are presented in sufficient detail and clarity to allow for replication or, at a minimum, offer the opportunity to build systematically on their findings; and
6. Has been accepted by a peer-reviewed journal or approved by a panel of independent experts through a comparably rigorous, objective, and scientific review. (§ 300.35)

INTEGRATION OF RESEARCH AND PRACTICE

The EBP approach aims for an integration of research and practice using the following clinical steps:

1. *Assessment of the Problem* using reliable and valid measures.
2. *Intervention Planning* using relevant, strong, and consistent research.
3. *Intervention Implementation* that adapts and applies the research in ways that account for client characteristics and complexity, clinician experience and expertise, and contextual constraints.
4. *Evaluation of Effectiveness* using the same reliable and valid measures from step 1.
5. *Documentation of Results* including dissemination to constituent groups (e.g., building principals, superintendents, and/or school-board members). (Raines, 2008a, p. 26)

It is important, however, to distinguish EBP from two other often-used phrases: empirically supported treatments and outcome evaluation.

EMPIRICALLY SUPPORTED TREATMENTS (EST) VERSUS OUTCOME EVALUATION

It is important not to confuse evidence-based practice with empirically supported treatments (Westen, Novotny, & Thompson-Brenner, 2005). A treatment is defined as the application of remedies to help a person recover from an illness or injury. Treatment assumes a medical model and presumes that the problem lies with the person, not the environment (Fonagy et al., 2002). The reason that ESTs do not qualify as evidence-based practice is that they cover only the first two steps of integrating research and practice and leave out the *final three steps* (Ruben & Parrish, 2007; Walker et al., 2007).

It is also important not to confuse evidence-based practice with outcome evaluation (Constable & Massat, 2009). Outcome evaluation is concerned with carefully measuring the results of one's interventions (Bloom, Fischer, & Orme, 2006). Outcome evaluation is a critical component of EBP, but it is not synonymous with EBP. The reason that outcome evaluation does not qualify as evidence-based practice is that it does not require practitioners ever to use the professional literature. It simply jumps to the fourth step in the integrated process and leaves out the *first three steps*.

In short, the problem with both of the positions above is that they commit a philosophical error called a "category mistake" (Meiland, 1999). Both the EST = EBP and the outcome evaluation = EBP advocates mistake a part of the process for the whole. Like the famous Indian story of the blind men and the elephant, they are partially correct, but cannot see the larger picture (Raines, 2008a). Evidence-based practice takes both elements equally into account.

EVIDENCE-BASED PRACTITIONERS

How do evidence-based practitioners differ from their peers who are conducting treatment as usual? Gibbs (2003) pictures them as follows:

> Placing the client's benefits first, evidence-based practitioners adopt a *process* of lifelong learning that involves continually posing specific questions of direct *practical* importance to clients, searching objectively and efficiently for the current best evidence relative to each question, and taking appropriate action guided by evidence.
> (p. 6, italics added)

Two parts of this description are worth noting. First, an evidence-based practitioner believes that there are no facts, theories, or research that practitioners can learn in graduate school and then depend upon for the rest of their professional careers. Good clinical practice requires that all professional helpers become self-regulated "lifelong learners" (Howard, McMillen, & Pollio, 2003; Masui & DeCorte, 2005; Slawson & Shaughnessy, 2005). Second, evidence-based practitioners seek satisfactory or "good-enough" evidence about current practice questions (Raines, 2008a). There is seldom unequivocal evidence so that clinicians can know that they are making exactly the right choices. At the very least, practitioners should be able to identify which interventions, such as Scared Straight programs, are harmful to children (Beutler, 2000; Petrosino, Turpin-Petrosino, & Buehler, 2003).

THE PROCESS OF EBP

According to the originators of EBP, there are five basic stages in the process (Ollendick & Davis, 2004; Sackett et al., 2000). Let's review each one in order (see Figure 13.1) and see how it fits into the integrated research-practice approach discussed above.

Answerable Questions

First, practitioners must convert their need for information into answerable questions. An important caveat, however, is that not all questions are answerable by science. There are two kinds of questions that science cannot

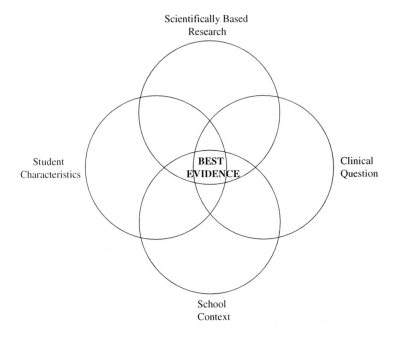

Figure 13.1   Four components of a search strategy.

answer. First, science cannot help us determine whether it is "right" for a pregnant 15-year old to have an abortion. That kind of question can be answered only on ethical or moral grounds (Raines & Dibble, in press). Second, science cannot help us determine the exact technique to use with an individual client. The best science can tell us is what works for most students, but never what works for all students. This stage is similar to the assessment step mentioned above: it requires practitioners to identify the crux of the problem by formulating intelligent questions that need to be answered before treatment planning begins.

INVESTIGATING THE EVIDENCE

The best investigators are both effective and efficient. To become proficient at both requires access to what Alexander and Tate (2005) call the private web. Unlike the public web accessible through Google or other search engines, the information on the private web is fee-based and edited for content. Efficient and effective investigators know how to search multiple databases and allow a computer to sift through mountains of data in a matter of minutes. This stage is similar to the treatment planning step; it requires practitioners to go beyond mere brainstorming and investigate which interventions are most likely to help the client.

This step will require access to professional books, computer databases, and Internet clearinghouses. Professional books differ from popular books by their level of rigor (Abel & Lyman, 2002). Typically, professional books are aimed at practicing professionals and will have textual citations and references for nearly every paragraph. Popular books, aimed at a general audience, rely almost exclusively on the author's authority (McRae, 1993). The key difference is the degree of peer review (Weller, 2001). An important tool is searchable databases that provide abstracts of scholarly journal articles, dissertations, and official reports. They require some knowledge of Boolean operators and wildcard characters (see Box 13.1). Internet clearinghouses are edited for content by the organization or government agency that supports them. They offer systematic reviews of prevention and/or intervention programs for clients.

Looking for the "best evidence" will lead to a multiple component search strategy involving four elements: scientifically based research (randomized controlled trials or quasi-experimental designs), the clinical issue (e.g., autism, behavioral disorders, or social skills), student characteristics

---

Box 13.1   Boolean Operators and Search Sets

Boolean Operator AND	Boolean Operator NOT		Boolean Operator OR
Child & Adolescent Terms	*Scientifically Based Terms*	*School-Based Terms*	*Intervention Terms*
adolescent*	clinical trial	classroom	Counseling
boys	comparison	school*	Intervention
child*	group	student*	Psychotherapy
girls	control group	teachers	Treatment
teen*	effectiveness		
youth	efficacy		
	evaluation		
	multiple baseline		
	quasi-experimental		
	random*		

Note: * is a wildcard character that enables databases to return any prefix or suffix, such as adolescence, adolescent, or adolescents.

(e.g., age, race, or gender), and school contexts (e.g., school, classroom, or teachers). Thus, the best evidence will be research that meets all four of the criteria. Occasionally, a search strategy will meet only two or three of the criteria and practitioners will need to adapt the evidence they find to fit student characteristics and/or contextual constraints.

Appraising the Evidence

Third, practitioners should critically appraise the evidence for its validity and applicability to the practice problem that motivated the initial investigation. This is one of the ways that evidence-based practice differs from treatment as usual: it requires critical thinking to determine what is the "best evidence." Practitioners need to keep their heads on and think critically about the "facts" that they uncover (Gambrill, 2006).

This book is especially interested in effectiveness studies of both prevention and intervention strategies. There are two major types of effectiveness studies. First, systematic reviews aim to systematically collect, cull, and compare all of the scientifically based research on a particular topic. These reviews should be rigorous, transparent, and auditable. *Rigorous* refers to possessing the most meticulous standards for inclusion in the review. Typically, this means that reviewers accept only randomized controlled trials and quasi-experimental designs. *Transparency* refers to the clarity of the reviewers' explanation for how the studies were located, the criteria by which they are judged, and the procedure by which the conclusions were reached. *Auditability* refers to sufficiency of details to enable another researcher to replicate the findings (Raines, 2008a). Second, efficacy studies include both randomized controlled trials and quasi-experimental designs. The U.S. Department of Education (What Works Clearinghouse, 2006) uses three criteria to judge the quality of these studies. First, *relevance* is determined by the study's topic, the adequacy of the outcome measures, and the adequacy of reported data. Relevance of the topic includes a relevant time frame (e.g., 20 years), relevant intervention (e.g., cognitive-behavioral therapy), relevant sample (e.g., school-age children), and relevant outcome (e.g., improved behavior). Adequacy of the outcome measure means that the measure is both reliable (consistent) and valid (accurate). Adequacy of the reported data means that the researchers have provided both means and standard deviations for both the treatment group and the comparison before and after the intervention. Second, *strength* is determined by whether the researchers conducted a randomized controlled trial (RCT) or used a quasi-experimental design (QED). The main difference between the two studies is that RCTs contrast a treatment group to a control (no-treatment) group and QEDs contrast a treatment group to a comparison (different-treatment) group. Third, *consistency* is determined by looking at the evenness of the intervention across different researchers, participants, settings, and outcomes. Ideally, the same intervention is tested by more than one group of researchers, using diverse samples (races, genders, and socioeconomic groups), different settings (urban, suburban, and rural schools), and different measures (observations, self-reports, or third-party rating scales).

Adaptation and Application

Fourth, practitioners should apply and adapt the results to their own clients. This step requires clinical practice wisdom. The process is also not top down. It assumes a collaborative relationship in which practitioners are familiar with more than one method to help a student (Kaslow, 2002; Nelson, 2002; Shapiro, Welker, & Jacobson, 1997) and offer informed choices to clients. There are three common adaptations that must be made to help empirically based interventions fit clients. These adaptations include developmental, cultural, and contextual changes.

DEVELOPMENTAL ADAPTATIONS   Practitioners should always take into consideration the developmental level of the child. This includes adjusting the intervention to allow for more therapeutic engagement (especially for involuntary clients), affective vocabulary, cognitive abilities, "homework" tasks, and parental involvement. First, since students seldom self-refer, most pupils should be regarded as nonvoluntary. This means that prior to launching an empirically supported intervention; group leaders should slow down and enable the group to engage with the worker and the other members (McKay et al., 1996). Second, many students may not have an affective vocabulary beyond obscenities. Practitioners may need to temporarily suspend ordinary school prohibitions about vulgar language while simultaneously educating students about categories and intensities of feelings (Ribordy et al., 1988). For example, "angry" can be nuanced for intensity by brainstorming other forms, such as "ticked off" or "enraged." Third, many cognitive therapy techniques require metacognitive skills that younger students will not have mastered (Kingery et al., 2006). A developmentally appropriate approach requires that these be modified to fit students' level of self-understanding. For example, the concept of cognitive distortions can be translated as "thinking traps" and cognitive restructuring can be termed "coping clues." Fourth, many behavioral therapy techniques refer to "homework." This is a loaded term for many children and should be neutralized by using terms such as "project" or "experiment" (Cooper, 2001). Finally, since externalizing children often require consistent structure and internalizing children often engage in social referencing their parents' reactions to events, it is important to educate parents about students' respective needs (McCart et al., 2006; Nock et al., 2004).

CULTURAL ADAPTATIONS   Practitioners should always address the issue of cultural sensitivity. This is especially important in schools that have the fewest minority students because they have the highest disproportional representation of minority students in special education (National Research Council, 2002). Turner (2000) posits that practitioners should attend to seven important factors when adapting programs for minority families. First, certain protective factors have greater salience among certain groups (e.g., church attendance among African Americans). Second, professionals should recognize that different families have varying degrees of cultural assimilation and comfort levels with majority traditions. Third, it is important to recognize intrafamily differences in acculturation so that children often adapt more quickly than their parents. Fourth, there are considerable differences in the reasons for migration. Families that emigrate from their homelands voluntarily have a much easier time adjusting than those who are forced to emigrate. Fifth, clinicians should be alert to the possibility of trauma for families that have left due to political oppression. Sixth, practitioners should pay attention to the family's work status and economic stressors. Many former professionals lack credentials to practice in this country and are forced to assume low-paying jobs. Seventh, schools should not assume that families are automatically literate in their native language (Jensen, 2001).

The research literature provides three different examples of culturally sensitive school-based group interventions. White and Rayle (2007) adapted the Strong Teens curriculum for African American male adolescents as part of a 12-session group. They used famous African American historical figures as role models to illustrate the theoretical concepts. Constantino, Malgady, and Rogler (1984) adapted Puerto Rican folktales to help children in kindergarten through third grade with cope with their anxieties over 20 sessions. Kim and colleagues (2006) used popular Korean music to help Korean adolescent school girls improve relationships and self-control. The groups met for 90 minutes over six sessions. These illustrations demonstrate that culturally sensitive practitioners can use pertinent heroes, stories, and songs to increase the relevance of group interventions.

CONTEXTUAL ADAPTATIONS   Finally, practitioners should consider the contextual constraints of delivering interventions within a public school. While schools have become the default providers of mental health interventions for children (Rones & Hoagwood, 2000), this does not mean that they are ideally suited to these purposes. Contextual constraints have a direct influence on two essential aspects of Tier 2 interventions: time and location.

Time considerations include the frequency, duration, and scheduling of Tier 2 interventions. The frequency of Tier 2 interventions can range from one to three times per week, but most psychosocial interventions will probably occur weekly. The duration of Tier 2 interventions will depend somewhat on the frequency, but most will last for one marking period or typically nine weeks (Mellard & Johnson, 2008). The scheduling of Tier 2 interventions can be done three ways, each with its own advantages and disadvantages (Burns & Gibbons, 2008). Many schools begrudgingly make room for Tier 2 interventions. Tier 2 services in these schools must be scheduled during regular class times. Since No Child Left Behind measures school performance on reading, math, and science, most schools would frown on using these class times. This restriction leaves other classes, such as technology, social studies, physical education, music, and art as the only possibilities. The strength of this approach is that students do not miss any of their core classes, but the weakness is that students often enjoy and excel at the other classes and would be reluctant to miss these. Practitioners would be wise to avoid always picking the same class from which to pull students on a regular basis and will probably want to choose those classes where the student is responding to Tier 1 instruction. Other schools have appropriately adopted a school-wide approach to RtI and this produces two other possibilities. Some of these schools have adopted a school-wide RtI time or a regular period in which all students either receive supplemental (e.g., gifted) services or targeted (Tier 2) services. The strength of this approach is that practitioners have a standard time for intervention; the weakness is that even if they conducted a different group every day of the week, they couldn't cover the entire school during this period alone and you would have to compete with other specialized support personnel if a particular child needed more than one related service. The final and perhaps best solution is to have a floating RtI time. This requires substantial centralized planning. In this model, each grade level would have its own unique RtI period during which supplemental or targeted services can be delivered. For example, Kindergarten may have 9 A.M. to 9:40 A.M., first grade may have 9:40 A.M. to 10:20 A.M., and second grade may have 10:20 A.M. to 11:00 A.M. The strength of this model is that it allows different support personnel to rotate the days of the week and still have time to reach every grade level; the weakness is that it assumes that a social worker, psychologist, or counselor is at the school five days per week.

The location of Tier 2 interventions has two main options. First, some school systems (e.g., Chicago Public Schools) require that most services occur within the classroom. This requires practitioners to "push-in" rather than "pull-out." If 5% to 10% of children need Tier 2 interventions, then the average classroom (~25 students) could have as many as five students served in this tier. The strength of this approach is that student support services gain transparency; teachers can observe effective group management strategies and emulate them. The weakness of this approach is that there is no expectation of confidentiality regarding student disclosures (Raines, 2008b) and there is no room for differentiated intervention; every group would need to be a cross-categorical or generic behavioral group. Second, practitioners can meet in a separate location, such as the social worker's office or other vacant space. The strength of this approach is that students can express confidential concerns and social workers can gather students from several classrooms for a targeted intervention. The weakness of this approach is that it assumes that the school building has sufficient space to accommodate small groups and this may not be true in overcrowded urban schools.

Outcome Evaluation

Finally, school social workers must begin to track and evaluate progress. It is this step that completes the circle and turns evidence-based practice into practice-based evidence (Barkham & Mellor-Clark, 2003; Evans et al., 2003). One of the major weaknesses of research by related services personnel has been the failure to link mental health interventions with improved academic outcomes. In a systematic review of 2, 000 studies, Hoagwood et al. (2007) found only 24 that examined this relationship. Educational outcomes included attendance, disciplinary actions, grades, special education placement, and standardized test scores. The good news is that 15 (62.5%) of these studies found positive outcomes for both mental health and academic success.

Outcome evaluation is important for two reasons. First, if we have adapted an EST then we must evaluate it to see if the evidence continues to support its use. Second, while ESTs have been established using another set of students, we really don't know whether they work for our set of students until we evaluate our efforts. Outcome evaluation and dissemination of results, then, is the culmination of an evidence-based process. We have converted our need for information into answerable questions; we have searched effectively and efficiently for the best available evidence; we have appraised that evidence for relevance, strength, and consistency; we have adapted and applied the evidence to the developmental level, cultural affiliation, and contextual constraints of a particular client; and now we must hold ourselves accountable for the results.

To determine effectiveness, data-based decision making demands that practitioners routinely collect and analyze relevant data. Malecki and Demaray (2007) use the RIOT acronym to summarize the various ways to collect data.

R is for Review records. Schools regularly collect an enormous amount of data about students, but they seldom analyze it to monitor student progress. Some of the best archival data that practitioners can use includes routinely recorded data, such as school attendance, grades, office disciplinary referrals, nurse visits, tardiness, and work completion rates.

I is for Interview informants. Gerber (2003) notes that teacher performance is still the largest factor in student achievement. Interviewing teachers about students' progress enables us to obtain an in-depth perspective. Another easy way to monitor progress is to interview students and ask them a scaled question. Scaled questions for pain are now one of the vital signs that nurses use by asking, "On a scale from 1 to 10, how would you rate your pain?" (Joint Commission on Accreditation of Healthcare Organizations, 2004). Raines (2008a) points out that the last word in this question can address any feeling state, such as sadness, anxiety, or anger.

O is for Observation. Volpe et al. (2005) compared seven observational coding systems. Most of these recommend that observers use an index peer (of the same age, gender, and race) to obtain normative data. Two of the systems could be used with a personal digital assistant (or Palm): Behavioral Observation of Students in Schools (Shapiro, 2003) and the Student Observation System of the BASC (Reynolds & Kamphaus, 2004). A social work observation form can be found in Massat and Sanders (2009).

T is for Testing. Aside from the standardized diagnostic measures, practitioners should become familiar with rapid assessment instruments (RAIs). Fischer and Corcoran (2007) have compiled almost 60 RAIs for children and adolescents, but new ones can be found by searching PsycINFO as well. For example, a group of school social workers recently approached me about how to measure the effectiveness of a social skills group for adolescents with autism. Working collaboratively, we found the Autism Social Skills Profile (ASSP; Bellini & Hopf, 2007), a strengths-based RAI designed for children 6–17 with autism spectrum disorder to monitor their progress toward IEP goals.

KNOWLEDGE AND SKILLS REQUIRED

School social workers will need to be proficient at a number of tasks before feeling competent at integrating EBP and RtI. These skills include model integration, systemic knowledge, team leadership, professional development, and systemic follow-up.

Model Integration

The problem-solving steps in RtI are shown in Figure 13.2. These five steps offer a natural place to integrate the EBP and RtI models. Each of the problem-solving steps requires modification to be considered evidence based.

PROBLEM IDENTIFICATION   Evidence-based problem identification requires social workers to determine whether there is a discrepancy between what is expected and what is actually happening. This means that social workers should be familiar with both academic and behavioral standards as well as know how to assess which students are not measuring up to expectations. A simple approach to universal screening is to calculate the class averages and standard deviations for common measures such as attendance, tardiness, office disciplinary referrals, nurse visits, and work completion rates. In a normal bell-shaped distribution, two-thirds of all students will be within one standard deviation (SD) of the center (mean or median), approximately one-sixth (16%) of the students will be 1 SD below the average. From an evidence-based perspective, this process helps the team define the problem in measurable terms.

PROBLEM ANALYSIS   Evidence-based problem analysis demands that practitioners understand why the problem is occurring and use a student-in-environment perspective to do so. Fortunately, RtI is ideally suited for the

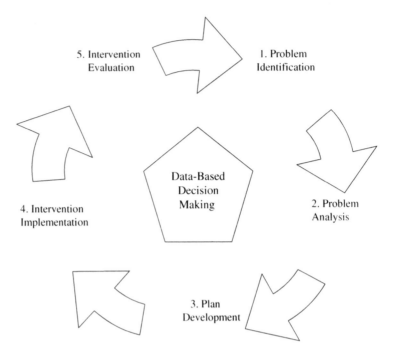

Figure 13.2   The problem-solving process in RtI.

ecological approach because there are four domains to consider. The first domain is *Instruction*. Instruction refers to how the content is taught. Assessment should inquire about the duration, pace, timing, groupings, teaching methods, and feedback opportunities provided to students. The second domain is *Curriculum*. The curriculum is what is taught. Assessment should ask about the alignment of the core curriculum with state standards as well as with adjacent grade levels. For example, a common problem regarding students' lack of social skills is the assumption on the part of the school that these have been taught at home when this may not be true (Gresham, Van, & Cook, 2006; Hawken, Vincent, & Schumann, 2008). The third domain is *Environment*. The environment is the social milieu of the classroom and school building. Environmental issues include student safety, classroom management, rules and their reinforcement, and physical arrangements of space (Doll & Cummings, 2008). Fourth, the *Learner* should be assessed last. When all of the above contributors have been adequately addressed, assessment should focus on the struggling student. Here assessment should consider behavioral, health, hearing, learning, motor, speech/language, and vision needs of the individual student. Diagnostic instruments can be used to analyze why the problem is occurring. From an evidence-based perspective, it is essential to obtain a baseline before developing a measurable goal (Raines, 2002).

PLAN DEVELOPMENT   Evidence-based plan development compels school social workers to know which interventions are research based and how to appropriately adapt them to fit the characteristics of students at their schools. Interventions should be distinguished from both accommodations and modifications. *Accommodations* are changes in the timing, formatting, setting, scheduling, required response, or presentation of an assignment that allows a student to achieve the same standards as their peers. Examples of accommodations include extra time to work on a test or preferred seating in a classroom. *Modifications* are adjustments to the assignment that enable a student to meet a lower standard than their peers. Examples of modifications include lower grade-level books to read or less complicated math to complete (deBettencourt & Howard, 2006). *Interventions* are specific strategies designed to teach or remediate an academic or behavioral skill. Interventions can target the students, their environment, or both. Examples include peer-assisted learning strategies or cognitive-behavioral therapy. From an evidence-based perspective, problem-solving teams can no longer simply "brainstorm" solutions to student problems and think that they have satisfied the requirement that interventions be based on scientifically based research. For a list of Internet resources of empirically supported inventions, see Appendix 13.A.

FIDELITY OF INTERVENTION IMPLEMENTATION   Evidence-based intervention implementation requires practitioners to be mindful of how faithfully the intervention will be carried out by teachers or other school personnel. Intervention fidelity or integrity, the degree to which an intervention has been implemented as designed, is critical in determining intervention effectiveness (see Chapter 9). While practitioners should adapt the scientifically based intervention before implementing the intervention, this should not be interpreted to mean that "anything goes." Some principles to follow in faithfully implementing the intervention are the following:

1. Remain faithful to the theory behind the intervention.
   Practitioners cannot use a cognitive-behavioral intervention from a psychodynamic perspective and expect it to work as effectively.
2. Be sure to implement the core components of the intervention. If practitioners are in doubt about which aspects represent essential elements of the intervention, they should contact the developer of the intervention (Pankratz et al., 2006).
3. Administer the full dose of the intervention. Just as schools would not consider giving a child half a dose of a psychotropic medication, they should not think about delivering a partial dose of an empirically supported intervention (Mokrue, Elias, & Bry, 2005).

From an evidence-based perspective, it is impossible to determine whether an intervention is effective unless it is consistently implemented.

INTERVENTION EVALUATION Evidence-based intervention evaluation obliges social workers to know how to collect and analyze their own data to determine whether students are responding to intervention. Data can be collected using any of the RIOT measures mentioned above. For all tiers, outcomes can be calculated using either a school-wide information system (SWIS) or an electronic spreadsheet program, such as Excel. From an evidence-based perspective, only interventions that have stood the test of local scrutiny can be considered research based.

Systemic Knowledge

School social workers should be able to read and understand the annual school report that is sent to the state education agency and available to public citizens. Typically, this school report details the number of students at each grade level that have exceeded, met, or failed state standards. It will also disaggregate these results by minority groups of sufficient size (usually 30–40 students). Such disaggregated groups may include student status such as gender, race, disability, low-income, and English language learners. The report may also include the poverty rate, mobility rate, and percentage of students receiving special education services. Raines and Ahlman (2004) recommend asking several questions about these data:

- Is the number of low-income students increasing or decreasing? How is this affecting the school's Title I funding? What programs currently exist to help these students?
- What families does the transiency rate represent (e.g., homeless, migrant workers, military, entertainers)? Is the transiency rate increasing or decreasing? How are these students introduced and integrated into the school?
- What languages are represented in the school? What type of outreach exists for these families? Does the school have any bilingual or English as a second language (ESL) classes?
- How is the ethnic and racial mix of the school changing? Is this reflected in the school staff as well? What kinds of positions do people of color hold?
- How is the school dealing with the increased focus on standardized testing? How is the decision made whether or not to include special education students? If they are included, what kinds of accommodations are made? (p. 39)

School social workers should also have some familiarity with the school's relational database or school-wide information system. Which variables are routinely tracked tells the practitioner the factors that the school administration regards as most important. Thus, it is helpful to monitor student progress using these variables as one way to check the effectiveness of the interventions. This becomes one way to demonstrate the relevance of social and emotional learning to academic achievement (Hoagwood et al., 2007; Welsh et al., 2001; Zins et al., 2004).

Team Leadership

Response to Intervention offers three opportunities for school-based practitioners to lead school-based teams (Hawkins et al., 2008; see Figure 13.3). There are building leadership teams that examine whole school issues related to Tier 1, such as location and scheduling issues. There are grade-level teams that peruse data and determine how and when to offer Tier 2 interventions (Gregory, 2008; Myers & Kline, 2001). Thompson (1997) used the Group Development Scale (Wheelan & Hochberger, 1996) and found grade-level team functioning was correlated with higher academic achievement. There are problem-solving teams that focus on individual students and how to help them with Tier 3 interventions. Each of these teams needs a designated leader with four skill sets: facilitating group communication, encouraging group participation, building trust and cohesion, and guiding group decision making (Iverson, 2002). While Burns and Gibbons' (2008) Problem-Solving Team Process Fidelity Checklist is primarily used for the individual problem-solving team, it could easily be adapted for the other two teams. For example,

Figure 13.3 Teams for Tiers.

one of the mantras that team trainers have used in Illinois has been "no data, no meeting." In other words, team meeting time is too valuable to be wasted listening to anecdotal complaints about students. Teachers are expected to come with hard data to document their interventions and students' level of responsiveness. Although the school principal is likely to lead the building assistance team, school social workers could easily facilitate group discussions at the other levels, making sure that members did not short-cut any of the steps in the combined EBP-RtI process.

Professional Development

Burns and Ysseldyke (2005) examined four large-scale implementation models and found that all of them required Response to Intervention to be phased in gradually. Burns and Gibbons (2008) provide a four-year process for putting RtI into action. Each year requires a "coach" to help school staff members learn about the process. The first year, the coach helps the school prepare for benchmark assessments, data interpretation, data-based decision making, and troubleshooting. It is essential that teams be trained in ecological theory (Rubinson, 2002), especially the influence of instructional, curricular, and environmental factors on academic success. The second year, the coach helps evaluate the fidelity of implementation for both academic and behavioral interventions. The third year, the coach continues to provide help on instructional and behavioral issues. The fourth year, the coach works with teams to establish criteria to determine eligibility for special education. Throughout the process, coaches from various schools or districts should network regularly to gain support and personal development.

Systemic Follow-Up

One of the reasons that school social workers are ideally suited to the RtI model is its inherent ecosystems perspective. As mentioned above in the Problem Analysis section, teams should examine instructional, curricular, and environmental barriers *prior to* thinking that the problem resides in the learner. While these barriers are best addressed in Tier 1, practitioners will discover that some teachers will remain attached to old instructional styles, familiar curriculums, and environmental routines that fail to support students. When this occurs, school social workers should use their systemic skills throughout the problem-solving process. Systemic interventions include assessing instructional, curricular, and environmental factors that create or maintain student problems; referring the problem to a team with greater governance power to change the location or scheduling of interventions; or advocating infrastructure changes to allow greater flexibility for meeting the needs of students. For example, Rubinson (2002) reports how one team obtained funding for a Saturday school program that provided remedial work in reading and writing as well as recreational and computing opportunities. Another team chose to implement block scheduling to allow teachers more time for individualized and hands-on work. As Rubinson concludes, "When the context in which the learner resides is ignored, systems continue to regard academic failure as solely a symptom of disability, eliminating the need for educators to question their conventional practices" (2002, p. 212).

CHAPTER SUMMARY AND CONCLUSIONS

The integration of evidence-based practice and Response to Intervention is a reasonable and natural extension of both models. The problem identification phase in RtI uses school-wide data to screen students at regular intervals to identify selected students for more intensive intervention. The assessment phase in RtI is decidedly ecological; it explores instructional, curricular, and environmental factors before assuming the problem lies within the learner. The biggest difference between evidence-based RtI and traditional practice will be in the plan development phase. Instead of relying solely on brainstorming to think up new approaches to helping youth, problem-solving teams must explore the professional resources to find interventions that are research based and matched to the identified problem. The implementation phase in RtI carefully balances clinically sensitive adaptation and fidelity to the empirically based intervention. The evaluation phase in RtI utilizes four data collection methods including reviewing records, interviewing informants, observation, and testing. Taken together, they provide practice-based evidence that students are responding to intervention.

APPENDIX 13.A
INTERNET RESOURCES FOR EMPIRICALLY
SUPPORTED INTERVENTIONS

American Academy of Child and Adolescent Psychiatry Practice Parameters http://
www.aacap.org/page.ww?section=Practice+Parameters & name= Practice+
Parameters

American Academy of Pediatrics School-Based Mental Health http://pediatrics.
aappublications.org/cgi/reprint/113/6/1839

American Psychological Association's Guide to Empirically-Supported Interventions
http://www.apa.org/divisions/div12/rev_est/

Campbell Collaboration Library of Reviews in Education, Criminal Justice, and
Social Welfare http://www.campbellcollaboration.org/frontend.asp#About%
20C2Ripe

Center for School Mental Health (University of Maryland) http://csmh. umaryland.
edu/resources.html/Summary%20of%20Recognized%20 Evidence%20 Based%
20Programs6.14.08.doc

Centre for Evidence-Based Medicine's Toolbox http://www.cebm.net/toolbox.asp

Cochrane Reviews of Evidence-Based Health Care http://www.cochrane.org/
reviews/

National Institute on Drug Abuse Principles of Drug Addiction Treatment http://
www.drugabuse.gov/PODAT/PODATIndex.html

National Institute of Health Consensus Statement on ADHD http://consensus.
nih.gov/1998/1998AttentionDeficitHyperactivityDisorder110html.htm

Office of Juvenile Justice and Delinquency Prevention's Model Programs http://
www.dsgonline.com/mpg2.5/mpg_index.htm

SAMHSA's National Registry of Evidence-Based Programs and Practices http://
www.nrepp.samhsa.gov/index.htm

School Success Online http://www.schoolsuccessonline.com

Treatment Manual for *Anger Management* http://www.schoolmentalhealth.
org/Resources/Clin/Anger%20Management%20Protocol.pdf

Treatment Manuals for *Coping with Depression* and *Coping with Stress* (free) http://
www.kpchr.org/public/acwd/acwd.html

U.S. Department of Education's Safe, Disciplined, and Drug-Free Exemplary
Programs (9 programs) http://www.ed.gov/admins/lead/safety/exempl
ary01/panel_pg2.html

U.S. Department of Education's Safe, Disciplined, and Drug-Free Promising
Programs (33 programs) http://www.ed.gov/admins/lead/safety/exemplary01/
panel_pg3.html

U.S. Department of Health and Human Services Agency for Health Care Research
and Quality http://www.ahrq.gov/clinic/epcix.htm

U.S. Department of Health and Human Services National Guideline Clearinghouse
(Mental Health) http://www.guidelines.gov/

U.S. Department of Health and Human Services, SAMHSA—Evidence-Based
Interventions for Children http://www.systemsofcare.samhsa.gov/header
menus/docsHM/MatrixFinal1.pdf

What Works Clearinghouse (Character Education, Dropout Prevention, ELLs,
Math, Reading) http://ies.ed.gov/ncee/wwc/

REFERENCES

Abel, R. E., and Lyman W. N. (Eds.). (2002). *Scholarly publishing: Books, journals, publishers, and libraries in the twentieth century.* New York: John Wiley.

Adams, T. (2000). The status of school discipline and violence. *Annals of the American Academy of Political and Social Science, 567,* 140–156.

Alexander, J., & Tate, M. A. (2005). *What web search engines won't find.* Retrieved May 19, 2007, from http://www3.widener.edu/Academics/Libraries/ Wolfgram_Memorial_Library/Need_Help_/How_to_Do_Research_/What_ Web_Search_Engines_Won_t_Find_/498/.

American Psychological Association. (2005, July). *Report of the 2005 presidential task force on evidence-based practice.* Retrieved January 29, 2009, from http:// www.apa.org/practice/ebpreport.pdf.

Barkham, M., & Mellor-Clark, J. (2003). Bridging evidence-based practice and practice-based evidence: Developing rigorous and relevant knowledge for the psychological therapies. *Clinical Psychology and Psychotherapy, 10*(6), 319–327.

Bellini, S., & Hopf, A. (2007). The development of the autism social skills profile: A preliminary analysis of psychometric properties. *Focus on Autism and Other Developmental Disabilities, 22*(2), 80–87.

Beutler, L. E. (2000). Empirically-based decision making in clinical practice. *Prevention and Treatment, 3* (Article 27). Retrieved May 19, 2002, from http://journals.apa.org/prevention/volume3/pre0030027a.html.

Bloom, M., Fischer, J., & Orme, J. G. (2006). *Evaluating practice: Guidelines for the accountable professional* (5th ed.). Boston: Pearson/Allyn & Bacon.

Burns, M. K., & Gibbons, K. A. (2008). *Implementing response-to-intervention in elementary and secondary schools: Procedures to assure scientific-based practices.* New York: Routledge.

Burns, M. K., & Ysseldyke, J. E. (2005). Comparison of existing response-to-intervention models to identify and answer implementation questions. *California School Psychologist, 10*(1), 9–20.

Constable, R., & Massat, C. R. (2009). Evidence-based practice: Implications for school social work. In C. R. Massat & R. Constable (Eds.), *School social work: Practice, policy, and research* (7th ed., pp. 140–151). Chicago: Lyceum Books.

Constantino, G., Malgady, R. G., & Rogler, L. H. (1984). Cuentos folkloricos as a therapeutic modality with Puerto Rican children. *Hispanic Journal of Behavioral Sciences, 6*(2), 169–178.

Cooper, H. (2001). *The battle over homework: Common ground for administrators, teachers, and parents.* Thousand Oaks, CA: Corwin.

deBettencourt, L. U., & Howard, L. A. (2006). *The effective special education teacher: A practical guide for success.* Columbus, OH: Merrill Education.

Doll, B., & Cummings, J. A. (Eds.). (2008). *Transforming school mental health services: Population-based approaches to promoting the competency and wellness of children.* Bethesda, MD: National Association of School Psychologists.

Evans, C., Connell, J., Barkham, M., Marshall, C., & Mellor-Clark, J. (2003). Practice-based evidence: Benchmarking NHS primary care counseling services at national and local levels. *Clinical Psychology and Psychotherapy, 10*(6), 374–388.

Fischer, J., & Corcoran, K. (2007). *Measures for clinical practice and research: A sourcebook. Vol. 1. Couples, families, and children* (4th ed.). New York: Oxford University Press.

Fonagy, P., Target, M., Cottrell, D., Phillips, J., & Kurtz, Z. (2002). *What works for whom? A critical review of treatments for children and adolescents.* New York: Guilford Press.

Gambrill, E. (2006). *Social work practice: A critical thinker's guide* (2nd ed.). New York: Oxford University Press.

Gerber, M. M. (2003, December 4–5). *Teachers are still the test: Limitations of response to intervention strategies for identifying children with learning disabilities.* Paper presented at the National Research Center on Learning Disabilities Responsiveness-to-Intervention Symposium, Kansas City, MO.

Germain, C. B. (1979). *Social work practice: People and environments, an ecological perspective.* New York: Columbia University Press.

Gettinger, M., & Kohler, K. M. (2006). Process-outcome approaches to classroom management and effective teaching. In C. M. Evertson, & C. S. Weinstein (Eds.), *Handbook of classroom management: Research, practice, and contemporary issues* (pp. 73–95). Mahwah, NJ: Lawrence Erlbaum.

Gibbs, L. (2003). *Evidence-based practice for the helping professions: A practical guide with integrated multimedia.* Pacific Grove, CA: Thomson-Brooks/Cole.

Gregory, R. J. (2008). Tier I response to intervention: Elementary school preparedness factors. Ed.D. dissertation, Indiana University of Pennsylvania. Retrieved February 3, 2009, from Dissertations and Theses: Full Text database. (Publication No. AAT 3308992)

Gresham, F. M., Van, M. B., & Cook, C. R. (2006). Social skills training for teaching replacement behaviors: Remediating acquisition deficits in at-risk students. *Behavioral Disorders, 31*(4), 363–377.

Hawken, L. S., Vincent, C. G., & Schumann, J. (2008). Response to intervention for social behavior: Challenges and opportunities. *Journal of Emotional and Behavioral Disorders, 16*(4), 213–225.

Hawkins, R. O., Kroeger, S. D., Musti-Rao, S., Barnett, D. W., & Ward, J. E. (2008). Preservice training in response to intervention: Learning by doing an interdisciplinary field experience. *Psychology in the Schools, 45*(8), 745–762.

Hoagwood, K. E., Olin, S. S., Kerker, B. D., Kratochwill, T. R., Crowe, M., & Saka, N. (2007). Empirically based school interventions targeted at academic and mental health functioning. *Journal of Emotional & Behavioral Disorders, 15* (2), 66–92.

Howard, M. O., McMillen, C. J., & Pollio, D. E. (2003). Teaching evidence-based practice: Toward a new paradigm for social work education. *Research on Social Work Practice, 13*(2), 234–259.

Iverson, A. M. (2002). Best practices in problem-solving team structure and process. In A. Thomas & J. Grimes (Eds.), *Best practices in school psychology IV* (Vol. 1, pp. 657–669). Bethesda, MD: National Association of School Psychologists.

Jensen, L. (2001). The demographic diversity of immigrants and their children. In R. G. Rumbaut & A. Portes (Eds.), *Ethnicities: Children of immigrants in America* (pp. 21–56). Berkeley: University of California Press.

Joint Commission on Accreditation of Healthcare Organizations. (2004). Assessment: Nutritional, functional, and pain assessment and screens. Oakbrook Terrace, IL: Author.

Kaslow, F. W. (Ed.). (2002). *Comprehensive handbook of psychotherapy: Integrative/eclectic, Vol. IV.* Hoboken, NJ: John Wiley.

Kim, S., Kverno, K., Lee, E. M., Park, J. H., Lee, H. H., & Kim, H. L. (2006). Development of a music group psychotherapy intervention for the primary prevention of adjustment difficulties in Korean adolescent girls. *Journal of Child and Adolescent Psychiatric Nursing, 19*(3), 103–111.

Kingery, J. N., Roblek, T. L., Suveg, C., Grover, R. L., Sherrill, J. T., & Bergman, R. L. (2006). They're not just "little adults": Developmental considerations for implementing cognitive-behavioral therapy with anxious youth. *Journal of Cognitive Psychotherapy, 20*(3), 263–273.

Malecki, C. K., & Demaray, M. K. (2007). Social behavior assessment and response to intervention. In S. R. Jimerson, M. K. Burns, & A. M. VanDerHeyden (Eds.), *Handbook of response to intervention: The science and practice of assessment and intervention* (pp. 161–171). New York: Springer.

Massat, C. R., & Sanders, D. (2009). Classroom observation. In C. R. Massat, R. Constable, S. McDonald, & J. P. Flynn (Eds.), *School social work: Practice, policy, and research* (7th ed., pp. 452–463). Chicago, IL: Lyceum.

Masui, C., & DeCorte, E. (2005). Learning to reflect and to attribute constructively as basic components of self-regulated learning. *British Journal of Educational Psychology, 75*(3), 351–372.

McCart, M. R., Priester, P. E., Davies, W. H., & Azen, R. (2006). Differential effectiveness of behavioral parent training and cognitive-behavioral therapy for anti-social youth: A meta-analysis. *Journal of Abnormal Child Psychology, 34* (4), 527–543.

McKay, M. M., Nudelman, R., McCadem, K., & Gonzalez, J. (1996). Evaluating a social work engagement approach to involving inner-city children and their families in mental health care. *Research on Social Work Practice, 6*(4), 462–472.

McRae, M. W. (1993). *The literature of science: Perspectives on popular scientific writing.* Athens: University of Georgia Press.

Meiland, J. W. (1999). Category mistake. In R. Audi (Ed.), *The Cambridge dictionary of philosophy* (2nd ed., p. 123).

Mellard, D. F., & Johnson, E. (2008). *RTI: A practitioner's guide to implementing response to intervention.* Thousand Oaks, CA: Corwin/NAESP.

Mokrue, K., Elias, M. J., & Bry, B. H. (2005). Dosage effect and the efficacy of a video-based teamwork-building series with urban elementary school children. *Journal of Applied School Psychology, 21*(1), 67–97.

Myers, V. M., & Kline, C. E. (2001). Secondary school intervention assistance teams: Can they be effective? *High School Journal, 85*(2), 33–42.

National Research Council. (2002). *Minority students in special and gifted education.* Washington, DC: National Academy Press.

Nelson, M. L. (2002). An assessment-based model for counseling strategy selection. *Journal of Counseling and Development, 80*(4), 416–421.

Nock, M. K., Goldman, J. L., Wang, Y., & Albano, A. M. (2004). From science to practice: The flexible use of evidence-based treatments in clinical settings. *Journal of the American Academy of Child and Adolescent Psychiatry, 43*(6), 777–780.

Ollendick, T. H., & Davis, T. E. (2004). Empirically supported treatments for children and adolescents: Where to from here? *Clinical Psychology: Science and Practice, 11*(3), 289–294.

Pankratz, M. M., Jackson-Newsom, J., Giles, S. M., Ringwalt, C. L., Bliss, K., & Bell, M. L. (2006). Implementation fidelity in a teacher-led alcohol use prevention curriculum. *Journal of Drug Education, 36*(4), 317–333.

Petrosino, A., Turpin-Petrosino, C., & Buehler, J. (2003). Scared Straight and other juvenile awareness programs for preventing juvenile delinquency: A systematic review of the randomized experimental evidence. *Annals of the American Academy of Political and Social Science, 589*, 41–62.

Raines, J. C. (2002). Present levels of performance, goals, and objectives: A best practice guide. *School Social Work Journal, 27*(1), 58–72.

Raines, J. C. (2008a). *Evidence-based practice in school mental health: A primer for school social workers, psychologists, and counselors.* New York: Oxford University Press.

Raines, J. C. (2008b). *SSWAA ethical guideline series: School social work and group work.* Indianapolis, IN: School Social Work Association of America.

Raines, J. C., & Ahlman, C. (2004). No substitute for competence: How to survive and thrive as a substitute school social worker. *School Social Work Journal, 28*(2), 37–52.

Raines, J. C., & Dibble, N. T. (in press). *Ethical decision making in school mental health.* New York: Oxford University Press.

Reynolds, C. R., & Kamphaus, R. W. (2004). *Behavior assessment system for children* (2nd ed.). Circle Pines, MN: Pearson/American Guidance Service.

Ribordy, S. C., Camras, L. A., Stefani, R., & Spaccarelli, S. (1988). Vignettes for emotion recognition research and affective therapy with children. *Journal of Clinical Child Psychology, 17*(4), 322–325.

Rones, M., & Hoagwood, K. (2000). School-based mental health services: A research review. *Clinical Child and Family Psychology Review, 3*(4), 223–241.

Rubin, A., & Parrish, D. (2007). Challenges to the future of evidence-based practice in social work education. *Journal of Social Work Education, 43*(3), 405–428.

Rubinson, F. (2002). Lessons learned from implementing problem-solving teams in urban high schools. *Journal of Educational and Psychological Consultation, 13*(3), 185–217.

Saari, C. (1986). *Clinical social work treatment: How does it work?* New York: Gardner Press.

Sackett, D. L., Rosenberg, W. M. C., Gray, J. A. M., Haynes, R. B., & Richardson, W. S. (1996). [Editorial] Evidence-based medicine: What it is and what it is not. *British Medical Journal, 312*, 71–72.

Sackett, D. L., Strauss, S. E., Richardson, W. S., Rosenberg, W., & Haynes, R. B. (2000). *Evidence-based medicine: How to practice and teach EBM* (2nd ed.). Edinburgh: Churchill Livingstone.

Shapiro, E. S. (2003). Behavioral Observation of Students in Schools-BOSS (Computer Software). San Antonio, TX: Psychological Corporation.

Shapiro, J. P., Welker, C. J., & Jacobson, B. J. (1997). A naturalistic study of psychotherapeutic methods and client-in-therapy functioning in a child community setting. *Journal of Clinical Child Psychology, 26*(4), 385–396.

Slawson, D. C., & Shaughnessy, A. F. (2005). Teaching evidence-based medicine: Should we be teaching information management instead? *Academic Medicine, 80*(7), 685–689.

Thompson, L. L. (1997). An investigation regarding the relationship between the effectiveness of elementary faculty groups as a whole and their respective grade level teams in kindergarten through grade six. Ph.D. dissertation, Temple University, Pennsylvania. Retrieved February 3, 2009, from Dissertations and Theses: Full Text database. (Publication No. AAT 9738007)

Turner, W. (2000). Cultural considerations in family-based primary prevention programs in drug abuse. *Journal of Primary Prevention, 21*(2), 285–303.

U.S. Department of Education, Office of Special Education and Rehabilitative Services. (2006, August 14). Assistance to states for the education of children with disabilities and preschool grants for children with disabilities: Final rule. 34CFR Parts 300 and 301. *Federal Register, 71*(156), 46540–46845.

Volpe, R. J., DiPerna, J. C., Hintze, J. M., & Shapiro, E. S. (2005). Observing students in classroom settings: A review of seven coding schemes. *School Psychology Review, 34*(4), 454–474.

Walker, J. S., Briggs, H. E., Koroloff, N., & Friesen, B. J. (2007). (Guest editorial). Implementing and sustaining evidence-based practice in social work. *Journal of Social Work Education, 43*(3), 361–375.

Weller, A. C. (2001). *Editorial peer review: Its strengths and weaknesses.* Medford, NJ: American Society for Information Science and Technology.

Welsh, M., Parke, R. D., Widaman, K., & O'Neill, R. (2001). Linkages between children's social and academic competence: A longitudinal analysis. *Journal of School Psychology, 39*(6), 463–481.

Westen, D., Novotny, C. M., & Thompson-Brenner, H. (2005). EBP? EST: Reply to Crits-Christoph et al. (2005) and Weisz et al. (2005). *Psychological Bulletin, 131*(3), 427–433.

What Works Clearinghouse, Institute for Educational Sciences, U.S. Department of Education. (2006). *What Works Clearinghouse evidence standards for reviewing studies.* Retrieved June 11, 2007, from http://w-w-c.org/review-process/study_standards_final.pdf.

Wheelan, S. A., & Hochberger, J. M. (1996). Validation studies of the group development questionnaire. *Small Group Research, 27*(1), 143–170.

White, N. J., & Rayle, A. D. (2007). Strong teens: A school-based small group experience for African American males. *Journal for Specialists in Group Work, 32*(2), 178–189.

Winters, W. G., & Easton, F. (1983). *The practice of social work in schools: An ecological perspective.* New York: Free Press.

Zins, J. E., Bloodworth, M. R., Weissberg, R. P., & Walberg, H. J. (2004). The scientific base for linking social and emotional learning to school success. In J. E. Zins, R. P. Weissberg, M. C. Wang, & H. J. Walberg (Eds.), *Building academic success on social and emotional learning: What does the research say?* (pp. 3–22). New York: Teachers College Press.

14

SUPPORTING THE ADOPTION, IMPLEMENTATION, AND SUSTAINABILITY OF RtI SYSTEMS

JAMES P. CLARK, MICHELLE E. ALVAREZ, WENDY MARCKMANN, & ANDREA TIMM

Developing, implementing, and sustaining the operation of a Response to Intervention (RtI) system is a daunting system development challenge. For school social workers as well as other educators, an imperative element is understanding the system change strategies and system supports that are needed to successfully adopt, implement, and sustain RtI in a school building or district and at the state level. The purpose of this chapter is to propose a role for school social workers in this process.

The ethical obligations and professional standards that provide a foundational rationale for why school social workers must play an active role in the system improvement efforts inherent in adopting a RtI system are discussed. The need for school social workers to act as change agents and to play a leadership role in facilitating multilevel systems change is also emphasized. Understanding the progression of large-scale systemic change is presented as a means of anticipating obstacles to implementation. Specific professional development procedures that have been used to enhance and refine skills needed for implementing RtI practices with individual students are described. Professional development supports are described as a means to ensure that practitioners acquire and maintain the knowledge and skills essential for practicing in an RtI system. Case reviews are proposed as an effective professional development process for giving continuous practice improvement feedback to practitioners providing individualized interventions to students. An example of a multiyear implementation of case reviews is presented as an illustration.

ADVOCATING CHANGE

School social workers have a fundamental ethical and professional responsibility to act as advocates for improved services to clients. Professional ethics and standards form the basis for this responsibility. Ethical principles that require a commitment to clients and a responsibility to the profession through the monitoring of policies, programs, and practices are explicitly stated in the profession's code of ethics (National Association of Social Workers, 1999). The professional standards for school social workers state, "School social workers, as system change agents, shall identify areas of need that are not being addressed by the local education agency and community and shall work to create services that address these needs" (National Association of Social Workers, 2002, p. 16).

With sound evidence demonstrating the effectiveness of the RtI process these ethical obligations and professional standards provide a strong rationale for the expectation that school social workers will act as change agents in advocating adoption and implementation. If systems theory and systems thinking are integral to school social work practice, it is reasonable to expect that practitioners will take seriously their important role in facilitating systemic changes that are essential for successful RtI implementation. For most school social workers this represents a significant shift in emphasis in the focus of their practice, from working with individuals and small groups to acting as system change agents at the school-wide or district-wide (macro) level. The need for this paradigm shift is documented by a recent statewide survey of 3, 000 school social workers in Illinois in which more than 88% of practitioners reported they primarily used individual and small group interventions with students (Kelly, 2008). At the national level this same pattern of practice was evident. Kelly et al. (submitted) surveyed 1, 639 school social workers and found that over 60% reported doing individual counseling and 31% reported doing group counseling all or most of the time. If these survey results are at all a reflection of typical practice, school social workers will have to take deliberate action to shift their attention to system-level interventions if they intend to have a role in improving the educational system.

BEGINNING WITH THE END IN MIND

It is best to begin changing systems with the end in mind. In the case of RtI, the end can be viewed as the totality of what has been described across the three tiers in the preceding chapters of this book. Though the focus here has been on addressing the social, emotional, and behavioral needs of students, a well-functioning RtI system will have comparable procedures and practices in place that also address student academic needs across the tiers. Differentiated instruction and supports are made available to all students. A potent set of universal supports or core curriculum will meet the academic, social, emotional, and behavioral needs of at least 80% of students. Screening procedures will accurately identify the 5% to 10% of students that have not adequately benefited from these universal supports and that will need targeted group interventions. Progress monitoring of the effects of targeted group interventions will provide data that will help identify the 1% to 5% of students that will need intensive individualized interventions. Responsibility for differentiating supports and instruction and utilizing evidence-based practices throughout this process lies with educators and professional support personnel as they strive to ensure educational success for all learners. This is the vision; it is the end to which change agents must focus.

With this end in mind it is critical to understand what is needed to adopt, implement, and sustain the successful operation of an RtI system that has these features. Strategies are needed that initially cause school buildings and districts to view an RtI system as a means for increasing efficiency and improving learning outcomes for all students. Strategies that support initial implementation of RtI practices and ensure sustainability of the RtI system are also essential. Adoption, initial implementation, and sustainability are best accomplished through a multilevel set of change strategies.

MULTILEVEL SYSTEM CHANGE STRATEGIES

With the end in mind, acting as a change agent and advocate for the establishment of an RtI system requires an understanding of the strategies needed to effect improvements at multiple levels of the education system. Because federal policy in the Individuals with Disabilities Education Act (IDEA) and the No Child Left Behind Act (NCLB) provides ample sanction for the use of RtI practices (see Chapter 1), the focus for changing policy, procedure, and practice will need to be at the local and state levels. Local change efforts will need to target intermediate education agencies (in states where these structures exist), school districts, and school buildings within districts. State-level change efforts must be targeted at the state department of education.

Systems change requires a shared vision for change, building consensus among internal and external stakeholders, and a declared willingness to adopt RtI (National Association of State Directors of Special Education, 2008a, 2008b; Slavin, 2004). Creating a shared vision requires beginning with the end in mind and communicating the vision at the district level to both internal (school personnel, families and students) and external (the community) stakeholders. In building consensus "RtI concepts are communicated broadly to implementers and the foundational 'whys' are taught, discussed and embraced" (National Association of State Directors of Special Education, 2008b, p. 2)

BUILDING-LEVEL STRATEGIES

Local change strategies should be targeted at school buildings since this is where instruction and supports are actually delivered to students. The National Association of State Directors of Special Education (2008b) has proposed that the school building is the unit of change when implementing RtI and that district-level and state-level supports must be systematically built to support implementation at the school building level. So, it is critical that policies, procedures, accountability expectations, and other guides established at a district level are directly supportive of RtI implementation by teachers, administrators, and professional support services staff such as school social workers, school psychologists, and school counselors at the building level.

CREATING READINESS AND ESTABLISHING COMMITMENT

Building-level change strategies begin with creating readiness by establishing consensus on the need for RtI implementation (Grimes, Kurns, & Tilly, 2006; National Association of State Directors of Special Education, 2008a). Initial interest and commitment to implementation are more likely if teachers, administrators, and professional support staff perceive compelling reasons for change and improvements. If staff or administrators have acquired an understanding of RtI or have witnessed positive results of RtI systems, adoption may have compelling appeal.

High levels of staff commitment and active support of administrators are critical to initial and long-term success. For example, an explicit prerequisite for implementation of School-wide Positive Behavior Supports is that at least 80% of the staff must agree to the need to implement and to be supportive of initial implementation activities. This level of commitment along with active support and involvement are also required of administrators (Office of Special Education Programs Center on Positive Behavioral Interventions and Supports, 2004). Slavin (2004) identifies high levels of initial commitment as one reason that an evidenced-based program has been sustained by 1,600 schools for over 20 years. "The whole school must make a free and informed choice to adopt SFA [the program/curriculum]; we require a vote by secret ballot of at least 80%" (p. 62).

If high levels of initial commitment cannot be obtained, initial implementation should be delayed while staff are provided additional information about RtI and how this approach can address problems in the current system. Student performance data may need to be presented to staff.

Time may need to be devoted to discussing, legitimizing, and summarizing the concerns of staff about how implementation might affect them and how they will be supported in the process, for example, with professional development and administrative support.

INITIAL BUILDING-LEVEL IMPLEMENTATION

Once initial building-level commitment and readiness are established, implementation can commence. In implementing School-wide Positive Behavior Supports, Horner et al. (2005) have identified six critical conditions that must be met to ensure successful implementation. The first condition is the creation of a representative school-wide team that engages in problem solving and data-based decision making. The National Association of State Directors of Special Education (2008b) proposes that a leadership team be formed to establish an infrastructure that supports school-wide implementation. Facilitator, coach, content specialist, data mentor, and staff liaison are identified as roles that team members will need to play throughout the implementation process. Detailed descriptions of specific functions carried out by staff in these various roles are also provided (pp. 15–17).

Other critical conditions that must be met include the provision of active administrative leadership and support, documented commitment to educating all students and improving the climate of the school, ensuring adequate personnel and time for planning and implementation, fiscal support for planning activities (e.g., materials, professional development), and the establishment of a data management system that supports data-based decision making (Horner et al., 2005). These conditions address many of the barriers to successful implementation that have been identified by Kincaid et al. (2007) including staff buy-in, data, inconsistency, and reward systems. The conditions may also address staff barriers such as lack of administrative direction and leadership, skepticism that the universal intervention is needed, hopelessness about change, philosophical differences, and feelings of disenfranchisement from each other, the administrator, or the mission of the school, that have been identified by Lohrmann et al. (2008).

The National Association of State Directors of Special Education (2008b) has proposed that the school-wide leadership team address the following 10 basic questions to inform the development of an action plan for implementation:

1. Is our core program sufficient?
2. If the core program is not sufficient, what led to this?
3. How will the needs identified in the core program be addressed?
4. How will the sufficiency and effectiveness of the core program be monitored over time?
5. Have improvements to the core program been effective?

6. For which students is the core instruction sufficient or not sufficient? Why or why not?
7. What specific supplemental and intensive instructions are needed?
8. How will specific supplemental and intensive instruction be delivered?
9. How will the effectiveness of supplemental and intensive instruction be monitored?
10. How will you determine which students need to move to a different level of instruction? (pp. 18–38)

Action plans must then be implemented school-wide across the three tiers. However, as is evident in the sequence of the questions above, graduated implementation typically begins with an assessment of how effective the universal supports (core program) in Tier 1 are in achieving desired results.

DISTRICT, INTERMEDIATE, AND STATE-LEVEL IMPLEMENTATION

Many of the same readiness and initial implementation steps must take place at the district and state levels. As noted earlier, district policies, procedures, accountability expectations, and other guides must directly support RtI practices at the school building level. Elliott and Morrison (2008) have proposed the development of a supportive district-level infrastructure including a district-level leadership team, clear identification of the roles that district/central administration will play in implementation, development of a district-level needs assessment, the establishment of a data collection system, development of a three- to five-year action plan, and an evaluation plan. These supports at the district level ensure that building-level implementation will consistently be nurtured and sustained.

Where intermediate educational agencies exist, their policies and procedures must also be explicitly aligned with and supportive of district- and building-level practices. In some instances such as in the case of Iowa's Renewed Service Delivery System initiative (see Chapter 1), intermediate educational agencies can actually play a leadership role in collaboration with the state department of education in advocating and supporting system improvements such as RtI. Professional development for staff and administrators to ensure their understanding of RtI and to acquire knowledge and skills required for successful implementation may be provided by intermediate agency staff. Technical assistance in developing and using data systems for collecting and analyzing information about student performance may also be a support provided by the intermediate agency.

State-level policies, regulations, and accountability expectations must also complement implementation efforts at the intermediate, district, and building levels. Acting on options now available in the Individuals with Disabilities Act to adopt RtI approaches for identifying students who are eligible for special education (see Chapter 12) is an example of a state-level policy that can be supportive of local implementation efforts. Allowing for the noncategorical identification of students eligible for special education can also be a helpful accountability support provided by the state department of education (see Chapter 12). Designing state initiatives including professional development priorities that support RtI adoption and implementation can directly enhance and support local implementation efforts. It is imperative that there are mechanisms in place for ongoing communication and problem solving that involve building level, district, intermediate agency, and state agency personnel as well as key stakeholders such as parents.

SUSTAINABILITY

Sustainability is the ultimate indicator of effective system change. Based on their experience with the Renewed Service Delivery System initiative in Iowa beginning in the 1980s (see Chapter 1), Grimes and Tilly (1996) note, "Schools have embraced an abundance of innovation and a thin history of long-term adoption of these innovations" (p. 465). In some circumstances the failure to sustain innovations in a system can be attributed to an overreliance on external funding sources that are time limited. Indeed, evidence-based programs/curriculums have sometimes been implemented and have produced successful outcomes but were unable to be sustained when funding was no longer available (Fuchs, Fuchs, Harris, & Roberts, 1996; McDougal, Clonan, & Martens, 2000; Shaughency & Ervin, 2006; Slavin, 2004). Additional challenges to sustaining evidence-based programs/curricula include change in staff who championed the implementation, district leadership, federal/state policy support or changes, or a shift in the emphasis of district initiatives (Slavin, 2004). Slavin (2004) points out that "in fact, even programs that do not cost much may still disappear when funds are cut" (p. 61). To counteract this phenomenon, sustainability must begin at implementation with the development of a durable infrastructure that can be maintained despite changes in the availability of funding (Stollar et al., 2008), which increases the likelihood of institutionalization.

The focus of funding evidence-based program training, materials, and evaluation efforts often relies on obtaining additional funds. George and Kincaid (2008) note, "External funds can sometimes create a barrier in capacity-building by causing districts to develop a reliance on an external source rather than building a district infrastructure to support their efforts. When external funds disappear, the infrastructure that was once supported by them may also disappear" (p. 24). What is overlooked is the reallocation of existing funds. The National Center for Mental Health Promotion and Youth Mental Health Promotion and Violence Prevention (NCMPYVP) (2008) developed a model of sustainability for Safe Schools Healthy Students grantees that provides a very detailed process for sustaining evidence-based strategies for students implemented in a school. Titled the *Legacy Wheel* (NCMPYVP, 2008), this model emphasizes the need to embed sustainability at the onset of implementation, examine the data regularly, and sustain the elements that yield positive outcomes for students (NCMPYVP, 2008). It also encourages schools to examine existing resources including monies received through state funding and the formation of community partnerships that include collaboration around use of existing agency funds and fee-based services (NCMPYVP, 2008).

The ultimate form of sustainability is institutionalization. Institutionalization means that innovations have become permanently adopted and have become woven into the fabric of the system. When institutionalization has been accomplished, sustainability is not dependent upon extraordinary resources because the available resources have been redeployed to support practices that have changed as a result of these innovations.

The process of implementing the RtI process has been addressed more specifically in the preceding chapters within each tier. However, overall implementation of RtI requires assessing what is already in place at each of the tiers within the school/district and utilizing that as the base from which to begin the implementation process. As noted in this chapter, creating a shared vision, gaining consensus, followed by developing an implementation plan with all stakeholders that is manageable and incorporates professional development and technical supports are essential. There will be challenges to implementation (Kratochwill et al., 2007); however, continuously evaluating the implementation process and maintaining what is working and discontinuing what is not producing positive student outcomes will lead to a higher degree of sustainability.

PROFESSIONAL DEVELOPMENT

Baker, Gersten, Dimino, and Griffths (2004) identified steps taken during the implementation phase of evidence-based practice that most contributed to sustainability. These researchers found that in addition to the policy mandate, professional development and ongoing technical support were predictors of sustainability (Baker et al., 2004). However, traditional professional development has been presented as one-time workshops on current issues in education with no follow-up or connection to other in-service trainings or building-based professional learning activities offered during that academic year. To implement RtI effectively, a comprehensive and intentional progression of in-service trainings must be offered to all school personnel, and systematic methods of evaluating the implementation of skills and the need for further technical assistance should be addressed (Brown-Chidsey & Steege, 2005; Stollar et al., 2008). Kratochwill et al. (2007) found that "it is no longer sufficient for professional development to simply enhance the knowledge and skill of trainees; it must also translate into improved student performance on outcome measures" (p. 629). Ongoing active learning opportunities beyond professional development training should be a part of a comprehensive progression of training and include developing teams or study groups, identifying and utilizing natural leaders within the system, providing coaches/mentors, conducting classroom observations, and making self-assessments (Kratochwill et al., 2007; National Association of State Directors of Special Education, 2008b; Stollar et al., 2008).

It is clear that many if not most school social workers will need to acquire new knowledge and skills to function in a RtI system. Therefore, professional development is a key ingredient in the system change process when RtI principles and practices are adopted. As an RtI system is implemented and refined, professional development becomes a potent force in ensuring the sustainability of the innovative practices integral to its ongoing and effective operation. As Stollar et al. (2008) have emphasized, "Successful system change requires a long-term commitment to high quality professional development that explicitly builds knowledge and skills needed for accurately implementing innovations that have been shown to be effective in similar situations" (p. 876). Many of the demands of operating an RtI system require skills that are familiar to school social workers but must often be reacquired and maintained. In some cases, new knowledge and skills must be intitially acquired. Thus, professional development procedures that provide continuous feedback on the quality and fidelity of practice must be established.

CASE REVIEW: A PROCESS FOR CONTINUOUS PRACTICE FEEDBACK

The multiyear case review process established at the Heartland Area Education Agency 11 in Johnston, Iowa, is an example of a professional development activity designed to provide continuous practice feedback to school social workers functioning in schools implementing RtI systems. Heartland Area Education Agency (AEA) is one of 10 AEAs that serve all schools in Iowa. AEAs are state funded and state mandated intermediate education agencies that provide a variety of general education and special education supports to local schools including school social work, school psychology, and speech-language pathology. Heartland AEA is located in the central area of Iowa and serves 54 public school districts and 32 nonpublic schools. When this case review process began in 2005 the agency employed 44 school social workers and a full-time administrative school social work supervisor.

The state of Iowa has had an established statewide RtI system in place for more than a decade. This system emerged from the Renewed Service Delivery System initiative that was launched in the late 1980s. (See Chapter 1 for more information about this reform effort.) AEAs have provided leadership in developing and implementing the problem-solving practices that are universally defined in state and local requirements (Iowa Department of Education, 2006). This case review process focused specifically on the application of these problem-solving practices to assessment and intervention development with individual students. It was viewed as a process that would continuously reinforce and improve the application of knowledge and skills that were presented in group training sessions and mentoring supports for new school social work staff, and other periodic in-service trainings provided to experienced staff to update practice expectations.

A group supervision model was used to implement the case review process in its first two years—from 2005 to 2007. During these first two years of implementation the process was led by a school social work supervisor with the assistance of a school social work professional development specialist. The professional development specialist was a school social work practitioner who devoted half time to providing professional development supports to the discipline. In the last year the process was facilitated by a school social work practitioner in the role of a *program assistant*.

The purpose of the school social work case review process was to improve the proficiency of school social workers in implementing problem-solving practices with individual students. Case reviews and training in the use of Microsoft Excel software were utilized toward this purpose. Case reviews were designed to provide an opportunity for documented work with individual students to be viewed holistically in a small group activity with peers. This included reflection and discussion of how data-based decisions were made, evaluation of linkages between various components of the problem-solving process, and consideration of the implications of assessments and decisions. Training in the use of Microsoft Excel software was provided in conjunction with each case review meeting. This software was used by school social workers in managing student performance data in the problem-solving process. School social work practitioners were expected to use this software for data collection, analysis, and display.

A group supervision model was used for case reviews. The school social work supervisor and professional development specialist facilitated a series of peer-based case review sessions. These sessions were designed to provide practitioners with the opportunity to present cases in a structured format with systematic feedback from peers and the supervisor. The intent was to create a collegial and supportive environment in which the focus was on improving practice.

Group sessions were held regionally throughout the agency with four to eight school social workers participating in each session. Each group met four full days throughout the year. The schedule was designed to provide an opportunity for each school social worker to present at least two cases during the school year. Each session was scheduled for a full day with two case reviews in the morning. Each practitioner was allowed 60 minutes to present a case and an additional 30 minutes was allocated for group discussion and questions. The afternoon was reserved for training and individualized guided practice with the Microsoft Excel software.

The school social work professional development specialist provided this training and support. A standard training curriculum was used to ensure that practitioners had acquired minimal proficiency in the use of the software. Practitioners were required to use actual data from cases presented in case reviews in this training.

Cases selected for review were required to include all elements of the problem-solving process contained in the "Innovation Configuration for Intervention Development, Implementation, and Evaluation" (see Appendix 14.A). Cases selected were required to be those for which the social worker had sole or primary responsibility for intervention development, implementation, and evaluation within the previous 12 months. A case review protocol and a sample case were provided to help organize each case presentation and to ensure alignment of the case content with the innovation configuration.

The innovation configuration was used for qualitative and quantitative assessment of each case. The innovation configuration identifies each major component of the problem-solving process and describes differential forms of implementation of the component on a continuum ranging from highly unacceptable (rating of 1) to ideal (rating of 5). Ratings of 4 or 5 are considered to be descriptions of acceptable practice for each component. Use of the innovation configuration provides continuity for case presentations as well as objectivity and precision in assessing the quality of case documentation and practice. Each practitioner was required to use the innovation configuration to complete a self-assessment prior to the case presentation and to identify the specific documentation upon which each rating was based. Self-assessment ratings were recorded along with group consensus ratings for each case. Group consensus ratings were established through discussion among peers and represent their collective agreement about which rating most accurately aligned with the case presentation and documentation.

Group consensus ratings were averaged with each self-assessment for each of the 11 components of the innovation configuration for 69 cases during the first year of implementation. Findings labeled "2006" are summarized in Figure 14.1. These data established a performance baseline for the social work staff and were used for identifying further professional development needs. Analysis of these aggregated data indicated that ratings of 3 of the 11 innovation configuration components were below the acceptable practice rating. These components included baseline, formative assessment, and treatment (implementation) integrity. It was not surprising that treatment integrity was the lowest rated area since the agency had just begun to provide staff with guidance, training, and tools for ensuring integrity of implementation during this first year of case reviews. These three components were targeted for improvement in the case review process the following school year. The goal setting component was also added as an area of needed improvement since it was exactly a 4 rating and the lowest area of performance among those components in the acceptable range.

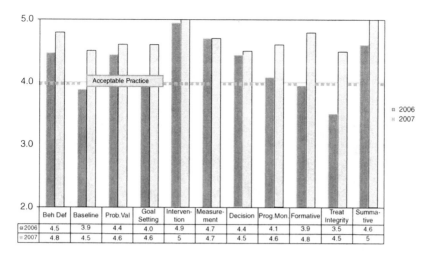

	Beh Def	Baseline	Prob.Val	Goal Setting	Interven-tion	Measure-ment	Decision	Prog.Mon.	Formative	Treat Integrity	Summa-tive
2006	4.5	3.9	4.4	4.0	4.9	4.7	4.4	4.1	3.9	3.5	4.6
2007	4.8	4.5	4.6	4.6	5	4.7	4.5	4.6	4.8	4.5	5

Figure 14.1 Case review aggregate ratings by components.
Source: Data collected, analyzed, and summarized by Heartland Area Education Agency 11, Johnston, Iowa. Used with permission.

The same group supervision format used during the first year of case reviews was used in the second year. Each regional group met four half days throughout the year. The same procedures for case selection and self-assessment were required. While practitioners were required to complete a self-assessment for all 11 components of the innovation configuration, group discussion and group consensus ratings focused primarily on the components targeted for improvement: *baseline, goal setting, formative evaluation,* and *treatment integrity.* If self-assessment ratings for any of these components were rated at 3 or lower, the school social worker was required to complete the "Case Review Improvement Worksheet" in preparation for presenting the case (see Appendix 14.B). This was intended to enrich the group discussion focusing on identifying practice and system challenges that are encountered in these areas along with posible solutions.

Training in the use of Microsoft Excel software was not included in the second year case reviews. However, the professional development specialist was available at each session to provide guided practice or troubleshooting assistance for any school social worker who requested it. Practitioners were encouraged to engage in further development of their skills in using Microsoft Excel by enrolling in agency-provided intermediate and advanced classes or by informally using the support and consultation of colleagues.

Findings for the second year of case reviews are summarized and labeled "2007" in Figure 14.2. These aggregated data showed that average staff performance was now in the acceptable range of ratings for all 11 components of the innovation configuration. Ratings ranged from 4.4 to 4.9.

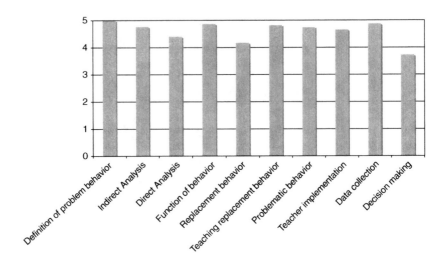

Figure 14.2   Average score on the FBA/BIP rubric of the items rated by the SSW group during case reviews 2007–2008.
Source: Developed by Heartland Area Education Agency 11, Johnston, Iowa.
Used with permission.

Though many school social workers expressed apprehension about the process in the beginning stages of the implementation, progress indicated by these summative data was viewed very positively.

During the third year of case reviews, various professional development supports were designed for school social workers who were new, those in their second year, and those considered veterans. Newly employed school social workers received new learning and guided practice on data-based decision making, special education policy, functional behavior assessment, behavior intervention planning, entitlement decision making, and school-wide positive behavior supports. Second-year school social workers were provided opportunities for guided practice in advanced data-based decision making, special education compliance, treatment integrity, progress monitoring, entitlement, diversity, and behavioral observation. Veteran school social workers were given the flexibility to determine their professional development needs from a catalogue of options. All school social workers were provided optional professional development opportunities to improve their skills in functional behavioral assessment and linking behavioral interventions to the function of the behavior. To provide opportunities for practice feedback, all school social workers participated in quarterly case reviews.

Case review groups were organized to ensure that school social workers provide valuable structured feedback to each other. Case reviews occurred four times a year in groups no larger than seven. Each session was scheduled for three hours. Each school social worker presented two intensive individual intervention cases. School social workers working in early childhood settings (birth to age 5) and school social workers serving kindergarten to age 21 were scheduled in job-alike groups to ensure that case examples would be relevant.

Case reviews focused on the components of functional behavioral assessment and intervention planning. This shift in focus was made because school social workers had demonstrated acceptable practice in all areas of the innovation configuration during the second year of case reviews. In addition to demonstrating acceptable practice, the agency had initiated the use of new functional behavioral assessment summary forms and increased expectations for documentation of functional behavioral assessment summaries. The functional behavioral assessment (FBA) and behavior intervention plan (BIP) rubrics were used for assessing cases. The assessment components that were focused on during case reviews included definition of problem behavior, indirect analysis, direct analysis, hypothesis of function of behavior, and definition of replacement behavior. The intervention components that were focused on included strategy for teaching replacement behavior, procedures for display of problematic behavior, outline of supports to assist teacher implementation, data collection procedures, and data-based decision-making rules (see Appendix 14.C).

Case review data for each case were collected on the components of the rubric. Each staff group reviewed documentation and agreed upon a rating for each component of the rubric. The group rating was recorded and averaged to determine group performance. Overall, cases were in the acceptable range (ratings of four or five) in all areas except decision making. The area of replacement behavior scored in the acceptable range, but during case reviews, Heartland school social workers expressed frustration with their ability to match replacement behaviors that were as efficient and effective as the problem behavior. As a result, it was determined that professional development for the following year would focus on matching effective and efficient replacement behaviors and decision-making plans for behavior intervention plans.

The case review process is an effective method for providing continuous practice feedback. Case review data are especially useful in targeting professional development supports for school social workers. In particular, these data help to differentiate supports needed for first-year, second-year, and veteran school social workers. These data also provide valuable information about progress practitioners are making in acquiring and maintaining skills that are essential for functioning in an RtI system.

KEY CONSIDERATIONS IN IMPLEMENTATION

The importance of consensus building and readiness has been stressed as a critical prerequisite to implementation as well as a predictor of implementation success. Creating this readiness for change requires both information sharing and the creation of opportunities for authentic discussions among staff members. Concerns and fears about the effects of pursuing a systemic change such as RtI need to be validated and responded to in supportive ways by colleagues and administrators.

Staff will benefit from an understanding that the complexity of system change required by adopting RtI demands persistence and sustained effort over many years. There are no quick fixes for most problems that exist in interdependent and complex systems. Staff will need to know that change can be frustrating because it is not neatly linear and always predictable.

Most educators and school social workers find it difficult to totally and abruptly abandon their current or preferred practices. Therefore, dual implementation of practices can be expected in most cases as innovations are introduced. Grimes and Tilly (1996) have explained that because some practices are routine and comfortable to staff, it is expected that for some time in initial implementation there will the need for a "dual system" where innovative or new practices "exist in the same system simultaneously" (p. 474).

School social workers might play a variety of roles in the process of adopting, implementing, and sustaining an RtI system. In building-level implementation, many school social workers will find themselves well suited to the roles of data mentor, content specialist, facilitator, staff liaison, and instructional leader. In most cases school social workers will need to intentionally inject themselves into or even initially create system change efforts designed to implement RtI.

KNOWLEDGE AND SKILLS NEEDED BY SCHOOL SOCIAL WORKERS

As states revise and align their special education regulations and procedures to comply with new federal requirements, school social workers should be active participants. While they have much to contribute to this process, informed and helpful participation will require a thorough understanding of RtI including its implications for school social work practice. Because RtI includes the development of school-wide supports for *all* students, school social workers will need to expand their repertoire of knowledge and skills beyond assessment of and services to individual students who are at risk or experiencing educational problems. For many practitioners, this represents a significant paradigm shift and requires a concomitant shift in practice that includes the development of knowledge and skills required to assist in the design and implementation of school-wide support systems. School social workers will need to be able to conduct system-level assessments and use these data to design differential interventions and supports that can be directly measured, monitored, and evaluated for their effectiveness. As discussed in Chapter 12, it will also be essential for practitioners to develop an understanding of how RtI can be applied to assessment and decision making for individual students who may be determined eligible for special education. In effect, RtI represents an opportunity to expand the scope of school social work practice by applying systems theory, functional assessment practices, and an ecological perspective to efforts to improve behavioral and academic results. As such, school social workers will need to effectively and efficiently integrate the principles and practices of RtI into all school social work practice.

CHAPTER SUMMARY AND CONCLUSIONS

This chapter has addressed the adoption, implementation, and sustainability of RtI systems. School social workers have a professional obligation and educational policy mandate to act as advocates for change by applying the skills in systems change they acquired in their graduate and undergraduate social work programs. These are knowledge and skills that school social workers have and can contribute to the process of implementing the large-scale system improvement challenge of RtI. Sustainability is the ultimate challenge in this process, one that requires vigilance and persistence on the part of change agents. Professional development supports will prove to be a critical element in adopting and sustaining the innovative practices required by RtI. The case review example provided here demonstrates a data-based strategy that school social workers can use to acquire and sustain skills they will need as active participants in an RtI system.

APPENDIX 14.A

INNOVATION CONFIGURATION FOR INTERVENTION DEVELOPMENT, IMPLEMENTATION, AND EVALUATION

Presenter: _____

Case: _____

Date: _____

Behavioral Definition

5	4	3	2	1
Definition is (a) <u>objective</u> — refers to observable and measurable characteristics of behavior; (b) <u>clear</u> — so unambiguous that it could be read, repeated, and paraphrased by observers; and (c) <u>complete</u> — delineates both examples and nonexamples of the behavioral.	Definition meets only two of the three criteria (i.e., objective, clear, complete).	Definition meets only one of the three criteria (i.e., objective, clear, complete).	Problem behavior is stated in general terms (e.g., reading comprehension, aggressive behavior, etc.).	Behavioral definition is not written.

Evidence Supporting Rating:

Baseline Data

5	4	3	2	1
(a) The appropriate dimension(s) of the target behavior (FLITAD) have been identified; (b) A measurement strategy is developed answering how? what? where? who? and when?; and (c) Data collected on the behavior prior to implementing the intervention consisting of repeated measures of the target behavior over several (at least three) sessions, days, or even weeks until a stable range of behavior has been identified.	All three parts are present, however, the dimension(s) addressed are not the most appropriate for the selected target behavior, and the measurement strategy does not answer all five questions. BUT the data were collected on the behavior prior to implementing the intervention consisting of repeated measures of the target behavior over several (at least three) sessions, days, or even weeks until a stable range was identified.	Data collected on the behavior prior to implementing the intervention; however, only two data points are reported. Dimension(s) addressed and the measurement strategy may or may not be present.	Information present indicates baseline data were gathered, but data may or may not be present. Dimension(s) addressed and the measurement strategy may or may not be present.	Baseline data not gathered prior to implementing the intervention.

Evidence Supporting Rating:

Problem Validation

5	4	3	2	1
Discrepancy determined by comparing the student's current level of performance, documented using baseline, to a typical peer performance (e. g., local CBM norms, peer comparison data)	Discrepancy determined by comparing the student's current level of performance to other local standards (e.g., teacher expectations, curriculum expectations).	Discrepancy determined using non-local standards (e.g., published expert standards, instructional placement standards, national norms).	Discrepancy described using unspecified standards.	Problem is not validated; discrepancy not described.

Evidence Supporting Rating:

Goal Setting

5	4	3	2	1
Goal stated narratively and represented graphically on performance chart specifying time frame, condition, behavior, and criterion.	Goal represented graphically on performance chart specifying time frame, behavior, criterion, and condition — not stated narratively.	Goal stated narratively specifying time frame, behavior, criterion, and condition — not represented graphically.	Goal stated narratively and/or represented graphically on performance chart but does not specify all four components (time frame, condition, behavior, criterion).	Goal not set.

Evidence Supporting Rating:

Intervention Plan

5	4	3	2	1
Plan stated (a) procedures/ strategies, (b) materials, (c) when, (d) where, and (e) persons responsible.	Plan stated procedures/ strategies. But one of the following components is missing: materials, when, where, or persons responsible.	Plan stated procedures/ strategies. But two of the following components is missing: materials, when, where or persons responsible.	Generic description of intervention strategy (e.g., behavior management) is stated. Materials, when, where, and persons responsible may be present.	Intervention plan not written. OR Generic descriptions of intervention (e.g., behavior management) only.

Evidence Supporting Rating:

Measurement Strategy

5	4	3	2	1
A measurement strategy is developed answering how? What? Where? Who? And when?	A measurement strategy is developed but only answers four of the five questions: how? What? Where? Who? And when?	A measurement strategy is developed but only answers three of the five questions: how? What? Where? Who? And when?	A measurement strategy is developed but only answers two of the five questions: how? What? Where? Who? And when?	Measurement strategy is not developed. OR The measurement strategy only answers one of the five questions.

Evidence Supporting Rating:

Decision-Making Plan

5	4	3	2	1
The decision-making plan indicates (a) how frequently data will be collected, (b) the strategies to be used to summarize the data for evaluation, (c) how many data points or how much time will occur before the data will be analyzed, and (d) what actions will be taken based on the intervention data.	The decision-making plan indicates three of the four components.	The decision-making plan indicates two of the four components.	The decision-making plan indicates only one of the four components.	Decision-making plan is not documented.

Evidence Supporting Rating:

Progress Monitoring

5	4	3	2	1
Data are collected and charted/graphed 2-3 times per week. Appropriate graphing/charting conventions were used (e.g., descriptive title, meaningful scale captions, appropriate scale units, intervention phases labeled).	Data are collected and charted/graphed once a week. Appropriate graphing/charting conventions were used.	Data are collected and charted/graphed irregularly and infrequently (less than once a week, but more than pre and post). Appropriate graphing/charting conventions may or may not be used.	Data are collected but not charted or graphed. OR Only pre and post information was collected and/or charted/graphed.	Progress monitoring data not collected.

Evidence Supporting Rating:

Formative Evaluation

5	4	3	2	1
There is evidence the decision rule was followed and visual analysis was conducted. This data was used to modify or change the intervention as necessary.	There is evidence the decision rule was followed and visual analysis was conducted, but the data were not used to modify or change the intervention as necessary.	Modifications or changes were made to the intervention based on subjective data.	Modifications or changes were made to the intervention but no indication as to what data were used to make these changes.	No formative evaluation was conducted

Evidence Supporting Rating:

Treatment Integrity

5	4	3	2	1
Degree of treatment integrity measured and monitored. Plan is implemented as designed, including decision-making rules. Intervention changes/modified as necessary on the basis of objective data.	Degree of treatment integrity addressed. Plan was implemented as designed and modified as necessary on the basis of subjective opinions.	Degree of treatment integrity addressed. Plan was implemented with variations from the original design with no basis for change stated.	Treatment integrity addressed, but intervention was not implemented as planned.	Treatment integrity not considered.

Evidence Supporting Rating:

Summative Evaluation

5	4	3	2	1
Outcome decisions are based on the progress monitoring data.	Outcome decisions are based on minimal data (i. e., pre and post tests).	Outcome decisions are based on subjective data.	Outcome decision stated but no indication of what data were used to make the conclusion.	No summative evaluation took place.

Evidence Supporting Rating:

Excerpted from Heartland Area Education Agency 11 (2002). Improving Children's Educational Results Through Data-Based Decision-Making. Johnston, IA: Author. Used with permission.

APPENDIX 14.B

Case Review Improvement Worksheet
School Social Worker Case Reviews 2006–07

1. Check innovation configuration components with a self-
   assessment rating of "3" or lower.
   ——— Baseline
   ——— Goal Setting
   ——— Formative Evaluation
   ——— Treatment Integrity

2. For each component checked, identify the **practice (knowledge
   or skill) challenge** (if any) contributing to a self-assessment rating
   of "3" or lower.

3. For each component checked, identify the **system barrier/challenge**
   (if any) contributing to a self-assessment rating of "3" or lower.

4. Identify potential **solutions/strategies** for addressing the practice
   and/or system barriers/challenges described above.

Developed by Heartland Area Education Agency 11, Johnston, Iowa. Used with permission.

FBA Rubric

1	2	3	4	5
ASSESSMENT:				
Definition of problem behavior:				
Problem behavior is not stated	Problem behavior is stated in general terms	Problem behavior identification meets 1/3 criteria (specific, observable, alterable)	Problem behavior identification meets 2/3 criteria (specific, observable, alterable)	Problem behavior identification meets 3/3 criteria (specific, observable, alterable)
Indirect Analysis:				
Record review completed but no direct interviews	Adult with minimum knowledge of behavior interviewed.	Adult with maximum knowledge of behavior interviewed.	More than 1 adult interviewed.	All adults involved with the child were interviewed
Direct Analysis:				
Observations were not based on interview data.	Observations were based on interview data but not conducted in a structured format.	Structured observations occurred in the problematic setting only.	Observations occurred in both problematic and non-problematic settings but different formats were used across settings.	The same or comparable structured observations were conducted in both the problematic setting and non-problematic setting.
Hypothesis of Function of Behavior:				
No hypothesis generated.	Hypothesis generated is not specific to a function of behavior.	Hypothesis generated is not supported by interview or observation data.	Hypothesis is supported by only 1 set of data.	Hypothesis is supported by both interview and direct observation data.
Definition of Replacement Behavior:				
Replacement behavior is not matched to the function of the problematic behavior.	Replacement behavior is the same as desired behavior.	Replacement behavior is matched to the function but requires a greater amount of effort than the problematic behavior.	Replacement behavior is matched to the function of the behavior, requires no more effort than problem behavior but is not efficient.	Replacement behavior is matched to the function identified, requires no more effort than aberrant behavior and is as efficient as problematic behavior.

1	2	3	4	5

INTERVENTION:

Strategy for Teaching Replacement Behavior:

1	2	3	4	5
No teaching strategies or SR+ schedule outlined.	SR+ schedule outlined but not in coordination with any teaching strategies outlined.	Teaching strategies outlined but no SR+ schedule.	Teaching strategies and SR+ schedule outlined but not in the same context as the problematic behavior.	Specific teaching strategies are outlined, to be taught in the same context as problematic behavior, and a SR+ schedule is outlined.

Procedures for Display of Problematic Behavior:

1	2	3	4	5
No procedures for display of problematic behavior outlined.	Procedures for display of problematic behavior are general school rules and not individualized to the student.	Procedures for the display of problematic behavior are individualized but too rigid (immediate restraint or expulsion from classroom)	Procedures for display of problematic behavior continue to allow the student access to identified function of the problematic behavior.	Procedures for display of problematic behavior deny the student access to the identified function of the problematic behavior.

Outline of Supports to Assist Teacher Implementation:

1	2	3	4	5
No supports outlined.	Specific people are identified to give support but definition of their role is not provided.	Definition of types of support is provided but people are not identified to provide the support.	Definition of types of support is provided with 1 person assigned to providing each type of support	Definition of types of support is provided with multiple people assigned to provide each type of support.

Data Collection Procedures:

1	2	3	4	5
No data collection procedures outlined.	Persons responsible for data collection are listed, but procedures are not outlined.	Data collection procedures are outlined.	Data collection procedures are outlined, dependent and independent variables are identified but data collection does not reflect the original target behavior.	Data collection procedures are outlined, dependent and independent variable defined, and data collection does reflect the original target behavior.

Data-based Decision-Making Rules:

1	2	3	4	5
No decision-making rules are outlined.	General decision-making rules are present.	Decision-making rules in 1 of 3 situations (student makes progress, stays the same, regresses) are outlined.	Decision-making rules in 2 of 3 situations (student makes progress, stays the same, regresses) are outlined.	Decision-making rules in 3 of 3 situations (student makes progress, stays the same, regresses) are outlined.

fort8

REFERENCES

Baker, S., Gersten, R., Dimino, J. A., & Griffiths, R. (2004). The sustained use of research-based instructional practice. *Remedial and Special Education, 25*, 1, 5–24.

Brown-Chidsey, R., & Steege, M. W. (2005). *Response to intervention principles and strategies for effective practice.* New York: Guilford Press.

Elliott, J., & Morrison, D. (2008). *Response to intervention blueprints: District level edition.* Alexandria, VA: National Association of State Directors of Special Education.

Fuchs, D., Fuchs, L. S., Harris, A. H., & Roberts, P. H. (1996). Bridging the research-to-practice gap with mainstream assistance teams: A cautionary tale. *School Psychology Quarterly, 11*, 244–266.

George, H.P., & Kincaid, D.K. (2008). Building district-level capacity for positive behavior Support. *Journal of Positive Behavior Interventions, 10*, 1, 20–32.

Grimes, J., Kurns, S., & Tilly, W. D. (2006). Sustainability: An enduring commitment to success. *School Psychology Review, 35*(2), 224–244.

Grimes, J., & Tilly, W.D., III. (1996). Policy and process: Means to lasting educational change. *School Psychology Review, 25*(4), 465–476.

Horner, R. H., Sugai, G., Todd, A. W., & Lewis-Palmer, T. (2005). School-wide positive behavior support. In L. M. Bambura & L. Kern (Eds.), *Individualized supports for students with problem behavior: Designing positive behavior plans* (pp. 359–390). New York: Guildford Press.

Iowa Department of Education (2006). *Special Education Eligibility Standards.* Des Moines, IA. Author: Iowa Department of Education.

Kelly, M. (2008). The Illinois example: Lessons learned from more than 3000 school social workers. *School Social Work Section Connection, 1*, 2–5. Washington, DC: National Association of Social Workers.

Kelly, M., Brezin, S. C., Frey, A., Alvarez, M., Shaffer, G., & O'Brien, K. (submitted). The state of school social work: Findings from the national school social work survey. *School Mental Health.*

Kincaid, D., Childs, K., Blasé, K. A., & Wallace, F. (2007). Identifying barriers and facilitators in implementing school-wide positive behavior support. *Journal of Positive Behavior Interventions, 9*(5), 174–184.

Kratochwill, T. R., Volpiansky, P., Clements, M., & Ball, C. (2007). Professional development in implementing and sustaining multitier prevention models: Implications for response to intervention. *School Psychology Review, 36*(4), 618–631.

Lohrmann, S., Forman, S., Martin, S., & Palmieri, M. (2008). Understanding school personnel's resistance to adopting schoolwide positive behavior support at a universal level of intervention. *Journal of Positive Behavior Interventions, 10*(4), 256–269.

McDougal, J. L., Clonan, S. M., & Martens, B. K. (2000). Using organizational change procedures to promote the acceptability of prereferral intervention services: The school-based intervention team project. *School Psychology Quarterly, 15*, 149–171.

National Association of Social Workers. (1999). *NASW code of ethics,* Washington, DC: Author.

National Association of Social Workers. (2002). *NASW standards for school social work services.* Washington, DC: Author.

National Association of State Directors of Special Education. (2008a). *Response to intervention blueprints for implementation, district level.* Retrieved September 28, 2008, from http://www.nasdse.org/Portals/0/DISTRICT.pdf.

National Association of State Directors of Special Education. (2008b). *Response to intervention blueprints for implementation, school building level.* Retrieved September 28, 2008, from http://www.nasdse.org/Portals/0/SCHOOL.pdf.

National Center for Mental Health Promotion and Youth Violence Prevention (NCMPYVP) (2008). The legacy Wheel. Retrieved October 10, 2008 from http://www.promoteprevent.org/Resources/legacy_wheel/.

Office of Special Education Programs Center on Positive Behavioral Intervention and Supports. (2004). *School-wide postitive behavior support implementer's blueprint and self-assessment.* Retrieved October 8, 2008, from http://www.pbis.org/tools.htm.

Schaughency, E., & Ervin, R. (2006). Building capacity to implement and sustain effective practices to better serve children. *School Psychology Review, 35*(2), 155–166.

Slavin, R. E. (2004). Built to last. *Remedial and Special Education, 25*(1), 61–66.

Stollar, S. A., Poth, R. L., Curtis, M. J., & Cohen, R. M. (2006). Collaborative strategic planning as illustration of the principles of system change. *School Psychology Review, 35*(2), 181–197.

Stollar, S. A., Schaeffer, K. R., Skelton, S. M., Stine, K. C., Lateer-Huhn, A., & Poth, R. L. (2008). Best practices in professional development: An integrated, three-tier model of academic and behavior supports. In A. Thomas & J. Grimes (Eds.), *Best practices in school psychology—V* (pp. 875–886). Washington, DC: National Association of School Psychologists.

15

RESPONSE TO INTERVENTION: A CALL TO ACTION

JAMES P. CLARK & MICHELLE E. ALVAREZ

As noted in our introduction, this book has been designed to provide school social workers with a working understanding of Response to Intervention (RtI) practices and systems. We have also presented a number of challenges to which school social workers will need to respond to ensure their active role in developing, adopting, implementing, and sustaining RtI systems that provide differentiated supports that effectively and efficiently address the social, emotional, and behavioral needs of all students. We conclude by summarizing these key challenges and issuing a call to action for school social workers to become more active agents of change in improving the responsiveness of educational systems to these critical needs. We fully acknowledge that meeting some of these challenges requires significant shifts in the assumptions underlying school social work practice and a willingness of practitioners to take on new roles, to engage in different practices, and to reconsider whether traditional, familiar, and perhaps more comfortable ways of practicing are still viable.

FOCUS ON THE PREVENTIVE EFFECTS OF SYSTEM CHANGE AND IMPROVEMENT

School social workers have much to contribute to the development of comprehensive, data-driven systems for efficiently providing differentiated social, emotional, and behavioral supports to all students. These contributions require a more balanced approach to service provision in which considerably more attention is directed to system improvements that use resources more efficiently and lessen the extent to which individual, group, and crisis interventions are needed. Maximizing the effectiveness of universal supports in Tier 1 is a particularly challenging systemic improvement in most schools. The greater the effectiveness of universal supports, the fewer targeted group interventions and intensive individual interventions will be needed.

An aquarium analogy is useful in illustrating this point. When fish in an aquarium are ill or begin to show signs of illness they can be moved to another environment, treated, and then returned to the aquarium. If this continues to happen to one fish after another, one can choose to continue to devote time and effort to nursing each ailing fish back to good health, or it may be time to assess the water quality in the aquarium to determine whether there might be a systemic cause for continued illnesses among the fish population. This same principle can be applied to school social work practice. Though school social work supports must continue to be made available to students who are in need, simultaneous attention to improving the school system will ensure greater educational health for more students and lessen the amount of intensive resources needed to support students with whom the system continues to be ineffective.

USE DATA-BASED DECISION MAKING IN A PROBLEM-SOLVING PROCESS

The implementation of RtI requires the use of a problem-solving process. Data-based decision making is an essential element of this process that demands the application of the scientific method to school social work practice. This methodology must be used consistently across all tiers in an RtI system. For many school social workers this will require an unprecedented and more intentional emphasis on the scientific dimensions of practice in order to demonstrate results. In particular, school social workers must become proficient in using data collection and management systems that inform the development of supports and interventions as well as ongoing progress monitoring that facilitates formative and summative evaluation of intervention effects.

USE FUNCTIONAL ASSESSMENTS TO DEVELOP SYSTEMIC AND INDIVIDUAL INTERVENTIONS

School social workers will need to be proficient in conducting functional behavioral assessments. This approach to assessment facilitates an understanding of the function or purpose of behavior and provides data that are useful in designing interventions. A functional approach to assessment also helps maintain a constant focus on problem solving and ensuring positive educational results, and it diminishes the need for labeling and categorizing students. In light of the profession's ethical stance on ensuring the dignity and respectful treatment of clients, eliminating the stigmatization resulting from procedures that label or categorize students is most certainly an appropriate advocacy challenge for school social workers.

Because of existing state and local policies and procedures, the use of functional behavioral assessments will be particularly challenging when used in full and individual evaluations for determining eligibility for special education. School social workers will need to become advocates for changing these policies and procedures to include improved approaches to assessment and decision making. This must include advocacy for the non-categorical identification of students requiring special education. School social workers will also need to consider carefully whether the social history or social developmental study is actually a functional assessment providing useful data for intervention development or a descriptive assessment that provides data for classifying students with disability labels.

USE EVIDENCE-BASED PROGRAMS AND PRACTICES

The emphasis on the scientific dimensions of school social work practice in RtI systems requires the use of evidence-based programs and practices. In light of recent findings documenting that school social workers are less likely to consider evidence-based sources when selecting interventions (Kelly et al., submitted), a significant change in practice is needed to address this challenge. School social workers must renew their appreciation for the importance of using programs and practices that have adequate scientific foundations. This will require proficiency with identifying and selecting programs and practices that have a sufficiently established research base as well as a willingness to use evidence-based programs instead of programs that may be more familiar or for which practitioners have a particular style or personal preference.

CREATE AND ACTIVELY ENGAGE IN ONGOING PROFESSIONAL DEVELOPMENT

Sustainability of RtI systems will depend to a great extent on the active engagement of practitioners in professional development activities that provide continuous practice feedback in relation to clearly articulated practice expectations. School social workers will need to assess their individual professional development needs by considering the knowledge and skills essential to practicing in RtI systems. They will also need to advocate access to the professional development activities that are needed to address these needs including the allocation of time and resources needed to fully participate. The use of case reviews is a particularly powerful learning process that allows opportunity for continuous practice feedback to ensure the appropriate application of knowledge and skills.

DEVELOP A WORKING UNDERSTANDING OF THE
OPERATION OF RtI SYSTEMS

To participate fully in the development, adoption, implementation, and sustainability of RtI systems, school social workers must acquire a comprehensive and deep understanding of the concepts, tenets, features, and critical elements of RtI. A working understanding of the operation of RtI systems and the role of school social workers in such systems has been the focus of this book. Though this foundation for school social workers seeking to become informed and active participants in RtI systems has been presented here, practitioners will need to expand their knowledge beyond the limitations of this book. The references cited throughout the book provide a rich array of literature that has increased significantly in the past few years. This literature should be scoured by school social workers as one means of becoming knowledgeable about RtI. Practitioners should also seek out the experience and expertise of school social workers who have been practicing in RtI systems as well as colleagues in other disciplines.

THE NEED FOR LEADERSHIP AND CHANGE

A national survey of school social workers was recently conducted (Kelly et al., in press) to describe the current state of school social work practice. Findings were compared to the results of similar past surveys, such as Allen-Meares (1994) and Astor et al. (1998). From a sample of 1,639 school social workers, Kelly et al. (submitted) concluded, "Findings from this survey indicate that the characteristics of school social workers, the context in which they practice, and their practice choices remain largely unchanged over the past 10 years" (abstract, in press). This is alarming. Continuing in this fashion will not position school social workers to be significant and meaningful contributors to the innovative practices needed to develop and sustain RtI systems.

Sadly, the virtual absence of innovative models, practices, and initiatives developed and published by school social workers noted in the introduction to this book is evidence of what is the profession's seemingly perpetual penchant for implementing the innovations researched and developed by other professions. This continues to force school social workers into the roles of follower and implementer, and away from the roles of developer and leader. Though the profession most certainly has much to contribute to the development of comprehensive, data-driven systems for efficiently providing social, emotional, and behavioral supports to students, leadership and a new approach are desperately needed.

THE CALL TO ACTION

The school social work profession must mobilize to ensure that school social workers are both active contributors to and participants in the development and implementation of RtI systems. School social work professional organizations must provide catalytic leadership in promoting the proliferation of RtI practices and in continued efforts to seek multiple avenues for generating school social work research and practice knowledge that contributes to the innovation knowledge base that is so desperately needed. Professional organizations and practitioners themselves must also work strategically to strengthen partnerships with schools of social work to more explicitly connect the practice, policy, and research that will improve the effectiveness of RtI systems and demonstrate the substantive contributions of school social work to these improvements.

School social workers should assume leadership roles in developing RtI systems in schools where they work and throughout states in which they work. They should challenge themselves to live up to the claim that the profession values the role of changing and improving systems for clients. This is an opportunity to fully realize the role of *change agent* and to apply our systems thinking to the development of innovative practices. This work also presents an opportunity to strike a more functional balance between the art and science of social work practice.

School social workers can and must take on the challenges presented here. Our reputation as change agents and advocates for students is at stake. The information and provocation provided in this book are intended to provide the inspiration for a new era of innovation, change, and unprecedented leadership by school social workers in improving education systems that serve our children. Let the innovation, leadership, and change begin.

REFERENCES

Allen-Meares, P. (1994). Social work services in schools: A national study of entry-level tasks. *Social Work, 39*(5), 560–566.

Astor, R., Behre, W. J., Wallace, J. M., & Fravil, K. A. (1998). School social workers and school violence: Personal safety, training, and violence programs. *Social Work, 43*, 3, 223–232.

Kelly, M., Brezin, S. C., Frey, A., Alvarez, M., Shaffer, G., & O'Brien, K. (submitted). The state of school social work: Findings from the national school social work survey. *Children & Schools. School Mental Health.*

INDEX

CPSIA information can be obtained at www.ICGtesting.com
Printed in the USA
BVOW04s1308080215

386796BV00004B/11/P